Contents

CONTENTS

Introduction

THIS is not an ordinary career book for one very simple reason. Becoming an artist is never an ordinary thing to do. Even in today's world, where the definition of "artist" has been expanded to include those who work in the graphic and commercial arts, the desire to create and having the talent to do so sets you apart from others. The drive to imagine and invent is such a highly personal process, it is often unexplainable in words. But it is this process, this quirky, original way of thinking and of seeing the world that gives us "art."

Art is satisfying, exciting, and involving. At the same time it is frustrating, aggravating, and depressing. The product, or end result—whether it be a painting, a film, an illustration, a design—is what the world sees and judges. But for the artist, the process—what it takes to achieve the product—may give far greater pleasure, lend to greater self-discovery, and be far more personally engaging than exhibiting or selling can ever be. Many artists would like to prolong this process for as long as possible. But producing the work, declaring the process finished is also essential. Not only does it allow the artist to get on to other things, completing and selling the product also makes it possible to pay the rent and buy more art supplies.

It seems paradoxical that at a time when making a living is more and more difficult and becoming an artist seems an impractical thing to do, art and film and video departments are flourishing in our colleges and universities. The desire to create has seemingly never been stronger. But pursuing a creative career has always been different from becoming a lawyer or businessperson. The clear-cut process that leads to career success in other fields—graduation from the right school, a good first job leading to a better second job leading to an even better third job, with more money and more success at every level—has little or nothing to do with the creative process most artists experience, whether they work on their own or work for others. The creative process is infinitely more complicated and more personal.

And its rewards are not easy to explain. Making money, having power, gaining fame and recognition—being successful in all these respects is possible, but the real satisfaction of living the creative life comes from its deep connection to a personal vision. When the world's conventional rewards are added to that satisfaction, art becomes possibly the most fulfilling of professions.

In recent years, the definition for "artist" has become far less narrow than it once was. The image of the smocked, bereted man with a palette, brush, and easel has been replaced by that of a woman or a man in jeans and a T-shirt, painting on a floor or a wall, using buckets and rags and hands, or focused intently over a drawing board, or leaning over a television monitor, or using a computer. You find artists in advertising agencies and design studios. You find them working on sets on the back lots of Hollywood, and you find them in small-town television stations.

But expanding the definition of artist doesn't change the fundamental reason you go into art. That remains the same: the need to create. How you satisfy that need is very personal. Artists who choose a commercial art field where it is necessary to meet other people's demands as well as to satisfy their own aesthetic sense understand that their work may undergo serious changes before final approval. In the fine arts, there may be no interference from others, but that freedom comes with no guarantee that the work will be exhibited. And even in the fine arts, many feel pressured to produce work they might not be inclined to produce except for the necessity of selling. Others find it easier to create within a structure, meeting the needs of a company or corporation, a studio, or another artist. The struggle there is to retain your own artistic personality and originality while doing work restricted by its purpose.

So you begin to learn the techniques of creative survival, techniques to sustain energy. For finding a way to sustain creative energy and excitement over the years is essential to maintaining a successful artistic life. There is no time in a creative career where you can "coast." You must remain passionate about what you do, taking risks at every stage. You must learn how to get more of what you want, how not to sacrifice the integrity of a creative concept while still fulfilling the requirements of the assignment, the client, the market, the collector, the dealer. The ability to do this, successfully, is often a major reason for what is termed a "creative breakthrough" in commercial fields, giving credence to the old adage about necessity being the mother of invention. It requires a full measure of patience, diplomacy, and tact. These characteristics aren't particularly important for the artist working alone in a garret. But in a business climate, having the social graces, having the ability to articulate ideas clearly, and being less self-oriented are advantages.

Today's artists who work in film, advertising, design, and even the fine arts are often in the position of having to explain ideas or directions or style to people who are inexperienced in looking at an artistic product and seeing what is there. Although the old definitions for "artist," and the preconceptions of what it means to be one, seem to linger on, today's artist is, for better or worse, tied to the marketplace.

This is a book for people who are interested in a life in the visual arts. It is designed to demystify and to clarify as we examine the many diverse careers available in the field. We'll talk about process, about talent, about money, about risks and satisfactions, schools, portfolios, first jobs—all the realities of becoming and being an artist. We'll talk about all the things you need to think about if you want to become an artist, if you want to change careers, if you're thinking about going to art school, if you want to know more about art as a career.

MOST PEOPLE STARTING COLLEGE ARE UNCERTAIN about what they want to do with their lives. Even if they want to become artists, in many instances they are unaware of what options are available to them. Finding direction and deciding on a satisfying lifework takes time and thought. Determine first your level of interest in anything, be it drawing, painting, taking photographs, or making films. Is it fun for you to do? Does it give you pleasure? Can it involve you for long periods of time? By age 17 or 18, you will have had a number of personal experiences in school that will have proved to you what you enjoy doing and what you don't. You know you're better in some areas than in others. Some things you can't do at all. Those you can't do you naturally reject as a basis for your life's work. But if you're not very good at a certain subject and yet you still enjoy working at it, don't give it up yet. If the subject or skill engages you and the process excites you, you may be better at it than you think—and you'll get even better, for that is one of the realities of life: If you keep doing something, you're bound to get better.

When you find something that you really like to do and that really interests you, focus on it. With further investigation, you may find the career exactly suited to you. Within the broad categories of art careers, there are many areas suited to special interests and special talents. A designer with an interest in video might do video and film graphics for a television station. A filmmaker who likes to draw might settle on animation as a career.

Conflicts in choosing a career arise when what you like to do, and are good at doing, doesn't seem to afford a very good living. Or when you like two things equally well and can't decide between them. This is a critical time. You often have pressures from family and friends to choose a direction that will offer security. Remember, however, that most people not involved in the art field are unaware of the options available to people with creative talents. And if they've never heard of some careers before, they will assume they are not viable choices. The only way to counter such objections is by educating others concerning your career choices. Few people realize that an artist can build a career on designing the books and magazines they read or on painting the illustrations that advertise the movies they go to see. People give even less thought to the kind of work involved in getting a television commercial or program on the air. They take for granted the symbol that identifies their bank or their insurance company or their supermarket, and never dream that some artist was probably paid very well to design that symbol.

Art careers don't have a very good press. They are either maligned or romanticized. Yet most people working in the visual arts are no different from other professionals; they are good at what they do, they provide a service, they're important to their communities, they earn a good living, and in most cases, they like what they do very much.

So if you're a bit uncertain about where your life is going, so are a lot of other people. Calm down and quietly begin the process of making the choice. Read books like this one and ask questions, but use your intuition as well. You know what you like to do. You know what you hate doing. Keep that very clear as you make your decisions. Don't worry about what the job is called or that no one in your hometown has ever heard about it. Just choose the job that gets you involved. Many people go through their lives working at jobs they don't like, jobs that give them no pleasure. You spend too much time working to make such a mistake. Since you're just beginning the search, go for what makes you happy.

ARTISTS TODAY NOT ONLY DRAW AND PAINT AND SCULPT, they make films and television commercials, they design fabrics, books, and interiors. They also take photographs, direct movies, and create sets for stage and television. If the definition of an artist has changed, the desire to create has not. The visually creative person simply has more directions to consider for a lifework now than ever before. The number of companies, corporations, and individuals needing the work and services of visual artists is growing everyday. Advances in technology are opening up entirely new occupations and providing new jobs for artists. When computers came of age, computer graphics became a career. The computer is important to the textile design industry, to fashion designers and interior decorators, and to many other art and art-related businesses. The videotape has also had impact. The once-not-so-interesting, clumsy relative of film has evolved into a full-fledged artistic medium with all the advantages of film and a few unique qualities of its own. So the decision to become an artist no longer wholly relies on a talent for drawing or painting, although for most visual people the introduction to art still begins with developing those skills.

As the need for artistic talent to serve business and industry increases, art schools and colleges continue to add courses, rethinking and reorganizing departments to bring them into line with the rapidly changing requirements for careers in art. Artistic careers have long been considered "glamour" careers because those who succeed in them are highly visible and well paid. To succeed in art, talent is requisite, and real talent always draws attention to itself. But no art school or college, no matter their advertising and promotion, can give someone talent who has none, and only a few from each class can hope to reach "star" status. But an art career is one way that anyone with a strong desire to create can find satisfaction. Ordinary talent, competent skills, and hard work are rewarded... one gets better. And that satisfaction can sustain an artist even beyond money and position. There are few careers that offer that kind of success to their practitioners.

LET'S TALK ABOUT WHETHER PEOPLE WHO BECOME ARTISTS ARE DIFFERENT from other people. Well, in many ways, they seem to be, that is if you believe their press. Artists are thought of as romantic, driven, gifted, eccentric, mad. A few certainly are, and many like the notion. However, the sensational stories of van Gogh cutting off his ear and Caravaggio as murderer are rare in the history of art. The life of most artists is quite ordinary. But the exaggerated image of the artist persists and distorts the reality. And we are left with the exaggerations that make it difficult for generations of would-be artists to convince their parents, spouses, and friends that becoming an artist isn't really such a foolish or impractical thing to do.

But it's easy to see where the misperceptions originated and why they continue. Artists create from imagination, and to the many who lack it, it seems like magic. In some sense, it is. A work of imagination can be analyzed, criticized, and appreciated, but where it comes from and how it appears on a page or a canvas is not easily understood, even by the artist. The ability to create something fresh or new out of nothing makes creative people "different."

Artists also generally possess some personal characteristics to a degree lacking in other people. They are highly sensitive and have a strongly developed intuitive sense. They are often more observant, seeing details others miss, sensing nuances in tone, attitude, and behavior. They are more original. But perhaps the idea that artists are different comes from those qualities they *don't* share with most people—like the ability to tolerate structure and bureaucracy long enough to make an impact on an organization; or to accept rules and regulations in order to advance group values; or to tolerate working in groups; or to be satisfied with simply getting a title, making money, and having security. Of course, there are creative people who have the ability to adjust to situations that go against their nature, but most eventually find themselves searching for a more accommodating or satisfying set of circumstances.

What is important about becoming an artist is to recognize the limits of your tolerance as soon as possible. It can save you much frustration and aggravation in the long run—time as well. Understanding that certain jobs and situations are not for you is not to fail but to face reality. To help you discover what is right for you is one of the aims of this book.

Art school may provide the first opportunity for a young artist to meet people who share the same sensibility, who value originality and invention, who understand the same process and want the same things. That is one of the benefits of going on to higher education after high school. You'll find the experience of meeting people who communicate on the same level supportive and exciting. You'll find that you feel less alone. It can change the way you handle the rest of your life.

THE PROCESS OF BECOMING AN ARTIST continues all through your lifetime. Unlike becoming a lawyer or a doctor, no certificate or ceremony marks the day you can begin practice. The real milestones in art are achieved day by day as your talent develops.

Becoming an artist, for many people, begins at an early age, with the way you see and the way you feel about what you see. Perception, intuition, and understanding are already present in childhood. But those artistic sensibilities are often challenged by the perceptions of the bigger, stronger, and more confident non-artists who generally surround you in childhood. And it is their perception that often controls the world, a reality that tends to make any artist-in-process doubt the truth of his or her vision. Since there's little reason to think this situation will change, your only recourse is to learn to trust your intuition.

The first step is to recognize that your ability to see clearly is a special talent, even though it comes naturally and easily to you. And when you find a way to make your thoughts and feelings concrete, the direction of your creative life will begin to take shape.

The artist is very lucky, for there is considerable personal power in creating and one need never be dependent on others to sustain that power. Perhaps the world won't recognize the power soon enough to suit you, but belief in yourself and your work is all you need to sustain it. Each time you try something, explore it, change it, and rework it, you learn more about who you are and you begin to harness and understand your power.

There are very few careers that can sustain for a lifetime the kind of consuming interest and excitement of discovery that a career in the creative arts can. There are, of course, negatives to becoming an artist, as there are in all professions. These become apparent when your process is incompatible with the way the world feels process should occur. Or when your product is not of the "mainstream." A career in art may not always provide the recognition you need in order to keep creating. It may not provide the means for your economic survival. Becoming a lawyer or doctor allows you to get a first job based on your education and training. But as an artist you must rely on the quality of your creative work. And that judgment is not yours alone, but often dependent on who's judging the portfolio.

Going into art for either money or recognition alone ensures failure from the start. If you achieve those goals, and many have, the world will applaud; but for the artist it is the small breakthroughs—knowing something you didn't know the minute before, understanding why something works—that keep you going. The process of becoming an artist confirms that real success, the exhilaration and satisfaction in creating what has never existed before, continues only by being free of other people's expectations.

In today's world, where the media hype on fame and money is evident everywhere, you as an artist must find ways to protect yourself from those distractions, simply because it affects your ability to work. It's useless to spend time and energy thinking about why other people, less talented, less skilled than you are, are successful. Spend that time and energy on your work.

MAKING THE RIGHT DECISION ABOUT WHERE YOU'RE GOING TO STUDY ART could make a difference in beginning your career. The right decision, however, is different for each person.

There are a number of things you should consider before making your final choice. What kind of artist are you planning to become? If you know that, you can eliminate some schools right from the start. For example, not all colleges have good film schools, so if you want to be a filmmaker, consider schools with full film programs, not simply film courses. In addition, the school's equipment and facilities should be a consideration. The department or college you choose should be well equipped. Today that means the newest technology so you will have the experience of working with cameras and editing equipment currently being used in the profession. Check out the faculty, either through personal contacts or by analyzing their bios in the catalog. You want to study with working filmmakers who can teach from their day-to-day experience—and who can recommend you for beginning jobs.

Or let's say you want to be a painter. Consider the school's faculty; it's important. Don't be seduced by important names alone. Name artists, it's true, are usually connected to good galleries and have strong connections that could be valuable to you, but equally important is the artist's ability to teach. Some can, some can't. Good painting and drawing teachers who have conviction and dedication are rare, but they can be found, even in schools with little reputation. Although it will require some effort on your part, visit the schools on your list of choices and talk, face to face, with one or more members of the faculty in your chosen field. That could be a deciding factor in your choice.

If you plan to go into the commercial art fields, such as advertising, graphic design, and illustration, you should do the same careful research before making your decision on a school. Many professionals teach at colleges or universities close to their studios or jobs. Visit them if you can. Working commercial artists, as part of their career maintenance, submit work to various art annuals. Go to the library and look through these books. Publications such as *Print, American Illustration, Communication*

Arts Annuals of Advertising Design, Illustration, Photography, and many others are available to you. Leaf through them and find work you like or that is in the direction of your own, and cross-check the artists' names in school catalogs. Write to them at the school, explain your situation, and ask for their opinions about educational possibilities.

Choosing a college is the first chance most students have to participate in a process that directly affects their future. You want to be able to make wise decisions with the information you have. Remember that the purpose of college is to learn all you can to be prepared for a career. And that you will learn better in an environment where you are comfortable. A school in a large city? A midwestern school with a campus? Fraternities, sororities—are they important to you? A small college where you can get to know everybody? A large college where you can get lost? Away from your parents? Near your parents? Out of town? In town?

Although financial considerations are important, you should first decide on your school or college with regard to other facts. Once you are accepted, then begin to find a way to pay for your education. Don't let the cart lead the horse. Most colleges and art schools offer scholarships and provide loan information for those who can't afford the tuition. There are work/study programs at most places, and any good institution has an effective placement program that can help you find part-time work while you're in school, as well as provide help once you graduate. If you will be needing financial assistance to get through school, begin investigating the possibilities early.

BECOMING AN ARTIST WITHOUT FORMAL TRAINING is certainly possible, but you have to be extraordinarily talented and highly motivated to overcome the problems and to become skilled enough to achieve excellence on your own. For most people, the discipline of school, whether full-time or part-time, is very helpful in focusing a talent and developing the skills necessary to achieve a personal vision. The working relationship with different members of a school or college faculty ensures you'll be exposed to many viewpoints and that you'll have the advantage of their collective experience and knowledge. You'll learn the history of art from various perspectives. You'll see techniques demonstrated and have the opportunity to apply them under close personal supervision. You'll begin to understand your own working process and to develop your talent.

On the other hand, should you be one of those unique and very rare young artists working without outside influences and producing work that's fresh and original and interesting, school is the last thing you need. If occasionally you feel out of touch, you can always drop by your nearest art school and talk with one of the teachers in your special area. I have seldom met an artist who teaches who didn't have time to talk with a talented young person.

But back to art schools. Most of them, in addition to being training centers, provide students with an introduction to the world outside. Students who do good work are usually "discovered" in the classroom, and on graduation they find themselves with strong entry-level jobs, with introductions to galleries, or with freelance work from professionals they've met while attending school. This, of course, presumes they've chosen a school with a working professional faculty.

Economics aside, becoming an artist today in any of the arts is easier if you take professional art courses at the college level, either during the day or in the evening, regardless of whatever other education you receive.

Along with developing your talent, structured curriculums offer courses that help refine your career skills—those abilities that enable you to present your work to best advantage and market it—and, in general, prepare you to be a working artist. In a highly competitive field such as the visual arts, being an extraordinary artist may not be enough to gain you the recognition you deserve.

THE REALITY OF BEING AN ARTIST TODAY IS THAT YOU ARE IN BUSINESS AS WELL AS IN THE ARTS. If you find yourself working in advertising or film for a corporation, your salary, tax deductions, overhead, and the like are handled through the machinery of the company. But most artists, at one time or another, find themselves as free agents in the marketplace, having full responsibility for handling the financial side of their work. Records must be kept and taxes paid, so its necessary to know something about how a business is run. Get professional help with your taxes if you need it. Get in the habit of keeping accurate records as soon as you begin to earn your own money. Keep receipts from all purchases of art supplies, office supplies, transportation to and from assignments or business-related meetings and lunches. If you work at home, a portion of your rent may also be deducted from your taxes. You should know how to bill a client. Many schools have specific courses in the "business of art," but if the one you attend does not, there are several good books with full information on pricing, marketing, and selling your work. We mention one in particular that is carefully researched and easily understood—*Selling Your Graphic Design and Illustration,* by Tad Crawford and Arie Kopelman (St. Martin's Press).

But don't make yourself crazy pondering your inadequacies as a financial wizard. Chances are your skills in that area won't measure up to the person who has chosen accounting as a lifework. After all, if you've made art your life, you should spend most of your energy on that. On the other hand, some artists find a certain satisfaction in organizing themselves, keeping records, and developing business skills. Using the left brain occasionally can be a welcome relief from the constant creative thinking activity of the right brain.

MANY ART CAREERS ARE STRUCTURED AS FREELANCE BUSINESSES, and for those who enjoy the freedom, it is the ideal way to work. However, if you need the security of a paycheck every week, the life of a freelancer would be a nightmare. Many designers, most illustrators, and all fine artists work freelance. Freelance simply means you work when you want and where you want, and if you want to earn more, you work more. You're in business for yourself, so you have to take care of your own medical insurance and pay the rent, gas, and electricity on your studio space, but you can also treat all your working expenses as legitimate tax deductions.

Within the art career field it is quite usual for people to work on a freelance basis. In the beginning, working this way may be rocky, but people who remain freelancers, and that's a great many people, earn very good yearly incomes. However, parents and people outside the art world are always somewhat anxious about freelance careers. They seem unstable, and most people feel it is not a lifestyle arrived at by choice—that if you could get a full-time job with a regular salary, you would do so. Banks, credit card companies, and department stores are hesitant to issue credit or loans to freelancers because there is no employer to back up their assertions that they are qualified for credit. But once you have established a relationship with a bank (that simply means you deposit money regularly and prove you can pay your bills) you can generally overcome their prejudice against your freelance status.

Artists who freelance have a chance to establish very personal relationships with their clients. As a freelancer you tend to work directly for those responsible for the job. The most important factor in finding success as a freelance artist is the ability to ward off anxiety when work is slow and to handle pressure when there is too much work. Because you're responsible for determining your own schedule and work load and for keeping track of all your expenses, it's important to be organized or else even the smallest freelance business can quickly get out of control.

Fine artists are a rather different kind of freelance artist in that they create for no specific client or market. If the artist is connected to a gallery, his or her paintings, drawings, or sculpture are sold through the gallery, which relieves the artist of some of the burden of marketing the work. However, if the gallery does not or cannot sell the art, the artist does not get paid. Having a gallery is not a guarantee of a living wage. Most artists also look for private patrons to buy their work. And some fine artists have non-art jobs to pay the rent, so they in fact have two businesses. As does any freelancer, the fine artist too must keep careful track of all expenses and of all sales, which are usually reported quarterly to the government.

DEVELOPING STRONG COMMUNICATION SKILLS is becoming more and more important for people in all areas of the visual arts. Today artists have to deal with many more people socially and professionally than they did in the past. No artist dependent on selling work for a living can hope to avoid communication with other people, so it makes sense to learn to do it well. (Visual people sometimes have to work harder at developing communication skills—perhaps because they are trained to let pictures do their talking.) The ability to articulate ideas, speak clearly and naturally, and write simply and directly can only help you in your career.

The commercial artist, illustrator, designer, art director, or photographer generally works with other people from the beginning of the creative process to the final product. In order to maintain a measure of control, you must be able to explain the strengths of your concept as well as to articulate the weaknesses of the concepts of others, and to do it persuasively. You will also have letters and memos to write. They should be written in good form, with no misspelled words and with careful attention to grammar and style. A letter that represents you should sound like you—and should say what you want it to say.

Those who have experienced difficulty presenting ideas verbally should take a basic speech course that focuses on speaking extemporaneously. It will help you overcome self-consciousness and will build your confidence. The idea is not to train to become a public speaker, but simply to get you used to the idea of thinking and talking on your feet.

The fine artist, too, although he or she generally works alone, must venture out into the world to talk with dealers, potential clients, clients, and maybe an occasional reporter or museum director. If you become successful, you could be asked to speak at public functions, to write an article, or to recommend a colleague for a grant. All of this is part of the business of art.

And on a personal level too, knowing how to express yourself can make a major difference in your life. In many ways, verbal and written skills can mean the difference between ordinary achievement and extraordinary accomplishment.

BECOMING AN ARTIST ISN'T THE EASIEST WAY TO BECOME RICH AND FAMOUS, but today there are more opportunities and possibilities to earn a living with your art than ever before. The reason lies with the expanded definition of what an artist is. In the past, an artist was someone who painted paintings or carved stone into sculpture. But with new materials and new technology, the market for art goes beyond private collectors to commerce, industry, communications, and business. Art of all kinds—film, video, photography, illustration, as well as painting and sculpture—is being used and appreciated.

The creative process has gone mainstream. Even the fine artist is freed from the limitations of traditional definitions of painting and sculpture—if the materials are conventional, the subject matter and form are less restrictive. Work exhibited in galleries can draw its influence from the streets, from media, from traditional crafts. Video art is earning credibility. Photography is now perceived as art rather than technology.

The fine arts, still regarded as the elite among the visual arts, remain the most difficult way an artist can earn a real living. Recently, there have been stories in the media about young artists and young art dealers who are making their fame and fortune in the fine art world, but most artists do not become rich from selling their art. A few can live on the income from their paintings and sculpture. But the majority of artists, young and old, inexperienced and experienced, show when they can, teach perhaps and sell a few paintings privately. The problem is that there are still too few galleries to handle the work of the number of artists who want to show.

But a new trend seems to be surfacing that could benefit all artists, giving them the opportunity to use their creative talents in many areas. The line between the fine arts and the so-called commercial arts is beginning to fade, and the crossover of artists to one field from another is more evident and certainly more possible than it was even a decade ago. Just as country singers are now singing mainstream pop music and young opera singers now perform pop and jazz in appearances on television—likewise we find the works of commercial artists being hung in fine art galleries and music videos being shown in museum exhibitions. Such trends usually evolve because the artists chose to ignore barriers. In such times innovation is prevalent and the arts flourish.

The elitism within the visual arts has been based on long-standing tradition. In art schools, the lines are clearly defined—the fine artist, even though poor, produces a product more "pure" than the illustrator, thus denying the illustrator entrance to the club of "real artists"—i.e., those who do no work for commercial sources. But today's young artists, brought up on video and film as well as printed matter, have different attitudes about the "purity" of their art. They feel that to gain money from their work—whether it is displayed in galleries or used by the media—is not dishonorable and that financial success can only add to their reputations as artists. Such beliefs change existing situations in the marketplace. If the artists do not maintain an elitist position, the critics, viewers, and dealers can't maintain it either.

In the future it is possible that artists will work in a variety of fields over a lifetime. They will have areas of major interest, and one or several areas of minor interest, thus giving them a variety of avenues by which to earn a living. Presently artists can earn a substantial living in the purely commercial fields. "Commercial" work is defined as that which meets the minds and needs of other people. This does not necessarily mean abdicating all creative control, but the commercial artist has nowhere near the same freedom allowed the fine artist. On the other hand the financial rewards for the majority of commercial artists are substantial. Is it any wonder that a fine artist on occasion is willing to forego artistic freedom for money to pay the rent?

As we said in the beginning, becoming an artist may not be the route to wealth, but you could be one of the few. It may not be the route to fame either, though fame may come more easily than wealth. Yet to become both rich and famous in art is no rarer that it is in music or law or medicine.

A FEW WORDS ABOUT SALARIES in the visual arts. As a visual artist your income will depend on a number of variables—such as the size of the city in which you work, the size and profitability of the company for which you work, your experience and talent, and the demand for your work.

In large cities salaries tend to be higher simply because the cost of living is higher. And typically, large companies pay more than small companies. In general, you can assume that if some one earns a salary above $40,000, he or she is experienced and has a record of successes. Women and men with two to five years experience generally command the salaries in the middle range—between $18,000 and $40,000. Starting salaries in art are relatively low, compared with jobs in other professions, ranging between $12,000 and $25,000. There are other factors involved in compensation, however, and they should be considered carefully before you decide on a job. For instance, some companies offer very good profit-sharing plans, medical insurance, and bonuses, while paying lower weekly salaries. Others pay on a very high scale but offer few or no benefits.

In the visual arts, the lowest and the highest incomes go to freelance artists. You can probably count on earning no more than $8000 your first year as a freelance illustrator. Yes, you could make more as a part-time waiter, and many do, subsidizing their art during those early years. Part-time work is often available in large cities, particularly where many businesses and corporations have instituted flexible working hours. Restaurants, banks, and telephone-answering services need help at all hours of the day and night.

Eventually you'll probably start to make more money from your art alone. The most successful freelance designers and illustrators earn yearly incomes above $50,000. A few earn above $100,000. But even their income level can rise or drop radically from year to year. Freelance assignments from advertising agencies, movie studios, and various promotional campaigns are very lucrative. The experienced freelancer knows the plum job is rare, but with a good agent it's possible to pick one up fairly regularly.

Even if you are beginning your freelance career, there are opportunities that can change your financial outlook. Often just one freelance assignment can net you more than a salaried person doing the same thing could earn in a week. That is one compelling reason for going freelance.

Some young artists may need to be subsidized for their first few years in the field. Within the last twenty years, the economics of this country have changed greatly. Twenty years ago, perhaps even ten years ago, it was possible for someone starting out to live, if not comfortably, at least adequately, on what she or he could earn on a beginner's job or on a few freelance assignments. But inflation has driven up the costs of rent, food, and transportation, and many young people, especially in cities, are sharing living space or studio space for a couple of years after college until salaries or assignments allow them to move out on their own. It's often an advantageous arrangement, especially if you share space with other artists. They will better understand your hours and working habits and needs. Even experienced artists share space these days, not only for financial reasons, but also because to work alone day after day is isolating and lonely.

THERE ARE EXCELLENT OPPORTUNITIES FOR WOMEN in the visual arts. There are female designers, art directors, film editors, illustrators, photographers, sculptors, and painters. Women hold management jobs in advertising agencies and studios. And in general, salaries for women compare favorably with those for men in the same categories.

Yet relative to the number of men working in the visual arts, there are still few women. The chairman of the illustration department of a large art college noted that his most gifted and talented students in school each year were women, but five years out of school, very few of those women were still in the field and even fewer had met the same success as lesser-talented men. It is not clear why this is so. Perhaps marriage and children become priorities for women, making it difficult for them to find the time for work that is needed for success in art. Creation takes not only time, but energy and focus. And if a person is to achieve excellence, work must sometimes take priority over other things—even so, the arts are an ideal field for women. Few clients care whether a man or woman designs a dress, an ad, a package, a poster, or a chair—or who creates a sculpture or painting. The criteria for judgment are the same. However, the visual arts *are* very competitive and only those who are aggressive in their pursuit find doors opening. Women who enter traditionally male fields like law or medicine gear themselves up for the competition they know they'll face. Women who choose a career in art will need the same kind of dedication and sense of competitiveness to succeed.

Women who do succeed in the visual arts can expect personal and professional rewards, particularly in fields such as advertising and design where their contributions have equal impact and where there is more of a tradition of assigning power and responsibility to whomever can handle it, regardless of gender.

If you are a woman and you want to become an artist, know that there are as many opportunities for you as there are for men. Set your sights high, develop your talent, get experience while you're in school, and go for the same jobs the men are after. (They're the best jobs or the men wouldn't want them.) Remember that it is as important for you as it is for any man in the field to have the opportunity for a creative life.

IT'S IMPORTANT FOR ANYONE WHO IS TRYING TO DECIDE ON A CAREER IN ART to hear the stories of those who have actually worked in the field and who have achieved success because of their talent. Knowing that, I have concluded each of the subsequent chapters in this book with excerpts from interviews I conducted with various professional artists who are highly regarded in some branch of the field of art discussed in the chapter.

It was fascinating to talk with such a broad range of creative people. Some went to art school, others learned on their own; some started their own companies, others have preferred to work for someone else. All of them were generous with their time, taking hours out of very hectic professional schedules to discuss both the practical and spiritual aspects of their lifework with me, and I am glad to share their views with you.*

I have chosen to include interviews that reveal a wide range of experience. I have not included an interview for *every* career category, though some career categories are represented by several artists. Note, in particular, the differences of opinion about their profession often expressed by people in the same field, and note how their perceptions of money and success, and the future, differ. There is obviously no one right or wrong way to see, feel, or think.

---

*I share their views if not their exact words. In the interest of summarizing many hours of discussion and long passages of transcriptions, I have often paraphrased the artists' words rather than always quoting them directly.

Consider the content of the interviews as tips from successful professionals, not as hard and fast rules. Even experienced professionals can be wrong and, as most of them will admit, they often are. Remember that, in the end, no matter how much advice professionals give you, you have to do it on your own. Personal qualities such as talent and ambition as well as opportunity and sheer luck are the major factors in anyone's path to achieving career goals.

I learned a great deal about each career field from the very candid opinions, observations, and experiences of the artists interviewed. I understand now why these artists have achieved so much in their professions. Their energy, enthusiasm, and commitment to the work they do is very impressive. My thanks to them all for their patience and consideration, for being interesting and fun to talk with, and for giving me the opportunity to spend time with some uniquely talented people.

1

Art Direction

CAREERS in art direction are exactly that—directing artistic products rather than personally creating them. Art direction opportunities are available in advertising and promotional work, editorial fields, and film. But the work is essentially the same in all these areas. Art directors are given a set of criteria within which they work. These criteria are usually determined by the client, the person or company who controls the product. Most large companies have marketing departments to help establish the criteria. Such companies have many fancy techniques for determining the market for their products. They use those techniques to determine how best to get their message across to the consumer. Who is most likely to buy the product? What kind of communication will reach the largest number of those consumers who will actually buy the product? Should they use radio or newspapers or television? Armed with the client's answers to such questions, an art director, often working with a copywriter, creates a concept, hires people to execute it, and then supervises the production. The product of an art director's skills is effective communication.

Marketing principles and sales jargon are as much a part of the education of the art director as they are of the corporate executive. The successful art director will begin his or her creative functioning from a business base. Talented art directors use their imagination and knowledge to satisfy the clients' requirements in fresh and exciting ways. Occasionally what is first perceived as a limitation can become the basis of a highly original concept. For instance, in the early sixties, Doyle Dane Bernbach became famous for the advertising program they designed for Volkswagen. At that time, large American cars were the order of the day. How would they sell a very small, quite undistinguished-looking German-made car to an American market? They did it by figuring out that as more and more people moved to the cities they would need smaller, less-expensive cars and that they would probably be willing to forgo Detroit styling. Doyle Dane needed to appeal to those consumers in a provocative way. They did so with a series of black-and-white ads in which the small, now-classic Volkswagen "bug" was introduced to a waiting public under a one-word headline: "Lemon." It was a headline that would go into the textbooks on advertising. The accompanying copy went on to allay people's fears about small cars and in very straightforward terms outlined all their advantages.

People bought the "lemon," and the entire automobile industry had to begin rethinking their approach to the American car market. There are many stories like this; they all begin with a creative idea, with a creative person who combined business principles with imagination, who risked moving in a new direction. These days the economy is tighter than in the sixties, and the innovative, creative person is in ever greater demand. But the challenges are more difficult. For all the talk about business background and corporate responsibility, art direction is still a career in *creativity*. Any artist who decides on it will do well to continue developing creative as well as business skills, to seek out people with expertise and talent in many fields—above all, the person who goes into art direction will do well to maintain a continuing interest in the creative process.

Art direction is a very demanding career; in addition to creative responsibilities and marketing skills, one needs social skills, communication skills, a knowledge of the production process (layout, printing, etc.), and a background in finance. But as we have said before, the creative abilities are the most important to the art director, and while you are in school you should concentrate on developing those. Get better at drawing and painting, try design and illustration and photography, learn to use a camera, make films and videos. The more you know about the different artistic processes, the more valuable you will be on the job.

Art direction is often combined with graphic design, so in most art schools, people studying either of these fields become skilled in both, though specializing in one. Advertising art direction focuses on selling. Other kinds of art direction usually require a balance of both selling and design, with design having slightly more weight. Some people feel more comfortable with one than the other. But with a background in both advertising and design, the artist has a measure of flexibility in the job market—and is also assured of the possibility of more than one career in a lifetime.

Advertising, or promotional, art direction ranks among the more highly paid of all the careers in the visual arts. But while the field is very lucrative, it also has high risk potential. Anyone in it can count on being out of work at least once or twice during his or her working life because of a management change, the loss of a client, or simply an economic cutback. But this should not be considered as a negative. Most people regard a career as a way to a stable life: Security is their guide in making choices. But for creative people, a change in jobs or environment is often a stimulus. It spurs them to challenge themselves. If you haven't been fired from a job by the time you reach a plateau in that job where your learning becomes minimal, you should be looking for a new position anyway. Naturally the best time to be looking for a new position is while you're still in your old one.

Advertising Art Direction

Advertising is a business created by other businesses to sell their products and their services. Selling is what advertising is all about. And this "selling" has created an entire industry of specialized communication. Corporations do a great deal of market research; they devise tests to try to determine what products people want and how best to advertise those products.

Based on this information, the advertising art director and copywriter create concepts for sales campaigns and produce the advertising materials. Because researchers are not always the scientists they should be and consumers are not always honest in survey responses, advertising campaigns do not always produce hit records, bestselling books, blockbuster movies or successful candidates.

A case in point was the introduction of the "new" Coca-Cola in 1985, a product designed to increase the company's cola market share. Research and testing had established what seemed to be a definite changing pattern in cola tastes, yet the new product failed to such a degree that the Coca-Cola company was forced to bring back the "classic" Coke after having taken it off the market. This is the long way of saying that advertising professionals must balance their business and technical training with strong doses of intuition—the most valuable of the artistic talents they bring to their job.

But while most successful people in the business rely strongly on intuition, they learn to express such feelings in ways that will be understood by more literal people. Advertising generates as many jokes about "them" and "us" as does the movie business, the record business—any industry that puts creative people in touch with businesspeople. It's important to recognize the differences in the approach to life that separate creative people from everyone else; it's especially important for anyone who works in a field where the product is the result of a creative process.

Advertising communication is a complete integration of the visual, the spoken, and the written. Such communication must be created and adapted for specific media—for television, radio, magazines, newspapers, and billboards. To be successful in advertising you should understand how each medium functions; you should appreciate the strengths and weaknesses of each. You may feel more comfortable working in one medium than in another, you may get greater satisfaction in working with the printed page than with film, but you should learn to work in all the media.

The role of the art director in advertising is a powerful one. Along with a copywriter, you hire all the creative talent. This means many people will want to present portfolios or videos or films to you in hopes of getting work. The art directors and copywriters who always take the time to see and consider new work are often those who are the most successful. No doubt, this success comes because they are continually exposed to new input and new ideas, and are presented with different solutions to some old problems. Those who regard the process of viewing portfolios as tedious often discover their own work becoming stale and uninspired. Advertising is like the fashion business. There are the trendsetters and the conservatives. The trendsetters make news; the conservatives seldom do. Exposure to new ideas of any kind, particularly for an art director, is essential.

BASIC RESPONSIBILITIES An advertising art director works with a copywriter in most agencies. The art director is primarily responsible for the visuals. A copywriter handles the words, or "copy." But it is really a collaborative relationship, where both work together to come up with a concept that can be developed into a successful print ad, television commercial, or complete sales campaign (that is to say, a series of print ads, TV and perhaps even radio commercials, and billboards).

Most agencies hire a creative director who is responsible for all the creative personnel (such as art directors and copywriters) in the company. He or she is usually an experienced art director or writer with management skills developed while working on individual accounts at one or more agencies. Depending on the size of the agency, a number of associate creative directors may be appointed in turn by the creative director. They can be selected from either the art or copy end of the business. Each of the associate creative directors is responsible for a group of accounts and for the people who work on them.

Although all art directors (and writers) must be knowledgeable about both print and electronic media (television, radio, and video), most prefer one medium to the other, and often that preference is reflected in their portfolios. One art director may have a reel with a few ads. Another may have a strong printed portfolio and just a few commercials. However, the reason for this may be circumstantial rather than preferential: The agency may have larger print accounts, or vice versa, and an employee's portfolio will reflect that. In designing your first portfolio, make sure it shows your major interest. If you want to work on television accounts, your storyboards need to be strong, and you would do well to apply for jobs at agencies whose strengths are in television. In general, if you enjoy doing one certain thing, odds are you do it better than you do most other things. Some people visualize in moving pictures. Others like their pictures to be still. In looking for a job, it's good to know your own strengths.

Advertising concepts developed by art directors and writers are usually based on research provided by the marketing departments of their agencies in cooperation with client specifications. Information about the market, about the likes and dislikes of consumers, is important in coming up with a concept, or a central idea, for presenting the product to the market it's designed to sell in. It may be as simple as getting a famous person to endorse a product or as complicated as getting cats to appear as if they are talking. Shearson–American Express has used provocative copy on the screen for thirty seconds as their total message. They have chosen a very inexpensive but impactful way of getting their message across. It works because their copy is strong and the direction fresh. On the other hand, both Pepsi and Coca-Cola have built effective ad campaigns using the production value of many people singing and dancing.

If the concept is for a print advertisement, the art director creates a layout, indicating headline and type, along with a choice of visual. This can be done very informally for presentation to the associate creative director, the creative director, and account executives. But the layout is presented to the client in a more finished form. In many agencies, the art director and the writer themselves will present their concept for an ad or campaign to the client, while in other agencies, the presentation will be made by the creative director or by one of his or her associates. The size and importance of an account often determines who makes the presentation. Smaller accounts entail less agency bureaucracy. Major presentations for large accounts are a team effort by top agency personnel, and the art director and writer are usually a part of that team.

When the concept and layout are approved, the art director and writer choose the photographer or illustrator who will best carry out the concept. The art director is responsible for knowing the work of illustrators and photographers working in the field, and must regularly look at portfolios and consult illustration, photography, and advertising annuals to discover new talent.

Once the client has approved the agency's concept, the art director works with the illustrator or the photographer to create the final visual. Usually, that artist is given a sketch to work from and some direction about the mood and spirit of the picture to be created. With a photographer, the art director is more involved in the process of getting the picture. He or she chooses or approves the model, the props, and the location and is usually present when the photograph is shot.

If the concept calls for a television commercial, the script and storyboard must be approved. The storyboard is a frame-by-frame visualization of what will be seen on the screen, with the copy indicated under each picture. Once the concept is approved, the writer and art director, along with a producer, screen reels of film put together by production houses to show the work of their directors. In many instances, the writer and/or art director act as their own producers. The more experience one has in film and video production, the more likely it is that one can serve the dual function.

Once a director is chosen, the production house, in consultation with the creative team at the agency, sets up the filming. The bud get is approved. Both art director and writer are present at the filming and work with the director to fulfill the concept sold to the client. The film dailies are screened, and both the art director and the writer work with the editor to edit the commercial.

If there is copy to be recorded, in addition to that on film (voice-overs, for instance), the producer reserves time at a recording studio and, together with the art director and the writer, chooses an announcer or actors. If music is necessary, the producer, along with the art director and the writer, chooses a composer to create the music, hires the musicians, and reserves a studio for recording purposes. If singers are necessary, the music production house arranges it. The music, copy, and picture are then "mixed," put together electronically to create a sound track.

The sound track and the picture are screened together as a rough cut. When the commercial is approved by the client, either the art director, the writer, or the producer sees the commercial through to finish with the production house.

SALARIES Advertising generates a great deal of money; therefore, the field tends to pay higher salaries, and also higher fees to outside suppliers such as photographers and illustrators. In general, an art director's salary is dependent on experience, portfolio, and/or reel and personal interviews, as well as on talent. Some agencies pay higher salaries but offer fewer, or less advantageous, benefits. When considering a job, ask about the benefits. These should include health and hospital plans, pension plans, and profit sharing. You may find the benefits justify taking a lower weekly salary. These days, for instance, an excellent health plan is necessary and expensive. The best plans include, in addition to good hospital and surgical benefits, provisions for dental care and psychiatric counseling. Salaries are negotiable, even in beginning jobs, so don't be afraid to ask for what you need or want. When you're starting out, however, remember you have no proven worth, so go easy. On the other hand, realize that all they can do is say no.

EDUCATION AND TRAINING Advertising art direction is a very specialized art career. It is not dependent on being able to draw or paint, although those skills can be useful in all art careers. But it does require a high degree of interest and education in how art is created. You need to know what's happening in all areas of the visual arts; it is also helpful to have a knowledge of theater, theatrical production, music, music production, and fashion. Also important is an awareness of trends in design, decorating, and the fine arts, as well as a genuine curiosity about things that are current in society and some knowledge of human psychology.

Developing computer skills is as essential for the advertising art director as for all art professionals. As the computer becomes more sophisticated, art directors use it increasingly for layouts and presentations, as well as for organizing billings and keeping files on suppliers (photographers, directors, stylists, etc.).

Art direction is also a very socially oriented career. You will be meeting new people constantly and interpersonal skills are invaluable. Public speaking experience is helpful since art directors often have to make presentations. Learn to express ideas clearly and persuasively. It is essential.

The formal education of an art director takes place in school. It's possible to work your way up to the job by starting as a secretary or a mail clerk, but barring extraordinary talent, the move up may take longer than you anticipate. Most advertising art directors are trained in specialized courses of study at an art school or university. These comprise a combination of graphic arts, advertising, and business courses, and an acquisition of practical skills in photography, film, and videotape. Courses in copywriting are usually required. Public speaking and acting courses help you gain self-confidence in presenting yourself to groups of people. The skill to sell your ideas may be as important as having those ideas.

Consider the following training: The most thorough is a four-year program at an accredited college or university with a strong reputation in the commercial art field. Check the catalog to make sure the courses are taught by people with professional reputations who are working in the fields they teach. There are also two-year associate-degree programs to help you begin to develop the skills you need. Beyond that, in large cities there are many competent evening courses taught by professionals. If you choose the evening-school method of getting an education, check with the guidance counselors. They can help you put together both a short- and a long-range program to help you achieve your goals.

LOOKING FOR A JOB You will need a portfolio when you enter the job market. It should contain sample ads, the best you are able to create. The number of ads to include is up to you. There should be enough to show the range of what you do, but not so many that the viewing experience becomes tedious or repetitious. The ads should be as professionally finished as possible. If you have any printed samples, by all means, include them. When personnel people and creative directors look at first portfolios, or "books," they are looking for your ability to come up with interesting, exciting, provocative ideas. They want to see how your mind works. Try not to simply duplicate what you see in the magazines and on the air. They want to know your potential and this may be your one opportunity to show them. Sometimes it is a good idea to create two portfolios—a "reality" book, those ads that show competence, understanding, and technical skill along with good ideas, and a second book featuring "ads I'd love to see," those fresh, innovative ideas that break a few rules and show your ability to design a page creatively.

Ask your teachers and professors for leads to possible jobs. Get names whenever you can. Call ahead for appointments and try to get personal interviews. Be there, if you can, when the person who's hiring looks at your book. Talk to him or her about what you're trying to do. Ask for opinions. Remember you are just starting out. No one expects your book to be perfect. Listen to what professionals tell you, and evaluate their comments. Do not assume that just because someone has a title that person knows what's right for you. On the other hand, do not assume that if the interviewer doesn't like your book he or she must be incompetent. Be open to criticism. If someone seems to like most of what you do, ask if you can return with the book when you've made some changes. Remember, interviewing for a first job is the one time you can play innocent. No one expects you to be a full-fledged professional and you won't be judged by standards applied to experienced artists. You only have to prove that you have the *potential* to be a creative art director.

Advertising is about selling. Make selling yourself the first order of business when you're looking for that job.

EDITORIAL ART DIRECTION

Editorial art direction deals only with print—books, magazines, and newspapers. Positions within those different media are generally interchangeable, although, as in all fields, there are special skills and responsibilities specific to each.

There was a time when editorial art direction was far more concerned with design than with selling, but in today's economy-oriented society, skills in design must be adapted to serve the marketplace. However, having said that, we reiterate that editorial art direction is still primarily concerned with design that is aesthetically pleasing and only secondarily focused on selling. Even though the art director knows magazine covers sell magazines from the newsstand, he or she also knows subscriptions still provide the base for a periodical's financial health. The art director in book publishing is pressured to produce covers that will attract readers, but the fact remains that covers alone do not determine the success of a book. Reviews, authors, and advertising are equally important.

BASIC RESPONSIBILITIES In the publication field, the art director's role is different from the same role in advertising. Unless you are fortunate enough to begin working on a magazine when it is new or when the format is in the process of change, design guidelines are already established and you direct the art product within those specifications. Editors in publishing houses share the responsibility for the final design solution. Unlike the relationship of the advertising art director and the copywriter, where both are specialists in one area but have knowledge, talent, and experience in the other, many editors are strictly word people, with little knowledge when it comes to visuals or design. But remember, the best editors, like the best people in any field, are open and knowledgeable about everything that affects their work.

Before mass-market television and certainly before video, magazines were a main source of information. The visual ones like *Look* and *Life* depended heavily on the skills of the art director to bring interesting, exciting images to the public. *Life* has now returned as a monthly, and other new magazines are constantly appearing to serve new needs and to replace magazines that have gone out of business. The field looks more promising than it has in years. However, the number of magazines is still relatively few compared with the number of art directors looking for a magazine to call their own. Special interest magazines such as *Spin, New Look, Cuisine* and *Ms.* have been a healthy addition to the field. Regional magazines such as *Southern Living* and *Sunset* continue to have strong followings, and it seems that every city, large and small, has its own magazine: *New York, San Francisco, Cleveland,* and *Atlanta* are among those holding their own.

The magazine art director is responsible for laying out the magazine, for accommodating all the elements necessary to the article or story—i.e., type, photography, illustration, and advertising, if there is any. The art director selects the illustrator or photographer to execute the visual and, on approval of the editor or some member of the editorial staff, commissions the work to be done. In some cases, depending on the structure of the magazine, an art director with seniority will make final decisions regarding art. The editorial art director must be knowledgeable about work done by the various illustrators and photographers and must remain informed of new people moving into the field. A good art director sees new work on a regular basis.

Carefully formatted magazines, such as *Time* or *Newsweek*, use computers to make the job of layout simpler and faster. Newsmagazines also need the flexibility to change stories at the last minute, and so the computer is an invaluable tool for both the art director and the editor.

The newspaper art director, and there are usually several on most large papers to handle the different sections, has most of the same responsibilities as the magazine art director. Many large newspapers are computerized, and in time almost all newspapers will be. Computerization makes the work faster and easier and can accommodate the many changes necessary for dealing with news.

Art directors on most papers commission relatively little original illustration. The few assignments made are generally handed out on a freelance basis. The *New York Times* op-ed (opposite editorial) page art director commissions at least one illustration each day. Photography is handled by staff photographers on a day-to-day basis, but occasionally a freelance photographer is commissioned to cover a particular story, generally for the magazine section. The magazine sections of a newspaper provide most of the jobs in art direction on a paper. At smaller newspapers, one person might be responsible for the art content of the whole paper. Like magazine art directors, the newspaper art director assigns a story, making sure the visual is appropriate. He or she is responsible for the layout. Because many newspapers publish on a daily basis, the pressure can be intense, particularly if there are last-minute developments in the news that have to make the deadline.

There are two categories of art directors in the book field, but we are primarily concerned with only one category—the art director who designs or supervises the design of the book covers. The other kind of art director carries the same title, but is concerned only with the type on the inside of the book. This work is very technical and detailed, and although it can be creative, it does not necessarily require a design background. However, the art director hired to oversee book covers must have a strong design education.

Exactly how much design work is required on the job is dependent on the kind of publishing house you work for. The book art director is responsible for hiring the illustrator or the photographer and directing that artist toward the kind of imagery that will best sell the book. As a designer, the director's responsibilities include evolving a concept for the cover that incorporates a type and an image compatible with the book's content.

Art directors in publishing houses that do trade books—fiction and nonfiction for the general public—concentrate on book covers. They may also design the seasonal catalog and advertising materials to promote books. In these areas, knowledge of marketing and advertising principles is very valuable. Mass-market paperback publishing houses, in particular, may look for business skills in addition to design talent in their art directors.

Some publishing houses specialize—in picture books, art books, design books, books on architecture, cookbooks, or gift books of various kinds. Such houses need art directors who are, in fact, graphic designers. Their portfolios should focus on innovative design concepts and should reflect a publication background.

Be aware that book art directors today are required to have many flexible skills.

SALARIES Salaries in the publications field are generally lower than those in the advertising field. The reason is simply lower profit margins. However, as with all salaries, they tend to fluctuate in direct proportion to the size and profitability of the company. Large companies with high profits pay wages that compare favorably with the salaries of experienced advertising art directors. Beginning salaries in publications, however, are lower, and in general, the median income for editorial art directors is about 10 percent less than that for advertising art directors.

As in most art careers, salaries in publishing are usually negotiable. Ask about the benefits. If the salaries are low, perhaps insurance, profit sharing, and other benefits are substantial. Check around to find out what the going wage is for your job category. In fields where there is strong competition, employers will try to hire you for the least money. Don't turn down a job on the basis of money alone. If they hold out the promise of interesting work, more creative control, and an opportunity to learn the business, explore the offer further. Working with top professionals who are willing to teach you what they know on the job is sometimes worth a little less money. If you want the job and the salary is truly ridiculous, try reasoning with your prospective employer. Maybe you can work part-time and get a job doing something else to make up the difference. Be creative.

EDUCATION AND TRAINING Editorial art direction is basically a career in graphic design; however, it could be very valuable to develop many of the skills of the advertising art director. If editorial art direction is your interest while you are in school, talk with your advisor about taking some advertising courses. Learn about marketing and selling. The editorial field is rapidly incorporating the language of advertising into its vocabulary.

Learn to use the computer. More and more magazines and newspapers as well as publishing houses are becoming computerized. Try some courses in computer graphics. In the future, such knowledge will be invaluable in these businesses.

As in advertising, social and communication skills are important here. Much of an editorial art director's job is dealing with other people—presenting ideas, explaining what is needed, explaining why something doesn't work, discussing money. Tact, charm, and persuasiveness are qualities that can make one's job easier and finally, more successful.

A four-year program in graphic design makes the most sense for someone considering editorial art direction as a career. Take some courses in basic advertising, photography, and illustration. Use extracurricular time to work with the college humor magazine, newspaper, or other school publication. Explore and experiment with new forms in magazines. They may never be published, but you'll learn a lot about what you like. Check out your library and the neighborhood magazine stands; read everything from comic books to the *Wall Street Journal*. Think about why you like some publications and why you hate others. Make the habit of looking at all printed matter a part of your life.

LOOKING FOR A JOB Pursuing a job in editorial art direction requires the same focus and planning as looking for work in advertising. You will need a portfolio. The work should include your best samples from class assignments as well as any printed work you might have done. Use all the connections you have—teachers, family, friends, and clients if you have any. Learn from the interviewing experience and apply what you learn to your next interview. Not getting a job need not be a rejection. Think of it as an opportunity for more polished future interviews.

FILM AND TELEVISION ART DIRECTION

Art direction in film and television is defined differently than it is in the other visual arts. The union definition places it in the category of scenic design, as in theater. In most film schools, the category of film art direction, per se, isn't designated as a major field of study; nevertheless, the student must be aware there is such a career and should choose course work that will support the interest. It is a limited field and most people who are successful in it get their education through practical experience, working as an apprentice to a scenic designer in summer stock or taking courses in scenic design at a college or university that offers a major in theater arts.

BASIC RESPONSIBILITIES There is much confusion about titles in this category. They do not always reflect the responsibilities of the job; compounding the confusion is the fact that in the visual arts people use titles interchangeably. So it is best to question a title, and ask what the responsibilities of the job are, even if you think you know. In a major studio that produces feature films, there is generally a distinguishable hierarchy. There is a production designer in charge of the total "look" of a film, including locations, sets, props, graphics, and costumes. Under the production designer is an art director with a staff and a costume designer with a staff. The art director is involved with budget, location, sets, and props. In smaller independent films, all the work of the scenic designer, costume designer, and art director is often done by one person who has a strong background in art and who chooses his or her own title.

SALARIES Salaries are dependent on your experience, your knowledge, and the quality of work in your portfolio and on your film reel. There are union guidelines for art directors on feature films and television films, but these guidelines simply determine minimums for a particular category. Many people beginning careers in this field work virtually for expenses and a credit.

EDUCATION AND TRAINING Although editorial art direction and advertising art direction are the two major career fields within art direction, the training for either can lead to other closely allied careers (as in film art direction). Colleges and universities tend to train people for established job categories. Special areas that might be a career possibility for the right person might not appear in a catalog, either because the institution feels the field is not sufficiently developed to warrant a course or because the institution doesn't know of its existence. In other instances where no specific curriculum or course exists and you *know* of career possibilities, a special program can sometimes be designed to meet the idiosyncratic needs of the job. Most schools will be happy to accommodate you and will be able to skirt the bureaucracy to allow you to take the courses you feel you need.

INTERVIEWS

ANDREW BONCHER

Advertising Art Director/Creative Director
Vice President, McCann Erickson, International

A graduate of Pratt Institute in advertising, Andrew Boncher began his career as a television art director at Grey Advertising where he worked for eleven years on such accounts as Ford, Greyhound, Howard Johnson, General Foods, Procter & Gamble, Gillette, Lorillard, Renfield Importers, and Mitchum-Thayer. In 1977 he was hired by Norman Craig and Kummel to work on Chanel, Colgate, Saab, and Olins. In 1979 Boncher joined McCann Erickson as an art director; his account responsibilities there have included Mennen, Gillette, and Johnson & Johnson. As creative director of McCann International, he and his group are responsible for about $75 million worth of billings on the R. J. Reynolds Camel account worldwide.

ON GETTING STARTED: I was interested in filmmaking. And when I was in school at Pratt Institute, the only area that offered filmmaking was advertising. So I kind of came in through the back door. On graduating from school, the jobs I was offered at the film studios were things like sweeping the floors. After four years of college I didn't feel I wanted to do that, so I started looking for jobs in advertising. I interviewed at two agencies and was accepted at both. After six months, I had my first commercial on the air. The first three years of my career were totally television. I didn't do any print at all.

ON PORTFOLIOS: When I came up for my first interview at Grey Advertising, I wanted to do TV and I told the creative director that. He said, "How come your book doesn't have TV? It's got record covers and mechanicals and things like that." That was on a Friday afternoon. He asked me to come back the following Monday. I did, with a totally different portfolio; it was nothing but television commercials. It's the advice I've given other people since then; your book has to reflect what you want to do. Especially because most of the books are looked at without the person present. So if you have a roomful of ten or fifteen applicants for a job, you have several assumptions. One—that the work in the book is what the applicant considers to be good work. That he or she wants to be represented by it. That the work reflects the kinds of things the applicant wants to do. Kids have come in for an interview, the same way I did, with a book that didn't represent their goals. They come in with what the Dean of Admissions says their book should be. They show bullpen skills, and that's the kind of job they'll get. Today in the agency, unlike in my day, we don't promote out of the bullpen unless it's a very small shop and it's a very intimate relationship and it's understood that a kid is going to progress on a line. A place like McCann Erickson does not train its people.

ON THE QUALITY OF TODAY'S PORTFOLIOS: I'm seeing kids coming in now, I admit most of them are coming to me from the School of Visual Arts, which has always been a professional school as opposed to being simply an art school. But I'd say most of the books I look at today are put together by some canny kids who know what they want to do. Their teachers and instructors tend to be professional artists, whereas when I was in school they were professional teachers. So they were giving assignments and they were producing students that were maybe ten, fifteen, twenty years behind the times. I don't get that impression now.

ON EDUCATION: I think a professional school is the best way to come into the business. However, I think you have to understand there is a limit to what you learn in a professional school. I would say that my first week on the job I learned more about the business than I did during the four years I was in college. That's not to say college isn't valuable, but as it relates to the business world, there's nothing like actually being in the business.

ON THE FUTURE OF ADVERTISING: I think this is probably the first time in history that this industry—and it may even be other industries as well—is not providing for its own future. Part of that is that the technology is changing so rapidly. I think if you went out of this door right now and talked with the first ten art directors you came to, I'd say nine out of those ten have never worked on some of the more contemporary and current pieces of technology, computers with animation and so on. It seems every time you're given an assignment now, you have to reeducate yourself as to what's available, if you're going to come up with a solution. It's mind-boggling how quickly it's changing. But I don't think the companies, and this is a criticism, feel it's their obligation to keep their people up to date.

The whole world is caught up in technology, and advertising is no different. I could take you to a writer, right now, who doesn't have a file cabinet in his room. He does have a computer. And everything he's ever written in the last fifteen years is on a floppy disk. That is using technology to make his life a little easier. There's also technology, at least from the art director's point of view, that is absolutely crucial in creating images.

ON SUCCESS: I measured it in a lot less money when I started out than I do now. I thought if I could make $20,000 a year I'd be set forever. Obviously, that's changed.

I didn't expect to stay in the business as long as I did. I really thought this was going to be a temporary stopover until I was able to get myself established enough so I could start working my way into films. But, I'm happy with my choices.

Today success is a constantly evolving thing. It's just a question of being happy at what I do. I can't think of anything I'd enjoy doing more. Success, I think, is within the work. Every time you're given a problem and you come up with a solution, it's a success—sometimes you have bigger successes than other times. I think I'm more successful at arriving at solutions than I used to be, and I hope I continue to have a better average.

ON THE SATISFACTIONS: I think that each stage in the development of an ad has its own satisfactions. Maybe the thing I love most about the business is that, as you go from one account to another, you learn about another piece of business. When you're working on cars, you get immersed in automobiles. I was working on a woman's contraceptive; I learned an awful lot about my wife, more than I did in the Lamaze courses we took together while we were waiting for babies. Because of the nature of the business, I feel I'm still in school. There's that constant learning. And, I must admit, it's fun.

There's also the challenge I find very satisfying. I don't think I ever had an instance where I've had the same problem twice. I've been in the business twenty years and I've worked on close to fifty or sixty accounts. The world is constantly changing, the people you're selling to are constantly changing, and even the way we sell to them is changing.

Then there's the recognition of your peers. There's a great deal of satisfaction in that. It comes in the form of salaries, and it comes in the form of titles and awards, although I don't think that's the chief thing. It's loving what you're doing. I guess that's true for any business you go into.

ON MONEY: It's probably one of the few businesses in the world where there is no ceiling on what you can make. I know a creative director who's making $45,000 a year. I know a creative director who's making $250,000 a year. They both work for the same company. Obviously, the guy making the quarter of a million is believed by the company to be very, very, very valuable to them. Not necessarily because of the work he does, but because of the client that stays with the company because of him. So, in his case, there's a cachet attached to his name that is worth those kinds of bucks. I don't think *any* art director (and let's face it, in his case, he's a creative director whose discipline is art) is worth a quarter of a million dollars! But if there is a client who is spending ten, fifteen, twenty times that much in commissions because of his presence, then absolutely he's worth that much.

ON THE CENTERS FOR ADVERTISING: I don't think New York is mecca any more. Maybe that's wrong. Maybe it is mecca, but it's not the only mecca. There are other places you can go. Obviously, the major companies are all still headquartered in New York. Even though McCann Erickson has offices in eight or nine cities in the U.S., this is still the flagship. There's a feeling that you've arrived if you're working for a New York agency. But I know many people who are much happier working out of New York than they were when they were working here. They're enjoying better lifestyles and they're doing great work. They have a much more intimate relationship with their clients.

ON HAVING A PERSONAL LIFE: I think the longer you're in the business, the less likely you are to lose control of your time. Certainly, when you enter the business, you cannot control the amount of time you spend at work. It's an axiom: You've got to pay for what you get. As you get older, you're still spending a lot of time, in some cases more time, on business; but you're at least controlling it. The guys who are the chairman of the board, the president of the agency, they spend six, seven days a week working.

ON ADVICE TO YOUNG PEOPLE: Don't ever present work that doesn't represent your best thinking and what you want to do.

RON TRAVISANO
Advertising Commercial Director/Art Director
Partner, Travisano DiGiacomo Films

In 1967, only seven years out of college, Ron Travisano became founder, along with Jerry Della Femina, of his own advertising *agency—Della Femina, Travisano and Partners. It became the thirty-fourth-largest advertising agency in the world under his guidance, with a reputation for creating advertising that was fresh, unique, and effective. But in 1985 Ron Travisano left the $205 million agency to pursue another of his artistic passions, directing. The new production company, Travisano DiGiacomo Films, allows him to devote full time to directing, a talent he developed at Della Femina, Travisano on such memorable commercials as Meow Mix, Tuesday Team's Statue of Liberty, Pacific Southwest Airlines, and Lloyds Bank California. Travisano has won every award in the advertising field, some many times. He has taught advertising design and concept on a regular basis for eighteen years at the School of Visual Arts and has taught in the master's degree program at Syracuse University. In 1985 he wrote and directed a seventeen-minute docudrama, "Africa, the Possibility," for the Hunger Project. He was a member of the Tuesday Team, which handled the advertising to reelect President Reagan, and was responsible for creating and directing much of the advertising for that political campaign.*

ON GETTING STARTED: When I was a kid, maybe 5 years old, I drew a picture of Mickey Mouse and it looked just like him. Everybody gave me a lot of praise. It's not that I understood what I was doing, but I guess when I saw how much attention I got for doing it, I said, well, maybe I should do more. At one point somebody called me an artist, and then I just understood that I was an artist.

I went to this private high school—no art courses, but again, I got a lot of attention because I was the only who could draw, and I used to have little exhibits in school. Wherever I went I always stood out as an artist, and it was very important to me. My mother wanted me to become a doctor, but as soon as I failed biology, we knew it was a wrong direction for me. I decided I wanted to go to art school. I applied to two—one was Cooper Union and the other Pratt Institute. I didn't get into Cooper, so I went to Pratt.

Between my junior and senior year at Pratt, I went for a summer internship at Young & Rubicam and I was lucky enough to be the one student they hired. What it really meant was you worked in this supply room and ordered paints and mixed rubber cement and cut mats, but at least I was in the right environment to get a feel for the business I might enter. When I graduated from Pratt, the next year, I went back to Y & R for a job. Actually, I went for two job interviews—one at a pharmaceutical agency who offered me $85 a week, and the other at Young & Rubicam who offered $75. But I was really turned on by the Young & Rubicam situation because they had never hired back any of their summer interns. I was the first one.

ON EDUCATION TODAY: My feeling is, when you want to do something, you'll do it no matter what. But, of course, the most sensible thing to do is go to an advertising school. To me, probably the best art school in the country is the School of Visual Arts—this sounds like a commercial, but it's not. There are actually a lot of good schools, but getting into the business is a little tougher now. It used to be that all you had to do was be a graphics person and make things look nice, but nowadays you have to be much more of a strategic thinker, much more of a marketing person. So you really want to go to school and get that kind of background.

I've been teaching at the School of Visual Arts for eighteen years, and when students come out of my class they know how to take a product, examine it, look at it in the marketplace, and decide how to position it. So when they begin to create an ad, it isn't something off the tops of their heads—it's advertising that is reaching out and looking to communicate to somebody for a specific reason. Can you learn that on the job and not go to school? Sure. But you have to get the job, number one. And number two, from 18 to 22, why not be in a place where you can get that kind of backing? Also, another wonderful thing about going to school, it's another experience in life. For you to be any kind of good creative person, whether you're doing advertising, painting, book or screenplay writing, whatever it is, you need to have observed and experienced life, so you can draw on it. I tell my students to think of themselves as a computer bank. The more information they can call on when they create, the better.

ON PORTFOLIOS: Mostly I'm looking for somebody who can think, who knows how to communicate to people on more than just a simple level. You have to be somewhat of a psychiatrist, you have to be somewhat of a lover of people, you have to be sensitive. And when someone has those qualities, it shows up in the work. Another thing I'm looking for is good design. You can have great thinking in advertising, but if you put it down on a page and it's not attractive, nobody's ever going to stop to look at it.

I'm looking for someone who's verbal, who can present himself or herself. This is the part that's not in the portfolio. Part of advertising is selling your work, presenting yourself and your work, because what good is having a good ad if you can't convince a client to run it in a magazine or on television? But basically what I'm looking for in a young person is good thinking and good design.

ON SUCCESS: What success meant to me when I first started was nothing. Because I didn't know what success meant. I told you the story of my starting out and getting a lot of attention. I needed attention, I really needed to get attention. So I was very lucky in one way to become very successful at a very early age.

Only seven years after I graduated from college, I had my own advertising agency. And within two years, I was "very successful." I had all the material things, all the pats on the back one could need in life. I had a beautiful family, a beautiful home. I had everything one could ever want, and I still wasn't happy. I began to realize that success is really in the eyes of the beholder. What I had didn't mean anything. I was looking, desperately, for satisfaction in life, and I couldn't find it. It was at that point, I began to take a trip into myself. What I discovered was you can't get satisfaction out in the world, you have to be satisfied inside, then bring it out. I went to swamis, I went to EST, I went to shrinks, I examined every possible avenue, and I really did find myself. I became satisfied with myself, and brought that satisfaction to whatever I was doing. I guess what I'm trying to tell you is that success didn't mean anything to me when I didn't know who I was.

ON MONEY: You can make phenomenal amounts of money. It's almost ludicrous and kind of gross when you think about how much money you can make in the advertising business. Everybody knows, anyway, that I've made millions being in advertising, and it seems there're more millions to make.

It's a matter of what you're willing to do, and how hard you're willing to dedicate yourself to make it happen. Any success story you've ever heard from anybody is that they went for it, man, they absolutely went for it. And when I say, "what you're willing to do," I don't mean illegal things, I don't mean stepping on anybody else. It's just a matter of putting yourself out completely, to absolutely live out every possibility you have. To me, life is possibilities. There are two ingredients: the wanting it and the taking the chance to get it. There are a million people who want something but who aren't willing to take a chance to go out and get it. I've always been willing to take a chance. I've given up ownership in the thirty-fourth-largest agency in the world to become a director. People thought I was crazy. They said, why would you want to do that when you already have what you have? It's because I want to direct and if I want to direct, I have to give up what I have to do that. There's this moment of being frightened that goes along with taking a chance, but it's so wonderful when you get to the other side. When you're committed and willing to take a chance, there isn't anything you can't do.

ON BECOMING A DIRECTOR: There was a point at which I decided I was a lot happier when I was on location shooting than I was when I was in the office. It's just a natural evolution. After having done something for eighteen years, we human beings get a bit tired of doing the same things over and over. So I got a little tired of it. The next $5 million account was no longer thrilling to me, and I loved directing. I really think that directing and the business of film is something I'll always be with because it really takes all of my talents, all of the things I love to do in life, and they all come together in this craft. I love to paint and draw still, and I can still draw Mickey Mouse and make it look like him. So the drawing and painting aspect has helped me create a visual that looks good and is designed well. I've always been a photography buff, so my camera eye is thrilled. I've always been a frustrated actor, so I get to play with that. I love being the center of attraction, and as a director, you're the center of attraction. I love designing sets; interior decoration interests me. I love music. I love sound effects. There's no aspect of the film business that I don't love.

ON WORKING FOR YOURSELF: What I love most about working for myself is that I can create the kind of company I want—a company where everybody gets an opportunity to express himself or herself, fully. To best explain what I'm talking about is to tell you what my purpose is in life. It is to use my creative talents to empower others to express themselves. When I'm teaching at the School of Visual Arts, I live out that purpose. I formed this company for that purpose. Everybody in this company and everybody I work with, the crews I hire by the day, everybody has that opportunity for expression. So to have a company like this is very thrilling.

ON THE CREATIVE PROCESS: The process of creating for me is really almost like not creating. An art director and a writer sit in a room, trying to come up with a commercial, and it's almost as if out of this computer bank somewhere these thoughts and feelings and images come out and you kind of review them, you pick and choose which are the right ones to do. It's almost like every advertisement I was ever going to create has already been created, and I just have to allow it to come up.

In advertising, things like client demands or needs—I never looked at them as limitations. They were guidelines. Very often I would create a commercial I thought was wonderful and it was killed. Very often when I came back, I came back with something better.

I think it's probably one of the most important things a young creative person should have, is to live out all the possibilities and to have no limitations. Creative people can't be bound up by practicalness and reasonableness; they have to be freewheeling, unlimited. At one point you're going to have to maybe pull back a little bit, but certainly not when you're at the point of creating.

STEVEN HELLER

Newspaper Art Director; New York Times Book Review

Steven Heller's multifaceted career as art director, editor, and writer have placed him at the center of the New York graphic-design community. Although the New York Times Book Review *is his major responsibility, Heller is also codirector of Push Pin Editions. Among the books he has edited, authored, or produced are* Man Bites Man: Two Decades of Satiric Art, Jules Feiffer's America, The Art of New York, Art against War, The Empire State Building Book, *and many others. He teaches in the M.F.A. illustration program at the School of Visual Arts, is editor of the* AIGA Journal, *and is a contributing editor for* Print, Graphis, *and* International Design. *He serves on the boards of the Swann Foundation for Caricature and Cartoon, the American Institute of Graphic Arts, the Society of Publication Designers, and the Poster Society. Currently he is working on several books, among them,* Innovators of American Illustration, The Literary New York Graphic Style, *and* Graphic Design and Illustration Handbook.

ON GETTING STARTED: I got out of high school with a drawing portfolio that wasn't even a portfolio. It was an envelope of drawings. I took the drawings to different newspapers, underground papers of the time, and asked them if they'd like to publish me. One of them, a magazine that later turned out to be the house organ of a killer religious sect, published the first ones because they were kind of apocalyptic—there were lots of Christs on crosses. I figured I was on a roll. I went to a few other papers and got some other assignments. Then I went to the *New York Free Press* and it just so happened that they needed a pasteup person. I didn't know what pasteup was. The art director had to tell me. I said I'd do it, so he hired me. He taught me how to use glue, they showed me the typesetting machine, and I started, just like that. I was pretty awful, but I learned on the job and I learned from the printer as well.

I liked newspapers. When I was a kid, I had done little newspapers. There was no great compulsion. It was really chance, chance that was pushed by some undefined force. I didn't know what an advertising agency was, and I didn't know what a graphic design studio was. But I knew what a newspaper was.

ON EDUCATION: I think a liberal arts education is the best thing. Ultimately a designer has to be literate and has to have a broad range of interests in the arts. I would think, not having gone to art school and having had a truncated arts education, I'm better for having that. Some schools, like the Columbia School of Journalism, offer courses in graphic design. At NYU, there's a course in graphic design for the would-be journalist. Whether the intention is to make a journalist into a designer or just to give a journalist some sense of what goes on in the design end isn't clear. But I think for anyone going into newspaper design, it's better to know the newspaper business along with design.

ON SUCCESS: Well, what I wanted to do once I decided to do drawings was to be as famous as Jules Feiffer. But I didn't have a clear idea of what success was. If I were to do it all over again, I'd be terrified. That's the good thing about being a student. Innocence. If I'd known the etiquette I probably wouldn't have gone up to the newspaper blind. The etiquette is, you call and make an appointment, and with luck somebody answers the phone. But, back to success. For the first year or so I didn't make any money, so success wasn't measured in terms of money. I measured it by how others responded to my work. The work became important, as something other than a job. It became a part of me. Even though I knew very little about graphic design, it was my means of expression and I invested a lot of myself in it. I wanted praise. That was success. Then the next step in success was to work on a publication I respected. But now I don't really know what success is. It still isn't determined by money. Maybe it's invitations to speak in California instead of Bridgeport, Connecticut.

ON MONEY: You can make a lot of money. It depends on where you are. The top-level positions will pay a lot. What's interesting about this field is that advancement isn't difficult. You can be an associate art director or an assistant or even a pasteup person one day and you can be an art director six months later. Once you've mastered some of the rules, and some of the procedures, it's not difficult because it's need that creates the art director. I took the pasteup job, and two weeks later, I was the art director because the then art director moved on to some other magazine. So there's a lot of change, there's a lot of flux, and in the flux you get pulled. If you're smart enough, ambitious enough, or energetic enough, you can control some of the pull.

Most major newspapers are union-controlled, so your salary is dependent on them. At newspapers like the *Times*, you could start at $15,000 and go to $100,000. If you're a great designer in New York and they want you in Seattle, you get paid what you want. Washington is a place they have a hard time getting good talent, so they pay high salaries. A small newspaper won't pay much of anything, but you'll get experience.

ON THE FUTURE OF THE PROFESSION: Well, newspapers will never die. It's getting more technological. There are computer systems that can be applied to the entire makeup of the page. So the traditional methods of newspaper makeup have changed, but the ultimate result of the newspaper is the same—printed matter designed in an attractive way to convey information, either hard or soft news. So I think it will just continue.

ON WRITING AS A SUPPLEMENTARY CAREER: The newspaper is confining when you're stuck with a format. It's flexible, but not totally changeable. In order to feed my own ego, I think that was a major reason—and when I realized what the options were out there—I developed the writing skill. I just do it and I have editors. It's the same way I got into the newspaper business. I did it, then I started writing, and then I got on a roll. And then I just connected with other people. At each step I learned more. I'd send in a manuscript, and when it was edited I'd pick up a few pointers.

ON INNOVATION: I wouldn't call what I do, in any regard, innovative. I respond. Mine is a responsive job. In the writing, I'm not creating a new form for the novel or for biography or anything like that.* What I'm doing is opening up a field, through writing, to a group that essentially has no literature. But that's not innovative. It exists and I'm just pushing it into our area. In terms of the *Book Review*, there are no measurable innovations. What there is is an opportunity to show some artists who, if they can run free enough, not only with the *Book Review* but

---

*Steve Heller's writing career has established him as a critic and historian of the graphic arts. He has edited many highly successful books on the field and is considered one of its most articulate spokesmen.

other places, could be innovators. But innovation is not what interests me.

ON WORKING FOR A CORPORATION: There are times I'm frustrated by the hierarchy here, but I like it. There's financial security. There's also a creative security, in the sense that I don't have to push as many barriers as I might if I were trying to make a name for myself on the outside. So I guess in a sense it may also be a creative lethargy. Since I'm supported by my job, I can take chances in the writing area. Of course, I enjoy that more, but if I had to do it alone I'd probably be scared and it might hamper me.

ON THE WORKING PROCESS: With designing the publication there's a format, so I follow the format. Being an art director means I'm an editor of other people's art. I buy other people's art and make assignments. I don't impose my value system, at first, on those people. The fact that I've made the choice of whom to use indicates some selection process has already gone on. Once they are given the manuscript, which I've read or skimmed, then it's up to them to come up with an idea. I'll edit their ideas, if necessary, or accept them without question once it's done. In designing the page, it's very procedural. I can only work with the one typeface we have. There's a prescribed format for that, and frankly only so many ways of using the picture. I'm constrained by space. The process on the *Book Review* is really procedure. Out of that procedure every so often something happens that's inspirational.

2

Film and Video

NEW and still-developing technology in film, and particularly in video, is providing tremendous job opportunities for young people. Almost all areas of the industry need trained personnel to help in the process of communicating facts, ideas, and entertainment for both specialized and mass audiences. But in the creative areas, where most neophytes envision themselves as producers, directors, cinematographers, and writers, the competition is fierce and the jobs limited. If one is to break into the field, such personal qualities as aggressiveness, patience, flexibility, and intense desire are almost prerequisites.

The film and video industry provides opportunities in movies (feature-length films for theaters as well as made-for-TV movies), broadcast television, (including the networks, local stations, and cable systems), television commercials, educational television programs, and documentaries. Each of these categories is an entire industry in its own right, and yet the skills required in one can be applied to any of the others. So for young people interested in entry-level jobs, film and video provide opportunities to learn the business. First of all, there are many ways to begin: The business needs assistants and assistants to assistants, so you can always get your foot in the door. Then if you work hard, learn fast, and have talent, the chances of your being able to make your way through the ranks toward your goals are good.

The problem with careers in film and video is that they are

fields where it's hard to grow old gracefully. There are always younger people coming up, with fresh ideas and energy. Traditionally film and video is a young person's business. For those who make a success of themselves early on, their careers can grow and develop, blossoming anew each year. But for those who work competently if not extraordinarily, there are few guarantees of seniority. This is primarily because it is a field of freelancers, and to keep working you must stay in touch and keep up your visibility.

There was a time, not that long ago, when film people were suspicious of that new development, videotape. No longer. Film and video are used interchangeably for different kinds of production. It is still true that each medium has very specific advantages and disadvantages, but recent technology is dramatically lessening the gap between them. The quality of videotape is vastly improved; in fact, with video equipment becoming lightweight and portable and with the advantage of being able to edit tape on location—video is beginning to look like the technology of the future. Diehard film advocates will deny this adamantly, but even they acknowledge that change is on the way.

Most people go to film school with the idea of becoming a director or a cinematographer, or both. Many leave film school having found a different direction. Film is a group effort. The creative thrust often comes from the director, the producer, or the writer, but you can't make a film completely on your own, unless it is a home movie or home video. Film requires the cooperation of every person on the crew. Anyone wanting to make a film should understand the role and function of each job, by experience if possible, and certainly by observation.

The directors and producers who manage to produce films that approach their personal vision are people who, if necessary, can do every job they ask others to perform—perhaps not at the highest professional level, but they *can* do the job. So when you decide to study film, you must choose a comprehensive program where you'll be able to experience each of the many jobs that go into creating a film.

Feature-Length Motion Pictures

Here we are talking about the Hollywood movie. This is the glamourous end of the business; Even the less glamourous parts are made to appear glamourous. On the silver screen, stars are bigger than life and the credits of filmmakers often shine above the title. The film business is, of course, competitive. It is, of course, difficult to get in. It is still primarily based in Hollywood. If you are serious about getting into the business of making full-length feature motion pictures you should consider moving to California. Recently, with more features coming out of New York City, filmmakers who prefer the east coast are trying to make it happen there, but at this writing, the majority of films being made come from Los Angeles. The directors and writers are unionized, as are most crewmembers. If it is difficult to become a director, producer, or writer, it is equally difficult to break into cinematography as a cameraperson or even as an assistant camera operator.

There is no one direct route. Some people make their own small films to start; some join with other people who want to make a film; still others try to get a job in any capacity on a feature film. A good piece of advice for young filmmakers or anyone on the outside wanting to get in is this: Know what you want, then start with the bottom job in the company where you want the top job. Once you're in, you have some basis for understanding who does what and how the system operates. You also meet the people whose jobs you'd like. Talk with them, volunteer your services. Often you can get to do a great many things if you don't ask to be paid. Once you're confident you can do the job, and they are too, you can negotiate for money. In film there are lots of ways to make yourself useful. Choose the one that most interests you.

Broadcast Television

Television at the network level is almost as difficult to break into as the movies. At any one time there are experienced professionals out of work who are looking for the same job you, with no experience, are looking for. The best way to break into broadcast television at the network level is to get a job in cable television or at the local level outside New York City.

Again the same rules apply to television as to movies. Get in wherever you can and, once inside, find the area that most interests you and make a pest of yourself. Volunteer your services, be ready to do whatever is asked. In television, like movies, there is always work for you if you do it on your own time for free. You may not get money, but you get experience, and you get to meet people and find out what's going on. Initiative—lots of it—in both movies and television is essential.

The networks still have a few entry-level jobs as production assistants, as secretaries, even as mail clerks. These jobs are in great demand, and most are given to college graduates who have had college television experience as well as summer experience with local stations—or to those who have contacts at the network. Television is a business of recommendations. Use any you can. Getting the first job is the most essential thing—in whatever capacity.

Television Commercials

This is a broader field than either the movies or broadcast television; however, it is also a very specific field. Many people who move into the directorial end of this business come out of advertising. They learn their skills as television art directors or writers. There are many small commercial television production houses, and again each of them has entry-level positions such as an assistant of some kind or a clerical worker. The jobs at every level except secretary are unionized just as they are in movies and network television. Camera people are hired generally through recommendation. Directors often choose to work with one or two camera people on a regular basis.

The commercial route is a very good way to learn film. Making short films of many different kinds offers a very broad experience in filmmaking, even if all the films are geared to the selling of a product. Commercials are often minimovies, and the cost of production for a thirty-second spot can be more than most people pay to make a feature on their own. The production quality is usually first-rate, and the creative talent at every level is very high.

Directors of commercials have gone on to make movies and television series, but crossing over from one field to the other is not easy. It takes intense interest, determination, and hard work. As always, a few manage to move back and forth, but they are the exception.

Getting to know people is the best way to get into this field, either from the advertising side or from the production-house side. If you know you want to direct television commercials, then you might knock on the door of any of the commercial production houses in the large cities—New York, Los Angeles, Chicago, Atlanta, San Francisco, or Dallas. If you have a reel of films you've produced, written, or directed, either in school or on your own, take it with you. It probably won't get you a directing job, but it could get you *some* kind of job. A person who wants to learn invariably gets the opportunity to learn, particularly in the film business.

Educational Films

There are public television stations across the country, a lot of them closely allied with colleges and universities. Often a young person's first production experience takes place at a public television outlet. It is solid experience and qualifies for a line on your resumé under professional credits. This is not a large field, and often people working in it have a real interest both in serious content for television and in film as an art form.

Whether you go to a film school or to a liberal arts institution for training in film, it would be wise to spend summers working in public television if you can. The actual job is unimportant. What is important is learning the different aspects of the field. If you can make a film on your own, that too can be a powerful tool in getting a job. Making a film indicates you have the initiative, the ideas and the ability to complete a job. It says as much about your possibilities for success as it does about your talent.

Documentary Films

This is the area of "actuality" filmmaking made so popular by the network news departments, where real-life situations are documented by the camera, where people are shown living out everyday experiences, even as they are being interviewed by reporters. Sometimes the documentary centers on crisis situations like a drought or war; at other times, a documentary explores the characteristics of small-town life in the midwest or it follows the fortunes of a high school football team or goes backstage for the Miss America pageant. The reporter is always after the inside story, what really happens to real people.

Public television made its splash in this area in 1973 with *The American Family*, a series of shows on the life of one American family who played out their story before a rapt public. The Maysles brothers took the documentary film to feature-film status with such classics as *Grey Gardens*, a documentary about a reclusive pair of sisters on Long Island, and *The Salesman*, a detailed examination of the work of a Bible salesman on his house-to-house route. A serious feature such as *The Sorrow and the Pity* by Marcel Ophuls managed to get some limited distribution, and recently the film *Pumping Iron II: The Women* was widely distributed. But at this time, the documentary form is not perceived by the "money people" as an entertainment investment, and we find network news departments cutting back on their documentary units. Even in public television, where documentaries were once welcome, the doors are, if not locked, at least closed a great deal of the time.

However, times are fickle, and no doubt the form will surface again. Those who believe in it will not stop making the documentary simply because there is no current market. It is a powerful form and a fascinating one.

For a young filmmaker, the documentary is a very good way to begin filmmaking. Since it is mostly photographed in natural light, using ordinary people rather than actors, the documentary is much less expensive to make. Many film schools begin their students on such projects. It is often here that young filmmakers develop a love for the medium.

It is not a field that leads to immediate fame and fortune. Still, a commitment to it, a passion for it can lead to the creation of films that will get noticed. Documentaries are not profitable, but they often communicate effectively and people respond to that.

Career Positions in Film and Video

Following are descriptions of the major careers available in both film and video. Both media use similar job titles. To avoid confusion, our primary focus here will be on the positions as they exist in the film industry, but the reader should understand that the titles and functions are the same in the video field unless otherwise indicated.

THE DIRECTOR The director, regardless of specialty, is the person who interprets and develops the script. He or she chooses the key crew: the director of cinematography, the assistant director, the editor, etc. The director casts the actors, selects locations, and coordinates budgets and shooting schedules with the producer. The director is ultimately responsible for most of the creative decisions and the final "look" of the feature, television show, documentary, or commercial. This responsibility extends to supervision of the editing stages of the project. The director is the key person on any production.

The director of feature films usually comes up through the ranks of filmmaking. It's not unusual for the director to have held such positions as production assistant, assistant director, and editor. Other directors begin as screen writers, art directors, or designers. A few directors have been cinematographers. And a few—who always knew exactly what they wanted to do—were directors from the very beginning.

In the field of broadcast television, directors often work their way up through the hierarchy of some local television station, beginning as assistants. Directors have also been known to have been in on the ground floor of developing a new program or a series, thus ensuring that the director's job ultimately belongs to them.

In commercial production, many directors emerge from the ranks of the advertising agency, most often through art direction. Since the work comes through the advertising agency, the creative team can direct their own commercials by hiring a production house who will supply the crew. This typically happens in small agencies where the bureaucracy is less institutionalized.

In public television, directors often come from the networks or from local stations. At each local public television station there are a few positions open for staff directors.

Much of the programming material seen on public television is produced independently and sold to the public television network. Because public television does not sell commercial time, the money for productions has to be raised through grants and through appeals to the general public. Public television stations across the country can allocate money from their station budgets to help fund a specific project they feel is right for their local market. Many independent filmmakers regard public television as an essential outlet, the only avenue they have for getting a film on the air.

In documentary films the director is often the producer as well as the writer and creator, and often the cameraperson.

Directors' fees are dependent on many variables. They are most often negotiable.

Hollywood film directors are very highly paid and all fees are negotiated with the studios by agents; the contracts generally provide for added fees to be paid to the director for such extras as television rights. Sometimes directors even receive a small percentage of the profits. A person directing his or her own film may choose to accept a nominal fee during production in return for a piece of the film. Directors who also produce their own films stand to make even more money.

Directors of industrial films and television shows have other fee schedules. Many commercial directors are on a staff basis with production companies. This means they work strictly for salary, though the salary is often negotiated by a lawyer or agent. Network and local station directors are often on staff too, hired on a contract basis or as freelance for one show or for the run of a series. These fees or salaries are also often negotiated by an agent. The Directors Guild has standard minimum fees, but these figures are seldom used except at the very beginning of a career, when you take what you can get. In general, if you make over $100,000 a year, you will get someone to negotiate the contract for you.

To become a director, the broadest film and videotape background is important. Experience in directing school plays, community theater, or your own films is very valuable. Studying acting, set design, dance, and music will also be of immeasureable use. Familiarity with videotape is essential for a broadcast director. A future director can benefit from a very strong background in graphic design and the fine arts, including composition, painting, drawing, and color. The Directors Guild of America, 110 West 57th Street, New York, New York, 10019, is the official union for directors and should be very helpful in supplying further information.

THE ASSISTANT DIRECTOR The assistant director's main responsibility is to help the director in any way. He or she works closely with the production manager to coordinate all phases of the shooting. The assistant helps the director with location scouting and daily shooting schedules, and issues calls to actors and extras. The position may be a stepping-stone to a career as a director or a producer.

In television broadcasting, the assistant has a slightly different schedule of responsibilities because of the technical differences in video production. However, here, as in film, the major responsibility is to assist the director, acting as an intermediary when necessary between crew and director.

On documentary crews, the roles of assistant director and production manager are often one and the same, in that on most documentaries there is not the budget to accommodate both positions. The reality is that, regardless of title, the director needs someone's help.

The education of an assistant director is the same as that of a director. However, in preparation for working one's way up the ranks, some courses in accounting and/or management can be very helpful. The assistant often has to keep track of many production details, including paying for props, meals, incidentals, etc. Being organized and paying attention to detail can be very helpful in keeping the second-in-command job.

Fees for the position are negotiable, although, as with the directorship, there is a Director's Guild minumum. Experience and the demand for your services are factored into the actual fee. There are staff jobs in this category at the network and at the local station level, but in these situations, fees are generally negotiated and there is no industry standard.

THE PRODUCTION MANAGER The production manager keeps the film going. Budget records of all technical and personnel expenses are among his or her responsibilities. The production manager arranges for permission to use certain locations, for traffic diversion during the proposed shooting hours, for police protection, if necessary, and for other such items. The manager hires or fires crew at the direction of the producer. Part of the job is supervising travel arrangements, providing for housing, and assuming the general responsibility for keeping the producer informed of all production expenses. (In television, the production manager's responsibilities are handled by the unit manager, who needs business and managerial skills along with production experience.)

The production manager's role is basically one of peacemaker and organizer. It requires tact, patience, and a strong sense of organization. Experience in a production manager's job can be good preparation for the producer's job. Although positions are limited in this area, independent productions have made the manager's job a key factor in filmmaking and more jobs are now becoming available.

Outside of a complete professional curriculum in filmmaking, the future production manager could benefit from courses in business, accounting, writing, acting, and directing. A network unit manager must have a business background, but any creative skills will help immeasurably in achieving success in the job.

THE PRODUCTION ASSISTANT These are beginning jobs in film and television. A production assistant works with the production manager, but is really the assistant for the entire film unit. The responsibilities lie in assisting in every phase of production—from handling phones, and getting props to going for coffee and keeping notes for directors and producers. You do everything no one else has time to do. Because it is a beginning job, performance of very basic duties determines advancement. This job is a way to learn all facets of production. In network-television production the assistant may also assume responsibility for timing rehearsals and shows and for script changes.

A background in film, or just simply a desire to be in the business, can be enough to get this job. Most people use this entry-level position as a foot in the door to reach their final goal of director, writer, or producer. It is definitely not a career position. No one stays a production assistant for more than a couple of years without moving on or out.

THE CINEMATOGRAPHER The cinematographer works with the director in hiring the key technical production crew, and often scouts and selects locations for filming. He or she works with the director to determine the lenses to be used, the camera position and movement, the proper film stock, and the proper lighting for exterior, interior, and day and night shots. It is not unusual for a director to consult with the cinematographer on light readings for every scene. Other responsibilities include follow-up in the lab and final processing of the film. But the major responsibility of the cinematographer is to realize the director's vision for the film—to establish the style, look, and feel of the story. The position is a pivotal one: The cinematographer is often a director and/or cameraperson in his or her own right and understands the role each person plays on a crew.

In feature films as well as in television films and commercials, a director often likes to work with the same crew, particularly with the same cinematographer. It is like a marriage, in that over the span of several pictures, each gets to know the other's strengths and weaknesses and works in a compatible way to compensate for them.

Over the years there have been cinematographers who have risen to star status, primarily because the directors with whom they work not only recognize their contributions to a film, but credit them publicly. Sven Nyquist who worked with Ingmar Bergman for many years, understood Bergman's vision and through his lighting skills gave Bergman films a "look" that was uniquely Bergman. But more often, the cinematographer's role is underestimated and misunderstood by the public.

In television commercials, broadcast television, and video, the cinematographer's role is not quite as comprehensive as it is in feature filmmaking. Lighting is handled by a lighting director who has that sole responsibility. Other technical details are handled by the technical director, who is primarily an engineer.

Becoming a cinematographer requires a thorough background in film and the other visual arts. Studies in literature, painting, writing, and the theater can be an invaluable supplement to a curriculum otherwise concentrated on film. The usual steps to the title of cinematographer consist of beginnings as an assistant cameraperson and then as a camera operator. Of course, that makes it seem an institutionalized path, where one job automatically leads to the next. It doesn't always work that way. Many would-be cinematographers take a variety of film jobs between those steps. Unions such as the American Society of Cinematographers, N.Y.C. Local 644, and the National Association of Broadcast Employees have training programs for qualified individuals.

Apprenticeships in film are by far the best way to become a cinematographer; unfortunately the opportunities for such positions are not many. The second best way is to go to the right film school, where you can meet professionals working in the field and can get the kind of training necessary to be competitive in a highly competitive field.

Like a director, the cinematographer is paid according to experience, reputation, and talent. The fees vary according to the medium. They are most often computed on a daily rate for the run of the production. The highest fees are paid to the cinematographer of feature films, whether they are produced for the theater or for television. Documentary and industrial films generate less income and consequently pay lower fees, but again money is negotiated with the producer and it's a matter of "whatever the traffic will bear."

THE CAMERA OPERATOR The camera operator is responsible for looking through the camera during the filming. The operator is directly responsible to the director for what the camera "sees." The camera operator is responsible for the proper functioning of the camera, and deals with all the technical aspects of that camera. It is a very responsible job, and the men and women who do it well are highly regarded.

For several years, now, the unions have been developing training programs in the industry for promising young people with the right film background. The number of independent productions has increased, giving more young camera people opportunities to practice their craft.

Video camera operators often come up through the ranks of the technical staff of the network or local station. Many get their first experience operating a camera in college, either in a workshop situation or on a campus television station. Often work in college can provide enough training to qualify you for a position at a local station. Organizations such as the National Association of Broadcast Employees and the International Alliance of Theatrical Stage Employees and Moving Picture Machine Operators of the United States and Canada, 1515 Broadway, New York, New York 10036, have helpful information on up-to-date programs.

THE SOUND ENGINEER The sound specialist is responsible for all sound recorded during the production of the film. Tape must be correctly "slated," or identified for editing purposes. The sound engineer needs a thorough knowledge of microphones, being responsible for the placement of mikes to achieve the desired sound. The sound specialist plans the sound effects, if any, that are to be used. It is essential that he or she understand the differences between recording outside and inside.

The audio technician, as the sound engineer is called in broadcast television, needs a strong background in engineering as well as video and broadcast experience. The skills needed are highly technical and require the ability to concentrate on details. A sound specialist needs a solid grounding in music and music theory, as well as in the science of sound. He or she will also benefit from learning the basic filmmaking skills.

THE PRODUCER The responsibilities of producers vary with each job. Some only raise money, others fulfill management responsibilities, but most of them are active participants in the creation of the film, television show, commercial, or documentary.

In general, a producer makes the major decisions on a project. He or she hires the director and recommends people for the staff, or delegates that responsibility. The producer approves the script, set, and costume design and supervises the budget. The producer often collaborates with the writers and the director on creative matters and decisions. It is not unusual for a producer to direct his or her own production—even occasionally to write, direct, *and* produce.

In broadcast television, the producer's role is much the same as in film, except he or she must answer to network or station executives for decisions particularly related to policy.

The independent producer also has the added responsibility of arranging for the distribution of the film when it is completed. Some choose to do that before initiating actual production. Others, who don't mind taking risks, will raise the funds to make the film, shoot it, and only then worry about who's going to see it.

Anyone who is considering producing as a career needs business, management, and accounting skills. It is also helpful to know about advertising and sales. It is in the producing area where the most money can be made, particularly in developing feature films and television series.

The producer of films is often a fund-raiser, and as in the theater, he or she will sometimes take a percentage of the profits in lieu of a salary. Sometimes the producer will just take expenses, or a small fee and expenses. If a producer is hired by a production company, the salary is negotiated by an agent. If a producer is hired by a network, there are salary guidelines, through even so, most producers' salaries are still negotiated by an agent.

THE ASSOCIATE PRODUCER For many people the title of producer comes only after they have had some experience as an associate producer, a job, as its name implies, that entails helping the producer with all his or her responsibilities. Depending on the project, it can mean doing research and keeping track of all records, budgets, files, and scripts. The associate producer should be a step ahead of the producer in planning, but should take a step back in decision making. The associate producer's job is usually a salaried one, the rate being negotiable. Associate producers on the prime-time network programs are often represented by agents who negotiate their contracts just as they do for producers. However, there must be enough money involved for the associate producer to justify paying an agent's fee.

THE FILM EDITOR The film editor organizes the footage, works with the director, producer, and sometimes the writer to select the scenes to be used, and then, with the help of an assistant or many assistants, depending on the scope of the film, puts it all together.

The editor is responsible for the final rhythm of the film, and many times determines its actual content. The relationship between the director and the editor, like that between the director and the cinematographer, is a delicate one. The editor is enormously important to the realization of the film. At its highest level, filmmaking is an artistic collaboration among the principals—the writer doing the script, the director having the vision, the cinematographer and cameraperson capturing it on film, and the editor making it all come together on the big screen.

The editor combines the picture and sound track, and sees the film through to completed prints from the lab. An editor's skills, creative ability, and imagination have often brought good film forth from mediocre footage, but most editors will admit that great films are made from great material.

Often in advertising editing, one finds highly skilled technicians in this job, people who simply execute a director's commands. Commercial editing is very frustrating to many editors as there are so many bosses—the director, the copywriter, the art director, and the producer, in addition to a client who knows nothing about film. However, as in all areas of advertising, commercial editors earn very high salaries. There are editing houses who cater only to advertising clients.

Editors are most often trained within the ranks of the film business, beginning as apprentices or assistants responsible for keeping track of all exposed film and sound. They catalog film and make a written record of the entire editing process. Preparation of the sound track is also part of the responsibility. Depending on the time factor, an editor may assign a portion of the film to an assistant to be edited. At the lowest rung on the editorial scale is the editor who functions as a pair of hands.

A background in film production—including courses in sound production and engineering—can be very important to an editor. A wide variety of interests is valuable. Film editing is always better when done by people who know a great deal about the content of the work. In film, that means not only understanding the technical process but also becoming involved in what the film is about. In a film editor's working life, the number of subjects he or she will learn thoroughly are many. The person who begins with a broad base of interests will find the work much more challenging and rewarding, and will have an opportunity to use what he or she already knows, even while learning more.

Videotape editing is not that different, in principle, from film editing, but the process is vastly different and it is disconcerting for film editors trying to make the transition. The hands-on aspect of film editing cannot be dismissed as one of the reasons film editors feel so passionately about their craft. As in any art, being able to touch the materials with which they work is an essential part of their connection to the content. In videotape, the entire process is technological; pushing buttons will accomplish more quickly and more cleanly what would take a film editor weeks or even months to do. However, it is the wave of the future in editing. Although videotape editing is expensive because of the equipment involved, in the long run videotape production saves time and consequently money. For the near future, however, because the stars of the editing business have worked with film all of their lives, much of the feature-film business will remain staunchly on film. Only in the areas of industrial film and commercials is video becoming the medium of first preference, and here videotape editing is an increasingly important process.

Film editing can be learned in most art colleges and universities; however, because of the cost, videotape editing is a less accessible skill. For anyone who wants to learn videotape editing, finding one of the few positions available in industry and learning on the job is one's best bet. Because technology moves so quickly—becoming outdated in six months to a year—classroom learning is almost no learning at all. No college or university can afford to present the state of the art in every area. However, industry cannot be without it. The jobs are limited, but if you are persistent, there are places where you can learn your craft. Do some research and find out where the best work is being done, then volunteer your services if necessary.

THE ANIMATION DIRECTOR Careers in animation are a blending of the disciplines of graphic arts and film, and serious animation professionals are often fine graphic artists as well as creative filmmakers.

Many new techniques have developed since the beginnings of animation with Disney, but, as in videotape editing with its roots in film, today's computer animation is also based in film. Interest in animation begins with an interest in still images that are coaxed into life through movement. Designers and illustrators often create the still visuals. From this, the animator creates the movement, i.e., gives life, or "animation," to the character. Illustration and design skills are the ones that are most important to the creation of animated characters and objects.

Recent advances in computer technology have made possible greater use of animation. There was a time when the costs of labor in inking and painting the hundreds of cells required to create even a few minutes of animated film threatened to eliminate the profession. But with the aid of the computer, animation has become a more viable field for an artist or filmmaker.

A basic film background, with additional courses in painting, graphic design, illustration, music, acting, and directing are essential to the animation director. Computer courses are, of course, invaluable, as is understanding video and video techniques.

For the traditionalists, there are still a few studios, mostly in large cities, where you can go to learn the "pure" process of animation. Even technology at its highest state of the art finds it difficult to match the quality, flow, and style of artist-created characters brought to life by other artists in the traditional way. However, it is prohibitively expensive these days, and there are few opportunities to learn with the "masters." If you should get the chance to work with an experienced animation director, it can be an invaluable foundation for any work in animation, regardless of changing technology.

Currently the only program for training future animators and animation directors is found at the School of Visual Arts in New York, which has a professional program in computer animation.

INTERVIEWS

DYANNA TAYLOR
Cinematographer, Freelance

Dyanna Taylor is one of a growing group of young women who have chosen to enter one of the more difficult career fields in film, that of cinematography. She works in both film and video and has spent twelve years producing, directing, editing, and working in still photography. Her early photographic influence came from her grandmother, Dorothea Lange. Her camera assignments have taken her around the world; in 1978 she was responsible for initiating the filming of the first women's expedition to Annapurna. On that project she acted as co-producer, director, and cinematographer. The film was awarded a Cine Golden Eagle and a blue ribbon from the American Film Festival. Among her other docu-

mentary credits are cinematography for Frontline *and* Women in India *for the Canadian Film Board and* Five Years with the Dolphins *and* Is Anyone Home on the Range *for PBS. Her television credits include* Real People *for NBC and* Hour Magazine, MTV, Ryan's Hope, *and* Superstars *for ABC. As director of photography she has worked on several feature films, most recently* Pumping Iron II: The Women. *Taylor lives in New York City but is most comfortable in northern California, where she grew up and began her career.*

ON GETTING STARTED: I got my start because someone thought I'd be the right person for a specific job. I'd been in college two years studying film aesthetics—nothing at all on technical film. I was terrified, and thought "Oh, I'm not qualified, I don't know what I'm doing," but I just sort of plunged in. It wasn't camera work, it was filmmaking, but through that experience I discovered camera work came quite naturally to me. I suspect that happened because I had so much visual experience because of my grandmother.

ON EDUCATION: If it's financially feasible, go to a film school—NYU, University of Southern California, University of California/Los Angeles, even San Francisco State. I'd say there are about five or six film schools that would be very good. There's a great film school in London. Stanford, even. In some ways, I wish I had been able to learn that way, because out of these schools comes an almost-qualified group of people. "Almost-qualified" in that they don't yet know what it's like to beat around the streets and work for a day.

But if you're not someone who can be a student full-time and you want to be a cinematographer, find a production house in your area that's doing commercials or documentaries or industrial films or anything that's related to camera work, and get in there and just start at the bottom. Let everyone know this is what you want to do, and just keep plugging away. I mean, it's really having a dream and just saying, "I'll take any opportunity,

I'll call anyone someone recommends." There's no easy route, no 1–2–3. Film school makes sense, because by the time you get out, you can start as a production assistant in some production house with knowledge, at least, of what they're talking about. I only finished two years of school and I took this job for no pay, made a ton of mistakes, took all my chances, but the film happened to be good enough. I learned enough from that experience to go to the next and then on to the next.

ON WOMEN IN FILM: It's harder for women, ultimately, to be taken seriously. I've been doing this for twelve years and I just had a meeting at ABC Close-up about shooting a documentary for them. Finally they're beginning to pay attention. I look like a 25-year-old hippie or something, and it's very hard for them to take me seriously. Once they see the camera on my shoulder and me moving around, commanding a crew, it changes. But it's difficult to get in that door. However, if you're good, they'll remember you because you're a woman.

There are opportunities for women in that many more projects focus on women—for them and about them. And often they want a woman to shoot it, or they want a woman who is quiet and sensitive and can go in subtly and do something. I went to India because they needed an all-woman crew to deal very intimately with women in India. But I always hate to be hired just for that reason. That's the other side. Another interesting thing: Men have given me more chances than women have. Women in equally high positions have often turned me down. I'd say 98 percent of the time the man will say yes and the woman no. I think a woman in a high place has worked very hard to get there herself and has an inherent suspicion of other women. She can't quite believe that another woman could work as hard, be as good as she is.

ON MONEY: When I'm working on a regular basis during the year I can make perfectly good money. I'm freelance, so there are dry periods for my equipment and myself. I'm very pleased with the money I can make. Some filmmakers make one film every two or three years and they're scrounging for the money to get the film finished. If you're a hired gun, which I am, you make money. I'm a cinematographer. People making films hire me. Networks hire me. They use me for my skill and my equipment. There's a price that goes along with that.

I don't think this is a career you go into specifically to make money. I've made it because I've specialized, because I'm good at it and committed to it. *Very* committed to it. I'm also willing to put up with what's involved. But if someone starts at the bottom and says, "Being a cinematographer will make me money," I'm not sure that's true.

ON SUCCESS: In the beginning I think I simply wanted to be recognized by my peers as someone who had a very strong, well-developed visual sense. And that, to me, was what success was. If someone who hires me can say, "I have a vision and I want you to see it through," that to me is being a success. Now, in the world of documentaries, I consider myself, finally, a success. At least in the last two years. But if I look at features, I'm sort of at the bottom. I've only shot one, so I'd have to say I'm a fledgling in that realm.

ON THE FUTURE OF FILM: Five years ago all of us in film were in a panic, saying, "It's impossible. Videotape has got to be the way it's going to go. We're dying." But what we've determined is that the "look" achieved in film still cannot be duplicated in videotape. And what's allowing film to stay in existence is that videotape editing was invented. Film can now be transferred to tape and edited, then put on television in a very efficient way, maintaining and keeping the filmed look. I think that will keep film alive longer. That and the fact that they haven't yet come up with a way to replace feature films in theaters.

ON WORKING WITH VIDEOTAPE: Someone who shoots videotape has to put up with what I consider to be a number of technical limitations in terms of achieving an image. It's getting more sophisticated, of course, and you can produce beautiful things on tape; they're discovering how to do that. But that's only if you're given a lot of time and a lot of money. It's a myth that videotape is cheaper and faster. I really don't think that's true. It's very expensive, and I think it has to be treated with kid gloves. Also in that it's electronic, it's out of your hands. It's not a medium that's tangible. Film is.

ON WORKING FOR YOURSELF: What I like about working for myself is that in doing documentaries, I'm thrown into situations I would never otherwise have a chance to be in. It's like a perpetual college education. An intense course in the aging, an intense course in the state of Wyoming, an intense course in ecology or in rubber plantations in Malaysia. Wherever I've been, all over the world, I feel free in terms of my living experience and my life experience. I have a certain control over my life in that I can say yes or no to jobs. I like having that control. But I don't feel I have exercised it enough yet, because I'm not willing to turn down more work.

The disadvantage of working for myself in film is that when you're working, your life is not your own. You're completely submerged, working twelve, fourteen, sixteen hours a day. You may go for six or ten or twenty-one days straight. You don't know. It's up to the production. You're essentially theirs. Although sometimes you're making very good money, sometimes you're not. And if you're making yourself available for productions throughout the year, you can't plan for anything. You never know when you're going to be working and when you're not. There's not one regular thing about my life. I'm frankly someone who yearns to have a home with a garden.

ON THE SATISFACTIONS: I'm finding out so much about the world. It's such an incredibly rich world that documentaries bring you. You meet very interesting people. You have a chance to go places and do things you normally could never afford—and you're thrust into the center of them, rather than seeing everything as a tourist on the periphery. And the creative part... when I'm shooting, I'm completely engrossed. I am that frame, the rectangular frame, and there's nothing more than that and the camera.

ON THE SKILLS NEEDED: To do what I do technically, the person has to understand the workings of a camera. Even knowing a still camera in and out and what its functions are will help anyone who is shooting with a 16-millimeter camera, because the principles are primarily the same. So knowing technically what the film image is and what happens when film goes through a camera is the first thing. You have to understand that very clearly so that when someone hands you a new camera or there are a variety of cameras to choose from, you have a basic understanding of what's happening.

Then, you need to understand light, and how light falls on things. And how to duplicate light. Spend time looking in spaces. For instance, here as we talk there are four lights working and a potential daylight source from the window, which is blocked off. If I came in to film you, I'd have to choose which ones I'd go with and which not. Understanding light comes from studying painters and photographers. The black-and-white photographs of the 30s and 40s, my grandmother's work, going back even further and studying the great painters—Edward Hopper, van Gogh, Vermeer, all the Dutch painters. Where they use light, how they use it. To understand how light works. It really pays.

ON THE WORKING PROCESS: I always begin with great anticipation and anxiety. It never changes. I've been doing it for how long, and I still have a period—whether it be an hour, or days, or a week before I start a job—of anxiety and trepidation.

Then I prepare all my carrying cases, figure out what lights I need, go through all my lighting equipment, talk with the producer about what's going to be required. I prep them all, make choices about the tools I'll need. On the job I'm doing now, it's basically lights.

Once we're on location, it's up to the director or the producer, unless I'm directing myself. My input ranges from everything to nil—that is, when someone just says, "Shoot this," and makes all the choices. So you have to be flexible. It's wonderful if you have a director with a great visual sense. Because people like that know what they want, I'm somehow free, within their structure, to do the best I can. When I am given a wide range, when someone just says, "Go out and cover it," then I have to run the full gamut to make sure I cover what they might want in the editing room, and the choices are almost too great. I'd almost rather work with someone who knows what they want, and then I can do my best. I don't want someone breathing down my neck, but on the other hand, I love working for someone I can really collaborate with.

The process at its best is fascinating because it is so collaborative. There are few people who make films, beginning to end, completely on their own. At some point, you have to give your film up to a lab, and you have to talk with a technician. So I see film as this giant painting which a hundred people work on. And everyone brings color to it. What I bring is the image. The lab develops my image. Later the lab timer will decide how much light will hit the image when doing the final printing work. The director cuts it up and juxtaposes it against different things. The sound person brings sound effects to it. It's just this enormous piece of work. And you have to be prepared to give up your immediate image, your vision of what you want, to be willing to have it changed, instantly. And that's the skill of being the best, it's being able to be fluid and to think on your feet and change.

It's frustrating too, because, for instance, right now, I just finished a feature. I worked very hard for six weeks on every composition. So hard. But now they've handed it over to the editor and the director, and I'm not really allowed in on that editing, so I can't say, "But this take was the best! Take #6. That was the one where the camera was perfect, the light fell right, the person fell in at the perfect moment." They're looking for different things, so I have to give up perfection for the whole. And that's what kills me. You have to be prepared for it. That's also what's exciting about it. Because my visual perfection may not, on its own, carry a movie.

ON SUSTAINING ENERGY: It's the moment of shooting itself. Time flies and there is no time; I am completely inside the camera and there's nothing but me and the subject and the camera. That's what keeps me going. That moment, and, of course, the finished product. When you're proud of it and when you look at it on the big screen finally finished with the sound effects, and it's clean and the lab did a great job, and the director is pleased and everyone is happy. And you can't believe after two years here it is finally up on the screen, and it looks splendid. That's also a primary moment. But I have fewer of those. The actual moment of shooting happens more often for me than the moment of finally getting it on the screen with everyone applauding and saying, "This is wonderful."

ON HAVING A PERSONAL LIFE: There's never been a question for me as to whether a personal life is important, because it is. It's a given. It helps to have someone who understands your work and what its demands are so he is personally not put off by whatever the requirements are that keep you out so late, or by the fact that you're never really home for dinner or that you can't plan a dinner party or whatever. I'm a woman and I sometimes wish I had a wife, but I don't. So I'm usually faced with the high-powered man I'm living with who has as many demands as I do. Sometimes we both arrive home at 9 o'clock at night and no one is cooking the dinner. We both sit and stare at each other wondering who's going to lift a finger first.

Relationships take work and they're worth it. But there's a lot of heartache too. I think the hard part is being away from each other, a lot, and not having a continuum you can count on. In film, I think there are more divorces, more split-up relationships, more impossible relationships, more people who are giving it up and living on their own. If I had to choose in the end between work or a long-term relationship, it would be impossible. What would I be bringing to the relationship if I'm not bringing myself and my career? So it's very difficult.

ON A PHILOSOPHY OF WORK: What I notice is that the more I give to my work, the more I begin to understand who I am in the face of that work, and the more integrity I'm able to bring to it.

JOANN GOLDBERG
Television Producer

JoAnn Goldberg began her career working as a researcher, associate producer, and field producer for NBC News political and cultural documentaries. She's produced Barbara Walters specials for ABC; she's also done NBC entertainment specials and has written, produced, and directed both adult and children's programs for Home Box Office. Her awards include an Emmy for documentary writing, a Christopher Award, and several Emmy nominations.

ON GETTING STARTED: I started in television by working my way up through the ranks, from secretary, through research, through associate producer, field producer, and then producer. At the time I came up—I started in television in 1960—it was most common for women to move up slowly through the ranks. Now I think it's easier to skip steps. But I began in the traditional way. I was hired by NBC the way they brought everyone in, either as a page or secretary, and then I moved up slowly.

ON BEGINNING TODAY: I don't think you need specific film or video training, although it's useful. Television breaks down, essentially, into sports, news, and entertainment. Within entertainment, there are several subdivisions, like sitcoms, dramas, movies of the week, variety shows, etc. Each area has a slightly different entrance way.

My advice to people I see now is to try to get out of school with some sample of your work. What the sample does is make people pay attention to you. It makes them see you and it gives you an excuse to get an interview. It puts you on a level to be taken seriously. My experience has been, with very few exceptions, that no matter what it is you've done before you get that first job, you're still going to have to begin on the very, very lowest level. I suggest that if you have an area of television in which you have a special interest, then find out who's doing the best work in the field and pursue them. I'd get in any way I could, on any kind of entry-level job. *Any kind.* Even if you had to save up money and work for a year for almost no money, even if you get in as a typist.

ON SPECIALIZATION IN TELEVISION: Moving from one area of television into another is second in difficulty only to getting into television to begin with. People who are very successful in one area of television can sometimes use this success to bribe their way into another area. "Okay, you want me to do this variety show? Let me do a movie of the week for you." And that way you strike a deal. At the moment, movies of the week based on reality are all the vogue. So if you have a strong background in news, you have a slight advantage. But it's very, very difficult to switch from one area to another.

ON SUCCESS: When I started in news, my idea of success was to become a news producer which meant, then, that you worked all around the world, with some of the most intelligent people, with a network entreé into any kind of situation you wanted to get into. I didn't think of it as business, but rather as journalism and a life experience that offered an opportunity second to none.

Success, in a funny way, now means essentially the same

thing. I enjoy television for the lifestyle it offers. I don't base my decisions as to what work I'll do on the amount of money I'm paid. So, in a sense, it still means getting into an environment with intelligent, interesting people and being allowed to practice my craft. However, as in any business, the nature of the business has shifted around. When I started at NBC, most of the people came from the original Edward R. Murrow unit out of CBS. And everyone was at such a level of excellence, it was very exciting to work around them. That's changed a little bit today. You can't move so easily through a news department and be assured of the kind of experience I had.

ON MONEY: Television is still a very highly paid profession. In some cases it seems to be overpaid. I mean, there are times in my career I've made as much as the President, which is sort of startling. On the other hand, there are only a few people who work steadily. Writers of a certain level of success and directors of a certain level of success work all the time. Producers, associate producers, researchers, etc., spend a lot more time between jobs. Therefore, what seems like a lot of money for the job they're doing actually has to cover longer periods of time.

However, there are a lot of business opportunities in television that are just beginning to open up now, and no one knows where they're going to lead. Home video is offering great possibilities. The people who made the Jane Fonda tape I'm sure are quite startled at the amount of money they made on what was probably a week's shooting. So there are areas of television which offer great business opportunities. That is not true of every area. If you're interested in documentary films and you're going into that for money, forget it. But there are definitely areas within television you can get into as a businessperson.

ON THE FUTURE OF TELEVISION: I believe video is where the future of the profession is. There are those who say that, in the not-too-distant future, even film will be made on video, after certain problems of resolution have been taken care of.

In fact, video exists in much better quality than we ever get to see. Our television sets have 525 scan lines per screen; there's the capability of having double that amount of resolution.

ON PRODUCING A SHOW: By and large, after you are successful, someone might come to you and ask you to produce something. But before that, you have to come up with an idea and present it to somebody. You don't have to be a producer, you can be a director. Most cable stations and networks have a very specific idea of what they're looking for. So you can do one of two things. You might have something you are dying to do, in which case you might try to find out what kind of market would be most receptive to the idea. If you're trying to simply work at your craft, it's a good idea to try to find out from programming departments what it is they are looking for at the moment.

Personally, I approach it in two steps. For instance, I was interested in doing something with Home Box Office. I made an appointment to find out what their documentary unit was looking for. What image did they have? What were they trying to project that particular season? They had a very clear-cut idea of what they wanted. In you go to them and make several suggestions. They'll give you feedback like, "I hate it" or "What if we thought about it this way?" or "What if you added this to it?" Then you'll go back and forth until you get something they'll spend some money for. They call it "development," and you're given X amount of dollars to prepare a treatment for television. The development deal places them under no obligation to produce it.

If they like it, and you decide to go forward, you the producer, or you the director who is also the producer, must put together a staff that can best and most efficiently and economically create the program. You hire writers if you're not also a writer. You hire an associate producer. You hire someone to take care of the budget and the books. In different sides of television, these might mean different things. An associate producer in entertainment television is usually, for instance, the person who hires all the crews and takes care of the money. In documentary television, the associate producer is more of a content person.

You figure out what format you're going to be shooting in. Is it 1-inch video or 3/4-inch video? Even before you start, you make arrangements as to where you would want to edit. You create a shooting schedule. The logistics of doing that efficiently are very important. Sometimes you'll have the luxury of being able to travel with the crews with whom you're used to working. Sometimes you can't do that, and you have to work with the technical people who are there.

Usually you do all the filming or taping within a given period of time. You begin your editing process afterwards. There are times they overlap. If your filming has to be done over a three- or four-month period, you might start your editing process while you're still taping. But usually, for efficiency in video, you first do all the shooting and then all the editing.

The period before which you actually begin shooting is called "preproduction." The amount of preproduction a program requires depends on the nature of the production. If you're going to be doing a Michael Jackson special, you'll need choreographers, dance halls, musicians, scores—all of this has to happen before the bulk of the shooting is done. If you're doing a documentary, the preproduction can be done by fewer people in a shorter amount of time.

Setting documentaries aside, most television is created in its preproduction stage. There might be lucky accidents that make things better than you expect. There might be better ideas that come up along the way. If you're organized properly, you go into a production knowing exactly what you want to do, what you want to photograph, and even exactly what time of day you wish to photograph it.

In documentaries and if you are doing what is called an "actuality," where you are just following people around and hoping you get something—obviously that's a whole different approach.

But even then, a lot of your creativity comes in making the selection before you ever start filming. Essentially you go into a production knowing everything you're looking for.

The amount of control a producer has, once the filming or taping begins, differs with the nature of the project being produced. If it's a project, for instance, like the "Twentieth Anniversary of Motown," which was an elaborate musical production, the director has enormous input into the creativity. And the producer will try to make his life easy, give him what he needs to do his job and to make sure things keep going in the right direction. In dramatic television, the producer might have a greater impact.

The terminology in television, or in film, is not consistent from one area to the other. A producer in documentary film is really the creator of the film. In entertainment television, the producer is usually the co-creator of the film, and therefore it's more of a collaborative medium. Also, in documentary television there are very few stars or celebrities. So the producer is the celebrity of the project, in relation to dealing with the press, etc., etc. In entertainment television, the producer takes a back seat, publicly, to the performers.

ON JOB SECURITY IN TELEVISION: There is almost none. As in any field, the very best and most creative work all the time and always will. The great number of people, even those who are extremely talented and enjoy what they're doing, will always have difficulty finding consistent work.

ON WOMEN IN TELEVISION: Each year television becomes more and more open to women. It still has a long way to go. My experience has been the lower the budget, the greater the opportunity for women. Money is still, by and large, controlled by men, and men seem to feel more comfortable putting $3 million into another man's hands. Whereas if you're doing a $400,000 project, that seems to be an area where women are making the greatest inroads. But it has changed a great deal already, and there is no reason to think it won't change more. By the way, everything I've said about women also applies to minorities.

ON OPPORTUNITIES IN VIDEO: Working in television at one time meant working in a local station or for one of the television networks. That is all changing quickly, and no one really knows what the opportunities in video are going to be. Music video has opened up a whole new field. Fashion videos are becoming a whole new field. Home videos, in which products are made directly to be sold in the home without ever being shown on the air, are opening up a whole new field. How-to video, in which you can look at recipes and some of the crafts, is being done directly for home sale. There will be libraries of video, just as there are libraries of books. The possiblities for video are changing so quickly. As equipment becomes lighter and easier to manage, high-quality work can be done by small numbers of people. I think the market can be anything you make it.

BOB GIRALDI

Director, Commercials/Music Films/Television;
Partner, Bob Giraldi Productions

Bob Giraldi is generally regarded as the country's leading commercial director, as well as America's leading music film director. Among his achievements in advertising are such memorable commercials as the Lite Beer from Miller ads featuring ex-athletes and screen personalities, Broadway show commercials for hits like Dreamgirls, A Chorus Line, *and many others. His PepsiCo campaign featuring Michael Jackson and the Jackson brothers and the new Pepsi campaign with Lionel Richie have become classics.*

In the world of music films, he wrote and directed "Beat It" with Michael Jackson, which won every top music film award in the business, including the Best Overall Video of the Year award from Billboard. In September of 1985, "Beat It" was included in an exhibition of video art at the Museum of Modern Art in New

York. His other music films have included hits by such stars as Pat Benatar, Diana Ross, Lionel Richie, Pia Zadora, Jermaine Jackson, and countless others.

His television work has included directing an hour film special for CBS, Kenny Rogers and Dolly Parton: A Christmas to Remember, *which first aired in December 1984. Most recently he completed directing an episode for the new CBS series* Hometown.

Bob lives and works in New York City.

ON GETTING STARTED: I was an artist as a kid. I mean I drew things and people could tell I was very artistic. So at least I had a beginning. Then I guess it was easy to find art schools, but for my mother and father to be able to afford them was more difficult. I tried Cooper Union* but was turned down because my grades from high school in Paterson, New Jersey, weren't very good. Pratt was out of the question. But as an athlete, I was, luckily enough, accepted to Wagner College on an athletic scholarship. When the athletic director saw that I had an aptitude for art as well as being an athlete, he asked me if I'd consider talking to his brother who was over at Pratt Institute. They were giving minimum scholarships to athletes who were proficient in the world of art or architecture or engineering. I said, "That's my dream. I always wanted to go to an art school." I went over to see them, and I passed all the art tests and was given a combined basketball and baseball scholarship. To this day, I still am the only artist in the history of Pratt Institute to have had his education paid for by the athletic department.

I had to play both those sports all the time, which was very hard, because art school in the sixties, maybe still today, was very demanding. There was always an assignment, a new project due the next day. And the competition among students was always so tough and bitchy. On the other hand, I had to leave

---

*Cooper Union, an art school in Manhattan, has a student body made up totally of scholarship students selected on the basis of artistic talent and academic achievement.

that at the end of every day and go to practice. For the first couple of years, I was a little ashamed of that because my teachers kept talking about athletics and art not mixing. But when I started to become a star in the school paper, I began to feel good about my second interest. I remember one teacher saying to me, "Are you the same Bob Giraldi that scored 25 points?" I said, "You're damn right I'm the same Bob Giraldi, pal." Anyway, it all worked and I graduated as an artist first and an athlete second. It was the way I got through school.

ON CHOOSING A CAREER: I chose advertising/design because I am basically a commercial person at heart. I'm more moved by communication, by emotional communication than I am by a beautiful piece of fine art. It may be sacrilegious in some quarters to say that, but it's where my body and my karma are.

One of the early things that influenced me was an ad for the Blind Institute of New York done by Len Sirowitz. A full black page with just a little white copy on the bottom that said, "This is how a purple sky and green grass, a red rose and a garden-full of chrysanthemums looks to a blind person." It was really stunning. That aroused in me a passion. I knew I liked communication. And it's a bit manipulative. I liked the manipulation. Whenever I do something, I like it if people cry or smile. And I die when people are indifferent. So I was drawn immediately to the advertising/design department.

ON TRANSITION IN CAREERS: When we were in school, and immediately after as young designers and art directors, we got off on doing print ads—headlines married to pictures. Print advertising then was so dynamic and stunning. Helmut Kron, George Lois, Steve Frankfurt created just wonderful, wonderful print advertising. Milton Glaser and Ivan Chermayeff influenced me with their design approach. Then, as a young art director at Y & R (Young & Rubicam, an advertising agency) about six or seven years after I entered the field, the television boom came. A man like Steve Frankfurt made the transition. It's almost comparable to the talkies and *The Jazz Singer,* where a man like Jolson never made the transition.

Television came, strong and fast, and a lot of us print art directors and writers wanted a chance to work on this new thing called motion and action. It just took us by storm and it captured some of our hearts. It scared and intimidated a lot of people, but it developed *my* career. It developed a whole communications system that this country is now a slave to, both positively and negatively. I've always felt that sound was the real emotion. I don't cry much at pictures, am not even moved much by pictures, but I can cry easily at words or sound or music. Sound to me is more devastating than picture, and when married with the right picture, it's the most devastating tool—propaganda tool—we have. So in those early years, I went right into heavy experimental stuff and tried to move people. I remember Steve Frankfurt telling me how incredible and hynotizing dripping water is, and how the ticking of a clock, when really played up a little bit, can be just so mesmerizing. All those little things really stay with me.

After I'd been a successful art director for a long time, having done many television commercials, I was working at Della Femina, Travisano and Partners as head of their television department. I was on a roll. I had just finished the hemophilia campaign, "We're So Close, Yet So Far." I'd won many awards with that. I had just started working on the Eyewitness News campaign, in the early years when Grimsby and Beutel—and Tex Antoine was still alive—and Frank Gifford were all part of that team, and it was new to have a team concept in news. I was doing commercials for them. But all of a sudden I said to myself, "You know what? I can do this probably better than most people I'm hiring to do it." So I started directing my own stuff. I was in a position to do it because I was the head of the department and also production people around knew I had talent and lent me their production support. I did a campaign for H & R Block that featured Henry Winkler, Tony LoBianco, Olympia Dukakis, and Dick O'Neil many years before they became stars. It was very successful. It got a lot of awards and recognition, which in our business you seem to have to have. And I was on my way in a career as a director. I decided to leave the agency business and pursue it totally. I did commercials for the first six or seven years and then branched out and did a movie, which was terrible, and came back and did more commercials, and did documentaries, and did a film for the School of Visual Arts. I always managed to work in different media, because I didn't want to just do television commercials. Then it just naturally grew. I've grown in the last fifteen years or so directorially, so I stay as a director and executive producer. My career hunting is over.

ON THE DIFFERENCES BETWEEN WORKING ON COMMERCIALS AND ON LONGER FILMS: It's really difficult to say. First of all, the technique is the same. I hire the same crew. When I walked on the set to do a one-hour show for CBS's *Hometown* series, I used the crew I'd done some commercials with a couple of months before. Exact. Right down to the hairdresser. The process is the same. The film stock is the same. The lighting is the same. The shooting is the same. The entire technical—which becomes conceptual—process of filmmaking is the same. What is different is the length of the narrative. What is different is that I have seven or eight to ten days of telling a story that has to follow a certain form. Commercials are much shorter. The reason why I don't find much difference, as opposed to other directors, is that all my work takes pretty much the same approach. I am most comfortable when I'm telling a story. Even my ten-second commercial has a little tiny beginning, middle, and end. My thirty-second one, the same. One of the reasons why I've been called a master at fast-form storytelling is that I somehow have the ability to gather momentum in a quick story. My videos do that. There's a beginning, a middle, and an end. "Beat It" is a story. "Say, Say, Say" is a story. "Love Is a Battlefield" is a story. My commercials for *Sports Illustrated*, the ones that are most talked about right now, are stories. Even the Miller Lite commercials, which are just men standing at a bar talking, almost have a story line attached to them. There's a reason they're saying something, which pays off eventually through a middle section to something. So even if I do it short, the transition is not so different.

ON STARTING OUT TODAY: I don't suggest that all people follow my sensibilities—obviously. There are those young people who do videos that are so unnarrative, they're fractured and disjointed and so experimental, that they are spectacular. The Japanese are going to be the next invasion. We've had our English invasion; they're still with us. But the Japanese will be here soon—directors, camera people, lighters, writers, whatever. And their influence will be felt. They bring a more abstract, surreal sense to film, like the English did. Frank Lloyd Wright and Moholy-Nagy were two of my biggest influences. I need the form to be inspired by some function, by some content. Then I can make it work. Most young people, I think, are away from that a little bit today. I think there's more daring stuff to be learned today than my kind of thing. Even though I am a contemporary man, living in a contemporary milieu, surrounded totally by contemporary things because of my music- and film-community affiliations, I still like to do very basic communication. I think if I were studying today, I'd be in the minority.

ON EDUCATION: Film school's a great idea. For one reason. Film schools today have so many more resources that they're just physically able to let students play. The worst kind of film school or art school you can go to today is a theory-oriented school. If you don't understand practical application, you're in trouble. It's like learning to ski. If you don't know how to ski, you can think about it all you want, but you can't do it. Making film is difficult. It's difficult for one large reason. It's expensive. You can't go get film today from the Kodak people of the world without paying a lot of money for it. Unless you steal it. Cameras are expensive. No matter what anybody says to you, still cameras, motion cameras are expensive. So the medium is an expensive one, unlike in the old days when paint or charcoals were less expensive.

The other thing is, there are certain contemporary applications that have to be met. You have to know your f-stop and know your lighting and know your stock and know how to physically load it, unload it, process it, edit it, mix it, and put music to it. Martin Scorsese is one of the best examples of someone who has done it in a bigger, higher-profile medium and done it pretty much the tough, gritty way, coming from the NYU film school where they talk about theory, but he put that theory into applications. And there are the art schools and film schools today, like Visual Arts, NYU, definitely like the west coast schools, which I think are even a little better right now. USC and UCLA. Like the North Carolina School of Art. North Carolina, where the film community is growing, is a wonderful place right now. Dino DiLaurentis just bought a major studio down there and is doing work out of there. The New Hampshire area, the New England area, obviously Boston.

No matter where I go, videos have brought a film form to young people. They can relate to it; it's not out of their reach. Commercials are out of their reach for the most part right now. And certainly feature films are out of the reach of the majority of young people in the world. But videos are not. Anybody can go out and rent that camera and do some form of music motion.

So I suggest an art school with a film curriculum, if you're interested in film. I suggest practical application. And then the hardest part. I suggest tenacity. The tenacity to bother your father's friend, if that's where it is, your mother's boyfriend's girlfriend, anybody, anyway, anyhow, where you can go hang on a doorstep and say, "I need to work. I need to work as a gofer, which means I will go for anything you want, and I will get into this business from the lowest angle." Because once you're in, you're in.

This business is good for young people in one way, there are lots of jobs to do. It's not a small business, like the fine arts business is a small business.

ON SUCCESS: Success to me was always sort of based on important people, which was not the best thing, but I don't know what else success can be. I'm not driven by money. Everybody thinks I make more money than anybody else in the whole world, which isn't true. I make good money, and I've always made it, based on my talent. A smarter, more passionate money man would have made more money. He would have parlayed the money I've already made into a lot more. That's not what excites me, and not what I do. I am driven by ego. I am driven by the desire to be respected in my community. I am also a man who has a major conflict with the concept of a commercial artist not being regarded as an artist. I've never been rejected by any community, but I've always had that problem inside me, which is hard to explain. One of the most satisfying things that has ever happened to me is having "Beat It," the Michael Jackson video I did, which is obviously a fine piece of work, admitted to the Museum of Modern Art collection. It makes me, in my own mind, an artist.

Now that I've achieved a lot of what I wanted when I was younger, it means maturity and responsibility. It means making a contribution to society, a good contribution.

ON THE FUTURE OF COMMERCIAL FILM: That's hard. It's headed where it's headed. Obviously, everybody thought the video business was going to explode. And it has not exploded. What it's done is made other fractured explosions; the music artist is one of the more important communicators we have, and the marriage of music and words is at an all-time high and something new. Just doing videos, though, and showing them over and over again on an all-night station is not where the future lies. VCRs and home videos and cable stations have all shown the world that we are still the leader in communication, and we'll go on being the leader in communication—for a very simple reason: We're the most thirsty for money and success. And we're going to go on searching out new ways. I cannot and will not predict where advertising, music, theatre, video, the arts are going. I will say that there has been a marriage of them all, an acceptance of them all, which is new, never before done. Just to see Live Aid in its own little world—it was spectacular to see Bob Dylan on the same stage with country and western and with pop artists like Lionel Ritchie. Before those people wouldn't appear together. Music used to be a very segregated field. The marriage of all the media has never been quite so promising. And that's fabulous. It opens it all up for young people. The future is so bright for them to get into the arts and this kind of communication field.

ON OPPORTUNITIES FOR WOMEN: There are, in my opinion, a lot of opportunities for women. My company is run by women. Well, that's not entirely true. My company is run by me and my partner, Phil Suarez. But from that point on, everybody who makes decisions here is a woman. My executive producer is a woman. My producer is a woman. Our A.D. I haven't found a lot of camerawomen yet, but that will change. I've found a lot of electricians who are women. They're called "gaffers" in our business; they're the people who light sets. I've talked with a lot of women directors and they don't get a lot of work. They feel there's still a quota. I'm not in position to give out those jobs, like networks or studios are. But I'm sure the bias is there. On the other hand, Madonna will only work with Mary Lambert or a woman director.

ON HAVING A PERSONAL LIFE: I make every effort to have a personal life, and I think I've done a pretty good job, through not a perfect job. I've always tried to be a good father and husband; I've not always been, but I've tried. I happen to be very lucky to be married to a woman who right from the early years was dedicated to the survival of a family situation. She wanted our children to be unique and free in spirit and heart, and I think she succeeded. I never would have been able to be where I am today without the family. This sounds a little pompous, but I don't mean it to be. I am probably one of the more-directed, connected, clear-headed high-profile directors in this country. I'm not a child. I know what the priorities are. It's very difficult. We stray obviously for ego and self. But one thing about maturity and age is that it brings you back. If you're lucky enough to still have good people around you, lucky enough to have family, you can be very old and still be very facile and keep going.

ON A PHILOSOPHY OF WORK: If you do quality, you will do quantity. It never works the other way around.

RICHARD MINCER
Television Producer
Vice President, Program Development, Multimedia, Inc.

Richard Mincer's career is unique in broadcasting. Beginning at a local Ohio television station, his success is linked to the development of the Phil Donahue Show. *The concept evolved as a local daytime show, and under his leadership became, over eighteen years, the celebrated daytime success it remains today. He was producer and director at the same time, then moved on to become the show's executive producer, winning not only regional Emmys, but five national Emmys for his contribution to a ground-breaking broadcasting story. As the program developed, his role changed, moving from the creative side to the more managerial. In 1985 Mincer moved the* Donahue Show *from the midwest to New York City, then accepted a major new responsibility as vice president in charge of program development for Multimedia, a conglomerate that owns cable broadcasting, newspapers, and television stations. They are also the owners of the* Phil Donahue Show. *Richard Mincer now works in New York City and commutes to Chicago on the weekends, but he plans to become an Easterner as soon as he has time to find the right house.*

ON GETTING STARTED: How I started: I went to Ohio State in 1956 in radio, television, and speech, working toward a degree in education in the College of Education. But I really didn't want to teach. I wanted to be in business. The education degree was something to fall back on, in case. I worked at Ohio State at the local radio station, but at the end of my junior year, I had an opportunity to work at a local television station in Columbus, WBNS-TV, a CBS affiliate. I was working in the film-editing department when they asked me if I would stay on and work a full load the following fall. The job was originally a summer job. My philosophy then, and my philosophy twenty-five years later, is, if you can get your foot in the door of a television or radio station, then take whatever job they have available and do whatever they want you to do until the right things open up. So I did that. I took my senior year and split it in two so I could continue on the job. About two months before my graduation in '61, I was promoted to producer-director and was doing local television programming. It wasn't very exciting as I look back on it, but it was good for me. I was drafted and was fortunate enough to be sent to a television production house in the army called the Army Pictorial Center in Queens, in Astoria, and I spent most of my two years in the Army doing television production. After the Army I went back to Columbus and continued to produce and direct there.

ON MOVING UP: Avco Broadcasting contacted me. They had stations in Cincinnati, Dayton, Columbus, and Indianapolis. They wanted me to work for them in Dayton. It was a real opportunity because the station I worked for in Columbus was a single station owned by the local newspaper. Most of the people in management had been there a long time and were relatively young. I didn't see an opportunity for me to grow in the business. I wanted to move up into production management—program director, general manager, etc. I saw getting in with a group station as a way of moving up in a company that could promote me either within the station where I was working or within one of their other stations. I'd have more visibility and opportunity.

ON THE EVOLUTION OF THE *DONAHUE SHOW:* About 1967 Avco decided to try a new concept, actually not terribly new, but in terms of television it was. A call-in program. It was being done successfully by Westinghouse in Boston, Philadelphia, and Pittsburgh with a program called *Contact.* And they had a guy in Dayton who had done very well with a radio show, very similar to that. People would call in and talk to celebrities or talk about issues. He had left the business because he'd been sending resumés to major markets and getting lots of turndowns. His name was Phil Donahue. They decided to try it as a one-hour local television show, and I was asked to be the producer/director. Quite frankly, when it happened I wasn't terribly pleased because I was in line for a promotion to production manager, a job I wanted. So I started sending out my own resumés. I really did.

Obviously, after the show got on the air, the excitement around the station for us was unbelievable. The show was doing things other local shows had never done, both in terms of ratings and audience response, and making the press, such as *Variety,* and getting national coverage.

From the very beginning, Phil and I decided the program would address issues. We were forced into it to some degree. Let's remember we were in Dayton, Ohio, so we did not have the kinds of guests that a New York or L.A. or Chicago audience would have. That is, we couldn't just pick up the phone and call Phyllis Diller or Bob Hope or whoever the local celebrities might be. They weren't in Dayton. We had to scramble to do programs that were different. We were forced to do issues more than anything else. But at the same time, we were comfortable with that. Phil's background is in news. And I'm much more a person who enjoys politics and history than someone who enjoys show business as such. So we were a pretty good combination in terms of the kinds of things we were comfortable in doing and knew about.

I stayed with the show and it remained a local program for about two years. Then Avco decided if it was that good in Dayton, they'd chance putting it on in Columbus and Cincinnati, and the show did very well there. But the major turning point for us was when the general manager of the Storer station in Cleveland, a CBS affiliate, bought the show for airing on his station. Storer owned stations in Atlanta, Detroit, Milwaukee, and Toledo.

The show began to slip somewhat in '73, and we knew if the show was going to survive, we'd have to be in a major market to get better guest availability, give it a better look, better sound, etc. So we moved the program to WGN, an independent station in Chicago, in early 1974. The progress in terms of syndication, selling a show to local stations around the country, was slow for about two years. Then Phil was nominated for a national Emmy and he won, on his very first nomination. That, because of the publicity it generated, opened up an awful lot of doors to our salespeople. When Phil won the Emmy, we didn't air in Los Angeles or New York, but right about this time WNBC, the local New York City O & O,* decided they would roll the dice and pick up the show.

From the fall of '76 to the fall of '77, the show grew dramatically. It went from 80 or 90 markets to 170 in just a year's time. All of a sudden we were the hottest program going. Then about 1975 or '76, Avco Corporation decided to sell off their broadcast properties. They sold the flagship station, WLWT in Cincinnati, along with the syndication division to Multimedia, who owned cable networks, newspapers, and television stations. And when multimedia bought WLWT, they also bought the *Phil Donahue Show*. So, Multimedia is now our owner and has been for the last decade. We were in Chicago until about '81 or '82 at WGN,

---

*"Owned and Operated by the network," in this case the National Broadcasting Company.

and it had become a superstation. That is, cable systems were picking WGN up across the country.

In December of 1984 we came to New York. We did that primarily because Phil had been living in New York since his marriage to Marlo Thomas. He had been commuting back and forth from Chicago to New York every week for two years. Finally he said, "Look, I'm either going to wear out or we're going to have to do something more accommodating for me." It was worked out with WNBC and with the NBC facilities, that we could move in there and produce the show from NBC.

ON SUCCESS: Back in 1959 and '60, I wasn't yet 21 years old and I'd suddenly been promoted to producer/director, and I was making a grand total of $450 a month! I thought that was success. I really did. But it changes with each thing. I suppose you look at something and say, "Now what's the next step?" And I suppose that's as much success as anything. One of the things in terms of success for me has been that you can really look at the *Donahue Show* and say, "This was a local show and it was successful." Then it became, in syndication, somewhat of a regional show in other cities around the midwest, and that was success. I think winning a couple of regional Emmys was a success. Then over the last eight years I've won five national Emmys with the *Donahue Show*. In our business you often think you'll never win even one. To have won five, to me, is an enormous achievement. I just never dreamed it would happen.

ON EDUCATION: I think two things apply today, as they did when I started. Certainly, a college education is a must. Initially, I'd recommend you have a major in the field of communications where you get as much as you can of television, radio, theatre, taking whatever courses will allow you hands-on production experience with the campus television or radio station. Develop whatever writing capacities you have, because from time to time that's certainly going to pay off. Secondly, I would recommend taking additional courses in business, even taking an M.B.A. I've never seen any indication, and this is strictly a personal opinion, that you get much in terms of a second degree, a master's or doctorate in Communications. If that's what you're going for, you're better off getting the experience working at a television or radio station. I really think I learned more in six months working at WBNS in the film-editing department, just because I was in the building. So experience is the first thing.

ON GETTING LOCAL TELEVISION EXPERIENCE: It's the old story of the dog chasing its tail. It's happened to me and it's happened to you and it's happened to anyone else in this business. When you walk in and sit across the desk, the first thing anyone is going to say to you, is, "What experience do you have?" It's a terrible question to ask, and yet there it is. And especially of a college student who has just graduated and who leaves, shaking his or her head, saying, "My God, how am I ever going to get any experience if no one will hire me?" What you should try to do is to take any position available in a local television station. What you want to do is work your way up. If you start in Des Moines, then move to St. Louis, then move to Chicago, you'll finally move to a top market like New York or Los Angeles. Pay increases are subject to the size of the market.

Most of the newspeople on the air today started locally. Jane Pauley began in Indianapolis, went to Chicago, then New York. And it works the same way for producers and directors and others. Try to establish yourself in a smaller market. I always say, "It's a lot better to be working and sending resumés out, than it is to sit in your apartment not taking the job for $400 a month, saying, 'I'll just keep sending out resumés until they recognize what a talent they're missing.'" Unfortunately, it doesn't work that way.

In the larger cities, there is more talent available. And that's tough for college graduates. Not only are they competing with other college graduates who want to get in on the ground level, they also have to contend with all the people from Columbus and Cincinnati and Indianapolis who have two years' experience before coming to Chicago or New York. Experience is a big plus.

ON THE FUTURE OF TELEVISION: I think we will see more diversity. I think that for so many years in our business, the local stations in this industry were controlled by three networks. Whatever they fed us, i.e., the public, was what we got and what we took. Because of cable and because of satellite feeds and because of independent stations and independent groups—which have grown dramatically—I think we're going to be more fragmented. There's going to be more opportunity to do things. The audience will have more to choose from. Cable systems, as well as the independents, are looking for programming. The cost of buying off network programming like reruns of *Dallas* or *Dynasty* or whatever has become prohibitive for them. They are now looking to create their own programs to go out and sell. So I think the decade is going to be very exciting for all of us in the job of producing new television shows.

ON OPPORTUNITIES FOR GETTING YOUR IDEAS TO THE RIGHT PLACES: When companies start doing a pilot for a new television show, the company is going to risk as much as $450,000 for a pilot, and certainly no less than $150,000. Obviously, it is much more comfortable for me to take a game show idea from someone who has been doing game shows for fifteen years than from someone who walks in off the street. So if you think you can create and produce a game show, get in with that company that does game shows. Take a job in the office if you can get in, so when someone's walking down the hall, you can say, "Hey, I have a game show idea I think you'd like." That's part of it. If you're 21 years old and you're walking around with a script, it's going to be much more difficult for you. It just is. That's not to say it can't be done. And it's not to say don't do it. But at least for the experience, go out and shop it, and see what you run into.

ON THE WORKING PROCESS: *The Donahue Show* is unique in that it was a local live television show. We examined the other programs that were like it, i.e., the Westinghouse programs called *Contact* in Boston and Philadelphia, and we looked at their tapes. It was really a relatively simple program to produce. It was a show that required a guest or a topic for one hour. You took telephone calls from the viewers, and the viewers asked the questions. The host moderated and the guest answered. It was pretty simple. We built a set and over a period of a couple of weeks got together a list of potential guests, many of them people Phil had already worked with successfully on radio, and started the program in that manner. There was no grand scheme—this was a local show.

In terms of programming now for syndication you start with an idea. It can come from either direction of the street. Someone will have an idea or a script. Either they will send it to you or program development will send it to you, saying, "This is potentially a good program." Where do you go from there? The next step is to contact them to say, "We like the idea and we'd like to discuss the possibility of shooting a pilot." In terms of syndication, unlike network, we would put up the money for that pilot, but it might not go any further than that. We would, however, have an option to do something further, i.e., a strip series (five days a week) or a once-a-week series, or whatever the case may be. The person who had originated the idea would come back to us with certain budget figures; in order to do this half-hour it's going to cost $150,000, or it's going to cost $200,000. And if we went to series with this, each additional program would cost $50,000 to do. While the creative element is going on, there is also the financial element. Your salespeople are looking at the cost and looking at where you would place the program in the daily schedule. What competition is out there? How successful do you think we can be with a new game show or with a new late-night comedy program? What are our odds if we try to place it just once a week on a Saturday afternoon or a Saturday evening? Would a network be interested in a program like this?

When the figures come back, if you see you're going to generate $40,000 worth of income per show and you know that it's going to cost you $50,000, the answer then becomes an economic one.

If it looks like you can, even in the beginning, break even or possibly lose only a little money, then you might go ahead and start producing that show. In syndication, the pilot is the most important thing. You give a pilot really your best shot. The worst thing you can do in terms of selling this to stations is to go to them and say, "Here's the pilot we shot. Now we didn't spend a lot of money on it. Don't pay attention to the set because we're changing it. Don't pay attention to the host because it's not the host we're going to have. And the game really isn't going to work this way, because we're going to make some changes." The person who wants to buy says, "Why did you bother me with it?" That's why the pilot is more expensive than doing a show. First you have one-time-only costs for the pilot. The set, the music. You're probably going to pay people on a freelance basis, so your costs are a little higher in terms of production, renting a studio, etc. But you make that commitment in terms of your program-development monies because the intent is to go on and do a series.

The exception might be if you're shooting a program from a different perspective, that is, strictly as a special. You shoot the show as a two-hour special and it will make money for you in that two-hour period of time. It may air once or it may air twice a year.

The other thing is to shoot one program, like a Christmas program. If you could go out and spend $450,000 to shoot a Christmas special that you knew was going to be what we call in our business "an evergreen," we could run it for the next five or six years. If it returned $200,000 on the $450,000 investment the first year, you're not really looking at a loss, because you know this is going to play five more years. And it eventually will recoup the investment and probably make money for you.

ON WOMEN IN TELEVISION: Like other industries, I think if you went back ten or twelve years ago, you'd see that the industry was pretty much male-dominated. Is that changing? I think it is. The *Donahue* staff, for instance, is primarily women. The person who replaced me was, in fact, the original secretary in our office. Her name is Pat McMillan, and she became an associate producer, then producer/director, then senior producer of the show during the years that I was executive producer. I think more and more we are seeing that women are becoming executives in this business. There are more women program directors today at local stations. There are more women general managers too. I think show business historically has had less barriers than others.

ON HAVING A PERSONAL LIFE: This is not a 9-to-5 job, and anyone who wants it that way should probably be in the financial end of it, i.e., the accounting department, rather than in the creative end. If the sun doesn't shine, you've got to wait until it does. Or if you're shooting something set at 9 o'clock at night, that's when you'll do it.

I personally think you have to give the company their money's worth, and you certainly never ever walk away from something until it's completed. But I also think the company has some responsibility to say, "Hey, we're paying you for forty hours a week or forty-five or fifty, and we don't think it's necessary for you to be working eighty hours a week, fifty-two weeks a year. We think you should be able to see your family on weekends and take a vacation.

There are rewards that go with this business. There are times when you don't have to come in at 9 o'clock. You can come in at 11. And you can travel and do other exciting things. There's a balance here. I think people are more lenient in this business. You don't have to be at your desk. It's not that kind of job. You can't sit at a desk and be told to create something. It's like telling a comic to be funny at a cocktail party. It just doesn't happen that way. And I think most people know that in this business.

RICHARD GREENBERG

Director/Designer; Partner, R/Greenberg Associates

Richard Greenberg's state-of-the-art film production company, which he owns with his brother Robert, has facilities unrivaled on the east coast. They produce from conception and design right through to the final optical negative, and they have everything and everyone necessary to create the most complicated special effects, graphics, and live-action film, all under one roof in mid-Manhattan. As creative director and designer, Greenberg's unique concepts, pared down to the essence of the message whether it's a commercial or a movie title, have made him one of the most sought-after directors in the field. Among his advertising clients are such companies as Atari, Newsweek, *Magnavox, American Airlines, Renault, MCI, Shell, Technics, Fuji Films, IBM, Timex, Sony, Whirlpool, Miller Beer, Mobil Oil, and countless others. He created the Tri-Star Pictures feature logo of a white winged horse flying through the air, the classic titles for* Superman *and* The World According to Garp, *the unique special effects for Woody Allen's* Zelig.*—and for* Educating Rita, Ghostbusters, The Right Stuff, Altered States, *and* An American Werewolf in London, *to name a few more.*

ON GETTING STARTED: I'm from Chicago originally. The summer between my fourth and fifth years of architecture school, I made a little film about the Chicago political convention. This was about 1970. I just used images pulled out of magazines and stuff. It was graphic, using very crude camera setups, getting the camera hooked into the floor, and moving these things around.

I had no interest in still images. I'd never used a still camera. Certainly I'd never had a film course. But I had this notion about working with time, and thought it might be fun. When I went back to school, someone I knew said he was sending a film into the New York Film Festival, which had a student film competition. It doesn't exist anymore. He showed it to me, and I thought, well, if he can send that in, I'm going to send mine. So I did, and it won. The film was simple and very crude, and it was nuts! With that under my belt, it sort of gave me a little more confidence to move into this area. I decided to get an M.F.A in graphic design so I could teach. At that point I thought I'd teach at a university and make these little private films so the university would provide the money to do them. Also, I was 22 years old and it seemed like instant status, the whole deal.

I taught from age 23 to 27. Then I realized that anything big, even though it could be initiated in Chicago, was always produced on one of the coasts. That's the nature of film. It's produced in New York or L.A. if you want to be privy to those kinds of major projects. I went to L.A., but there was something about the place. I just got this feeling that if you weren't really well connected it would be awfully hard to break in. So I came to New York and worked for somebody for awhile, always with the idea that I could go back to teaching if things were really horrible. Then I freelanced, doing a lot of work for *Sesame Street,* developed by The Children's Television Workshop, which provided income and also opportunity. It was a neat place in those days, with Edith Zorno, because it gave young people a chance to direct and produce small, manageable sequences. They didn't pay a lot, but you could take a concept and develop it. I don't know if options like that are available to people starting now. Then my brother joined me in New York, and we began the company on one floor of a brownstone on 38th Street.

ON A PARTNERSHIP: The neat thing about the way our business has worked from the beginning, and still works, is that we divide our responsibilities. I'm the creative director and I oversee everything that goes through. Bobby, my brother, handles the management and financial aspects. So it's very good, because as an artist I could never have made the necessary capital expenditures. I don't think most artistic people can do it. Some of the equipment we have here is *very* expensive, and I personally could not deal with spending that kind of money.

ON THE WORK OF THE COMPANY: We do opening title sequences that we design and then produce. We do promotion for feature films, where we're designing the advertising or shooting what's known as a "teaser trailer," where we actually shoot material that is then used to represent the film. To wit, on *Back to the Future* or *Alien,* where it is not footage from the feature itself, but is shot specifically to create a metaphor for the film.

We do television commercials, and in some we have a lot of creative freedom. Bell Atlantic, for example, came to us with certain basic copy points and we took it from there. We also simply act as a production company doing storyboard concepts. There's a range there, in terms of our creative freedom.

ON THE EVALUATION OF GRAPHICS: It became apparent to me maybe seven or eight years ago that graphics was moving into another phase, that of the integration of a live image with a graphic image, and the manipulation of the two. And that animation as such, and live action as such, that those separations were going to break down. And essentially, that's what happened. For instance, it's very difficult now to look at a television commercial and see what part of it is graphic and what part of it is live. There are no longer these hard lines between things anymore. It's because of an advance in technology, but also because we expect things that are more and more sophisticated. The need that American advertising has to generate this stuff so quickly and be new all the time—it comes from a lot of interest in innovative stuff, as well as a lot of junk.

ON SUCCESS: If someone predicted all this would happen, I just wouldn't have believed them. It's probably more of a surprise to me than anyone else. A lot of success is just luck, and drive, the right combination of things. I don't feel successful, so it's hard to say. I'm not just saying that. These things have all seemed external to me. I gave a lecture up in Cambridge a month ago. I was surprised to be greeted by an audience of young people who seemed to perceive me in a certain way, in a way I don't see myself. They perceived me as having made it. All I see are the day-to-day problems, and what we're going to do, and where this all leads. You hope success allows you to do what you want to do. It's not always that simple, unfortunately. But perhaps it will allow you to do what seems to elude most people, to become a whole human being. If success means you can afford a fancy sports car and stuff, then what is it? It's not much.

ON GETTING STARTED TODAY: You need practical skills. One of the things that makes it difficult for a young person in this business is that it's so capital-intensive, and you can lose money so easily and you can spend money so easily. As an employer, when you look at a young person's work, you want to see what they've done. If you want to be a filmmaker, make a short film. Get it done by whatever way, just to do it. It's seeing the film, something physical, that would make me want to hire somebody. The thing you want to prove is that you have enough drive to pull this thing off.

I once read a beautiful little article that Ingmar Bergman wrote. It was actually part of a speech he gave when he received something called the Erasmus Prize, and it was reprinted in front of a screenplay of *Persona.* He was saying how he felt this necessity to show things, even as a child. I think I have that need, too; certain people have it. He said he knows there are certain people who have probably done much finer films than he has, but the films are "behind their eyelids." In order to make a film, you've got to take them from behind and put them out front and show people. It's very easy to talk about great things, it's very hard to do them. So I would say you just somehow have to get it done.

ON BEING GOOD AT WHAT YOU DO: When I started making my first film, I realized that I had this strange ability to be able to work with an image over time. Again, I don't know where it comes from. And I realized I was particularly good at it. In other areas, conventional graphic design, architecture or industrial design, I think I was just average. But in this area I was very good. It was a real strange thing to have happen when you're 20. It was great! I was very lucky. I think maybe there are a lot of people out there who never do find that thing they're really good at. Film became this strange thing for me, which it is still to a certain degree. It's a way of performing, but without having to be there. But you have to want it an awful lot. Even in this kind of colorless, crass world that we're part of, it still is a personal vision. You've got to have that.

ON THE SATISFACTIONS: Nothing is ever as good as a dream. Nothing is ever as good as when you first sit down and start planning something out. But there is a point where I can look at something and say, "Gee, that came pretty close to what we originally thought about and it's pretty good." Yeah, there's a lot of satisfaction. In fact, that's the only satisfaction in the work, since I'm not really dealing with the money side of it. It's good. I like it. And ultimately you've got to satisfy yourself. You can't try to second-guess a client. That doesn't mean you throw out their idea. But you make it work for you, and then most likely it will work for someone else. If it doesn't work for you, it isn't going to work for anybody.

ON THE NEW TECHNOLOGY AND CREATIVITY: What's beginning to happen that's interesting is that creative people can now work with the new vocabulary, because it doesn't require an engineer to do it. So you're getting it out of the hands of the strictly technical people and into the hands of people who can deal with it on an emotional level. I think we're going to see wonderful things come out of this.

ON THE REALITIES OF COMMERCIAL FILMMAKING: My brother and I are in this together. If there are certain ideas we know the client will never pay for, we throw those out! Film is expensive. I may have an idea for a title sequence that would cost $200,000 to film. Well, they're not going to do that. Film is a business. You can't get away from that. It's a big business. But on occasion it all works. You have a great idea, and you make someone want it. They go for the money. All those pieces fall together and something really interesting comes out of it. Other times, the work is compromised. I wish it weren't so, but it often is.

ON THE WORKING PROCESS: If we're working on a title sequence for something, I try to find the central metaphor for this two-hour movie. That's the first thing I look for. You try to address that. You try to synthesize the problem and figure out what is critical to this whole thing, what is to be thrown away and what isn't. If you try to define what is important, you're eliminating a whole lot.

A good idea is a good idea. If you have a great idea for something it's going to be a better project. The opening title sequence for *Garp* is done with this baby.* Technically that was very difficult to do, to pull off, because we couldn't actually throw a baby in the air. But the important thing was what the audience got from it. The way it was done gave you a macro-sense of the baby.

Then take one of the first major things we did, or at least the one that got us a lot of notoriety in Hollywood—the opening title sequence for *Superman*. Everything had to be done by hand. It's all easy to do now, but at that time, it wasn't. The notion of streaking titles was a very good idea for *Superman*, since it's a

---

**The World According to Garp* opens with an award-winning title sequence where a baby is continually thrown in the air, laughing and cooing.

movie about a man who can fly. So the flying titles were a good metaphor for the whole movie. Right there, you have a good idea. At that point, just to physically get it all done and get it cut into the film in London, where it was being put together was incredibly laborious. There were mistakes in it, lots of errors where things didn't link up. That was all I could see. But I went to the opening, which was at the Ziegfield. It was filled with every sort of luminary in New York. It's a very large theater. And I sat down and watched those titles flip an audience. I realized it didn't matter that there were technical problems; the audience was just soaring with it by the end. They went with it, because the concept was right and the execution was good enough to pull it off. It didn't *have* to be perfect.

ON SUSTAINING ENERGY: You've got to be self-protective where you can. We're in an industry where you can abuse yourself and your creative energy. I think you have to have interests outside of what you do, or your focus becomes too narrow and you begin to lose it. If you lose what you are as a person, then maybe you've lost it all.

ON WOMEN IN FILM: One thing I think that's very strange, which I'm going to go on record for, is why in the seventy-year history of film have there been so few women directors? I think if you ask yourself that question, it becomes obvious that directing is a kind of closed club. It's opening now. There are women directors who are beginning to do commercially viable things. When we're hiring somebody, whether it's a woman or a man, it makes absolutely no difference. It's the way a person thinks that I'm interested in. But I think it's going to take a long time before it really changes in Hollywood, especially on commercial features, because the money people out there still think of women as secretaries to bring them coffee.

ON ADVICE TO YOUNG PEOPLE: Try to be true to yourself. If you really want to do film, just do it. There's always a way. You don't need sophisticated equipment. Don't try to make a Hollywood film with $5000. Produce something else, and maybe that will be a lot more inventive than what a Hollywood film is. I think that's where students often fail, because they're looking at all this slickly produced television stuff and feature stuff, and then when they go out and try to do it. They're almost reinventing the wheel. They're trying to do that same thing without the means. It's a terrible predicament to box yourself into that corner.

3

Fine Arts

THE fine arts—drawing, painting, sculpture, and printmaking—attract very special kinds of people. Often they are women and men who reject traditional career goals and economic security, for exploration, self-expression, and self-discovery. Today, however, it is far more difficult to make the choice for a life in the fine arts. Living is expensive. Materials are expensive. And even when artists are willing to sacrifice most comforts other people take for granted, they still cannot afford to pursue only artistic goals.

Art is unappreciated by most of the world unless it sells for a great deal of money. But critics and commentators constantly lament the passing of that simpler time when artists, poor and unacknowledged, dedicated themselves to putting their visions on canvas. This places the artist in a double bind. A society that otherwise applauds a "go for the gold" philosophy respects the purity of poverty when the choice is for art or principle. An artist who becomes rich in his or her lifetime is suspect. But today's artist, growing up in a society with such schizophrenic values, sees the idiocy in romanticizing poverty; it only complicates the process of continuing to make art.

Artists are now far more sophisticated about the economics of the fine art world and are taking responsibility for their own economic well-being. This begins with a simple awareness that the work they produce has value, not just value from a pure aesthetic or historic sense, though that may exist, but value in the marketplace. This awareness gives artists more power over their artistic lives. They know they have the means of production in their hands. Until the artist produces the work, neither the dealer nor the collector has anything to exchange money over. Taking one's art seriously means not only creating it with integrity and passion, but believing in its financial value to other people.

If much of the art that is being produced today is criticized for its lack of substance and lack of technical excellence, more artists have become rich and famous within their lifetimes than ever before, and many are earning at least a part, if not all, of their living by their art. This is a major change in the status of artists. Young people considering a career in the fine arts should understand that however this change came about, the artist has only gained by it. When young artists begin to sell paintings for a lot of money, it is good for all artists. It means there is a market for art. As long as there is a market, everyone, including the artist, benefits.

Much of the talk of the art world revolves around "good art, bad art." That's talk for media and critics. It's not talk for artists. Valid judgments are rarely made by the creators and it is better not to be involved in critical politics.

The fine art world's traditions have been held together by nonartists—writers, historians, critics, museum executives, collectors, all those people who, while not producing the art themselves, have established the ground rules, the standards, the aesthetic. It has always been to their advantage for artists to be dependent on their values, their system.

Most artists by nature want only to work, to be left alone to put their vision on canvas or paper or to carve it out of steel or stone, or whatever. Artists traditionally have been grateful to have responsibilities for everything but their own work handled by others. They no longer enjoy that luxury. They live in a world that has become increasingly savvy about advertising, marketing, financial planning, promotion, and image making. Artists should understand that some involvement in these areas, though not their ultimate goal, can often help them achieve artistic success.

Today's professional art schools are teaching young artists to question what has gone before, the old systems and traditions that no longer apply in this less stable world that has gone advertising- and promotion-crazy. Granted, they are teaching them that what has always been important for an artist continues to be true today—that creating a work that is unique and personal and is the truest representation of the artist's vision is the first stage of a fine arts career. But they are teaching them that that is only the *first* stage.

Not long ago, the first stage was *it* for the artist. After that, the work was up for grabs. Maybe a gallery would give the artist a show, maybe not. Maybe someone's aunt would buy it. Maybe it could be exchanged with the landlord for this month's rent.

The art schools today—particularly those with faculty who are professional artists experienced in the ways of the art world—are teaching stage 2. Stage 2 demands a more aggressive stance for the artist. Showing the work is a legitimate part of the creative process. If the work is not seen, it is not complete. Ideally, it should be seen and sold; however, for most artists, the first is difficult enough to achieve. At one time galleries became less and less inclined to take chances on showing younger/or unknown artists; it was a period when the art market was tired and jaded. It is no longer. Artists are breaking the once-universal rules that said that there were only a few galleries worth showing in, that certain places were inappropriate for showing art, that the fine artist does not do commercial work because it diminishes the image. Today's artists are showing in discos, and store windows, they're showing on magazine covers and on the street. And they're getting responses and they're selling. Galleries and museums are no longer their only outlets.

One of the great lessons of the recent art boom in New York's lower East Side galleries is that when artists take their own careers in hand, make their own rules, they create excitement about their art and people begin to come to them: collectors, galleries, and museums.

The best schools for the fine arts are those with a professional faculty in touch with such change in the art world, who will teach beginning artists the fundamentals, will help them develop strong skills, and will then free them to move in any direction that will further a personal vision.

EDUCATION AND TRAINING The most common route to becoming a fine artist is art school. For four years you'll study painting, sculpture, drawing, color, and art history, among other things, usually declaring a major field of study sometime in your sophomore year. Art school is a time for exploration and experimentation and self-discovery. By the end of your undergraduate experience, you should have found an area of interest, if not specialization, to continue in.

Few students are ready to show immediately after graduation; they need more time to develop. This is one of the reasons why many students go on to graduate school, where they enjoy two more years in a studio setting under the close supervision of one or several artists who work in their medium. Working artists make the best teachers for young artists. The teaching relationship becomes an apprenticeship where you learn not only about technique, but about the world you'll live in as long as you continue to create. A graduate degree in fine arts also makes you eligible to teach in those colleges and universities with undergraduate programs in the fine arts.

When choosing both your undergraduate and graduate programs, visit the schools and talk with the heads of the departments. See if there will be freedom for you to explore as many avenues as you like, and whether the environment has the kind of energy, enthusiasm, and freshness that will make you take your art seriously.

In undergraduate school you will choose a major from among three areas: painting, printmaking, or sculpture. But because many new media now exist, the three areas are no longer clearly defined. Many new materials and methods are used to create art. Oil on canvas is hardly out of fashion, but works with textural elements, collage elements, and sculptural elements are now also categorized as "paintings." The definition of sculpture has expanded as well. Wood beams, rocks, sand, plaster, and iron join stone as suitable materials for use by sculptors.

In a sophisticated art program, the basics are taught, the principles of traditional art defined, and the uses of materials and methods explored. With these tools at hand, the artist can mix and match to find the medium, the material, and the method that best reflects her or his vision.

THE GALLERY SYSTEM

There are many changes going on in the gallery system today, with many newer galleries opening, not only in the large cities but all across the country. As people have more leisure time and more disposable income, they can afford to buy art, perhaps not "Art" with a capital A, by established painters, sculptors, and printmakers, but art by artists as yet unknown, who can be collected before they become famous.

The gallery system exists as a hierarchy. The top galleries handle only name artists—famous living artists and/or the estates of famous dead artists. Your chances of exhibiting with these galleries are slim, unless you become very famous first at a lesser gallery. If so, they will no doubt come to you and offer to raise the price of your paintings with the move. A middle range of galleries handles some well-known artists of lesser stature, but will also look at work of new artists and take on some of them each year. The top and middle-range galleries function not only as dealers, many become career managers, arranging promotion, editing articles, and negotiating exhibits, international sales, and public appearances for the artist. This kind of activity is, of course, dependent on the particular gallery and the ambition of the person in charge. Lesser galleries may do these things as well, but building an artist's career takes time, energy, and commitment, and most galleries simply sell art.

Below the top and middle-range galleries come the rest. They are of various different sizes. Some may be family-owned businesses that were once frame shops; some are run by people who are in it simply because they like art. Galleries generally have a group of clients, although they also count on making some sales from street traffic.

Financial arrangements vary, but most often the gallery functions on a percentage basis with the artist. Most take 50 percent on each work sold. At one time, established galleries would pay the artist a monthly allowance to meet expenses. It was seen as a payment against future sales. But this is rare in today's dealer/artist relationship. When a show is mounted, the artist often pays for half of the framing and half of the cost of the catalog or brochure. The gallery generally pays for advertising in newspapers and magazines.

One of the most important benefits an artist gains from a gallery show is the reviews. Unfortunately, getting reviewed, particularly in a large city like New York, is chancy. There are many, many shows opening every week, and the most newsworthy shows get first exposure. "Newsworthy," of course, applies to artists with established reputations. However, because of renewed interest recently, more column space is being devoted to arts, and more artists' shows are being reviewed. In smaller cities and towns, where there are fewer galleries, a show opening is an event and consequently has a better chance for a review.

Group shows are becoming more and more common. In a group show, an artist who may or may not have any formal relationship with a gallery shows anywhere from one to several pieces in an exhibition with other artists. The gallery takes its usual commission, but only on the pieces exhibited in the show. New artists are often discovered in such shows, which are frequently reviewed, particularly those in established galleries, because they afford an opportunity to see many artists' work at one exhibition.

In several large cities, there are artists' cooperatives, an arrangement whereby a group of artists rent space together so they will be assured of a place to show their work. Commissions from sales are returned to the cooperative to pay expenses and advertising. Occasionally, the cooperative will offer to show someone who is not a member. In such a case, the artist may have to pay for all expenses incurred for advertising, promotion, etc., and, as with members' sales, a commission is taken by the cooperative.

A recent phenomenon on the New York art scene, one we touched on earlier, is the sudden appearance of a new gallery area on the lower East Side, where several hundred small art galleries are now housed in what used to be storefronts and small shops. Some are run by established gallery professionals tired of the high rents and the formal atmosphere uptown. Others are run by people in their early and late twenties, some of them artists, others entrepreneurs wanting to strike out in new areas for a small investment. In the beginning, rents were inexpensive; but with the area's success, they have doubled and tripled. Prices being asked for the art, once very cheap, are also climbing though they are still affordable. The lower East Side is the ideal place for new artists, and in fact, many young artists have had their first shows there. A few of them have since been "discovered" by Soho—once itself a new area for unknown artists and now quite established—and uptown galleries and museums.

Museum Exhibits

Museums, primarily nonprofit organizations, invariably have expenses above their operating costs; these often have to be met with funding from corporations, foundations, and governmental sources. The large exhibitions that draw great public attention—and money—are a recent phenomenon. The money raised from a show like the van Gogh exhibition at New York's Metropolitan Museum can be used in turn to mount more scholarly or special interest exhibitions.

Many museums across the country are making an effort to show new work on a more regular basis. The most well-known of exhibits dedicated to such work is the Whitney Biennial. Curators make great efforts to move across the country and look at as much art as they can. Sometimes they come up with shows which, though uneven, represent one museum's view of the most significant art currently being produced in this country. Artists may apply for consideration for these shows by submitting slides of their work to the curatorial staff of museums that mount such exhibits.

Other Careers in the Fine Arts

Some careers in the fine arts field are based on showing or writing about the art created by others. Museum directors, curators, conservators, art historians, and art critics, though not fine artists themselves, are directly involved in the field.

THE MUSEUM DIRECTOR In today's complex museum world, the job of museum director is primarily an executive management position, and the operating style of each director is very different. Although the curatorial path is a route to this top job, often the most creative and talented scholars find the burden of fund-raising, promotion, and entertainment difficult. Though most museum directors today are men, there are signs that women are moving into the arena, just as they are in many management postions in other businesses.

THE CURATOR Careers within a museum are basically curatorial: research assistant, assistant curator, associate curator, and curator. Curatorial work involves assembling art for exhibitions, supervising the installation of exhibitions, writing exhibition catalogs, and lecturing on an exhibition or on a particular area of specialization.

Those who plan to become curators usually major in art history in college. By their junior year, most future curators have chosen a specialty, whether it is in African art or twentieth century American art. The course work for all four years focuses on reading, research, and scholarly writing.

Many colleges also offer majors in museum administration, and for anyone who is considering a long curatorial career, it might be wise to take a few courses in such areas as fund-raising, business administration, promotion, and finance.

All things being equal, a prestigious museum will choose as its curator an art historian with a doctoral degree. That degree can open a great many doors, especially if it is from an outstanding liberal arts institution. The job of curator combines creativity, scholarship, and administration. The decision to mount a show on a particular period or artist, or to create a show around a theme, begins with the curator, in consultation with the director. The works of art have to be collected, sometimes from around the world. The curator with his or her assistants arranges for shipping, insurance, and the installation of the exhibition. All of this, of course, has to be done within a fixed budget and on a certain schedule.

THE CONSERVATOR Most large museums have a conservation department. Conservators are highly skilled artists with strong backgrounds in art history, in the science of materials, and in the techniques used in past and present art. They also must have skill and experience in cleaning, restoring, and reconstructing works of art.

There was a time when conservation was a simpler matter, although it was always painstaking work. It was handled as a master/apprentice experience, where the apprentice worked with the master, learning basic techniques until ready to work on his or her own. But with the new materials and techniques used in art today, the demands for technical knowledge have become far greater. Although the job opportunities in this field are limited, there are programs available at a few colleges and universities, and a college education with at least a master's degree is now recommended for the position as well as apprenticeship with a master (if you can still find such a person).

THE ART HISTORIAN Like the museum curator, the art historian majors in art history, but with a focus on an academic career. This means becoming an expert in one particular area, and invariably going on to graduate school, since a doctoral degree is mandatory to achieve any status in a university structure. Teaching, research, lecturing, and writing compose the work of an art historian. It is a life of intellectual pursuit. Academic salaries, even for tenured faculty are not high, but can be supplemented by fees from lectures and articles and by advances and royalties on books.

THE ART CRITIC Although technically one might consider this a career in writing, art criticism is a profession that evolves from a passion for the appreciation of art. The art critic can remain within an academic environment and write as part of the teaching experience. Or the art critic can take on curatorial responsibilities at a museum, responsibilities that involve the writing of catalogs for shows and exhibitions in the museum. This kind of writing can require original thinking and in-depth research, although just as often catalogs simply present information, with little assessment or critical analysis involved.

The art critic can also enter the field of journalism and write for a large daily newspaper or a mass-market magazine. Criticism on this level wields a great deal of influence, and these positions are highly regarded by dealers, consumers, and collectors of art—and, of course, by artists, who rightly or wrongly feel controlled by the power of the press. Art critics are the most visible professionals in the field, since their perceptions and opinions appear regularly in papers and magazines. Their opinions can establish the career of a young artist and can easily influence the career of a well-known artist as well. Presently, because New York is still the country's major art center, the

New York Times senior art critic holds the premier position in the field. In fact, any position in criticism and reporting for the *Times* wields influence. *Time* magazine with its wide distribution also has major impact.

The work of a newspaper or magazine critic consists of reviewing exhibitions as well as presenting the various worlds of art, past and present, to the general public.

The art world is a very small one, with limited career opportunities, but those who write about it—the world itself, its politics, economics, and marketing trends—are at its center. It is a world that respects knowledge, acknowledges influence, and is impressed by money. The successful writer will be conscious both of the limitations of his or her position and of the opportunities he or she has to further truth, beauty, and creativity.

INTERVIEWS

NANCY GROSSMAN
Sculptor/Painter

Nancy Grossman's reputation was established during the mid-seventies when she was represented by Cordier and Ekstrom in New York City. Since then, her powerful drawings, paintings, and sculpture have been exhibited at the Whitney Museum of American Art, the Brooklyn Museum, the Corcoran Gallery of Arts in Washington, the Larry Aldrich Museum of Contemporary Art, the Dallas Museum of Fine Arts, the National Museum of Art, the Phoenix Museum, and the Albert Loeb Gallery in Paris, as well as in private collections both here and abroad. Her work has gained the attention of both the popular and art media. She was awarded a Guggenheim Fellowship in 1965 and received the American Academy of Arts and Letters/National Institute of Arts and Letters Award in 1974 and the National Endowment for the Arts Fellowship in Sculpture in 1984. She is listed in Who's Who in American Art, Who's Who of American Women, Contemporary Artist, *and others.*

ON GETTING STARTED: I went to school in the late fifties. I was very young. I started art school when I was 16 years old. I worked my way through school. It wasn't as if my parents were able to help me, although they did. There was a kind of admiration and some kind of support. I'm sure that's why I became an artist. It was something I did that made me very special to other children and my parents.

I went to Pratt Institute. They didn't even have a fine arts department then. The closest thing I could get to being an artist was a department called Graphic Arts and Illustration. It was only when I met people who were actually studying with abstract expressionist painters who taught at Pratt at night that I realized there was such a thing as the secret life of the painter. I mean, for me it was a secret life. I had a boyfriend who used to come home and give me all the problems that Adolph Gottlieb would give him. They were space problems. They were abstract expressionist vocabulary problems. And I would fail miserably. But it was an orientation to work, which in a way I still have. Even though I use big, heavy materials, very often my approach has very much to do with accident and it has to do with discovery.

While I was at school I met a couple of people who were very influential in my life. One of them was a painter teaching at Pratt named Richard Lindner. He was very smart and wonderful with students. He was also one of the few people who was not particularly sexist. Maybe he was in his personal life, but on a very deep, personal artistic level his contention was that his best, most creative students were women. He thought it was kind of tragic that they would get married, have children, and stop painting.

I left Pratt, but I went back to finish. I felt I owed it to my parents. I fought so hard to go there. I went to school on academic scholarships. I could have gone to an academic school, not an art school. It was so much in left field that I had chosen to go to art school. By the time I finished up at Pratt, I already knew. I was painting and painting. I was going to be an artist. I was very straightforward.

And I was very clear about what to do. You needed to pay your rent and you needed materials. And your work was going to bring you those things. So there was no problem with starting at one end of Madison Avenue. It was filled with galleries in those days, in the early '60s. I went to every single gallery with a portfolio of drawings and couple of slides and things. I wasn't the least bit interested in "Gee, you're good" or "You're not good." It was irrelevant to me. When I think of the places I walked into and how ultimately inappropriate they were. I wouldn't say I was an overly secure person, but I had a sense of conviction about my work. And finally I walked into the 9,998th place. Oscar Krasner. He said, "You got any drawings?" He was very condescending. "Your drawings are really nice, kid. Your paintings? I can't show your paintings. I'll take the drawings, but not the paintings." I said, "If you take my work, you have to take all of it." I'd stubbornly maintained that position until very recently, when I realized it's a waste of my energy, and who cares anyway. It's saying, "Love me, love all of me. Love my dog, love my landscapes." Everything has changed so much that if you have some red paintings and some blue paintings and someone is interested in only the red ones, I don't know, maybe it's all right to just show red paintings, then.

ON BEING A YOUNG ARTIST TODAY: I think there's a burden, overload, because being an artist has become a viable profession. It became recognized somewhere in the middle sixties as a profession. Artists began to appear with models in the pages of *Vogue* and *Harper's*. It's the cult of personality now. It's OK to be an artist. People began to imitate artists. And somewhere during that time, Americans began to collect American art in a big way. The collectors and museums and the artists began to make it a viable profession. So students now who want to become artists, they have to sweep away a lot of burdensome ideas about it. I tell students that they are the ones—that while the marketing, the style, and the fashion in collecting and selling and the fashion in galleries will change, they are going to be artists until they die. This is a real thing to be! It's like having a special horn that you can blow. It's your life. The best thing you can do is to do what you can't help doing. It's usually the easiest thing, too.

ON COMPETITION: When you're an artist, you're not competing with other artists down the street. You're competing with all of art history and you're competing with yourself. Your own best efforts. That's what you have to get better than. And you have to get better than Michelangelo, you have to get better than Rembrandt. You have to get better than the very best there ever was that ever made a visual gift to all of civilization. You take everybody on. So the idea that there are only so many spots in a gallery is complete hogwash! This is a very devastating concept for students. Even if it's advantageous for dealers to kind of run that line past students, it's simply not true. And the part of me that made it possible for me to walk into one gallery and then another gallery and then another was a conviction that it was not true. And it's proven to be right!!

ON MONEY: Until you love your work so much that you feel you're really making a big breakthrough with your own work, it's worthwhile to try to make money in another job. I did odd jobs. Then a friend offered me an illustration job which was beneath his consideration; it didn't pay well enough. But it was better than what I was making painting houses. But I felt very threatened, like I would be compromised and seduced by making a lot of money at something which was not my real desire and my love. So I never got my passion involved in illustration. I did many children's books. I treated them sort of at arm's length. They look it, too. I had an agent. I never told the agent I was really a painter. Then in 1965, I won a Guggenheim Fellowship in painting. The agent was horrified and stopped getting work for me.

ON THE PROCESS TO SUCCESS: I had my first exhibition in 1963. The critical attention was immediately good. I can't say I could support myself. I couldn't, even though the whole show sold out. I was with Oscar Krasner. Brian O'Doherty from the *New York Times* gave me a wonderful review. You could say that was success, in relation to what artists expected in those days. Two years later I won a Guggenheim Fellowship in painting. That gave me the luxury of time. And it was so heady and so exciting. I didn't have to worry about paying the rent and having all these odd jobs. So I reapplied, but they didn't grant second fellowships. So I took on, I think four or five different jobs, books, children's books to do. I calculated that they would take me just a month or two months each. It dragged on and on. And I was sitting while I was doing it. With my own work, I was always standing. This is very important because it changed my whole metabolism. And it changed my work. I got slower and slower. The kind of excitement and enthusiasm I always had was ebbing. It was more than nine months before I finished these jobs. Now I had my time, but I walked into the studio and I no longer cared. I had been away from my work too long! I didn't know who had been doing all that noisy work before. All I had in my hand for nine months straight was a pencil and a rapidograph. But even so I had done two years' worth of work in nine months. And I had changed in the process. I began making drawings. And those drawings led me to these head sculptures. And they were really self-portraits. The work had been abstract before, and now it was figurative.

I want to say this, it's very important. Everything you do comes out in your work. In some way, being a visual artist, you're kind of a sponge. Not to say that you're not just as intelligent as anyone else, maybe even more so. Some day they'll know exactly what parts of the brain are coming into action. Whatever it is, it's very complex and very different from a straight, linear kind of pursuit.

When I was doing these little figurative drawings for books for nine months, I didn't consider them related to my work at all.

Still they seeped in somehow. The figures seeped into my work I did them for so long. And I had always felt close to drawing from life.

I was still with Krasner when I began to do these drawings that led me to do sculpture, which I taught myself. I went to see him, having done all this work and not having shown him any of it. I said to him, "I want you to sell my work." He said, "What do you want, kid? Egg in your beer?" I said, "I can't do illustration any more." I was really depressed. I had these fabulous sculptures at home that I had done and not shown to anybody. I decided I was going to find a different gallery. It was a big challenge. He said, "If you find somebody who can do it better than me, good, go, go! You're free!" And I said, "Okay," and I did. So I went to Arne Eckstrom and he was very good. When he finally decided to handle the work, he made it very visible. Out of his gallery, Cordier and Eckstrom, it became very collected. He was cautious with prices. There was nothing to get rich about right then and there. But tremendous visibility. You can't say that you're rich and famous these days, but you can be famous without being rich—sadly enough.

ON FAME: It made me very self-conscious. It was very sudden. And it completely put into jeopardy my secret life as an artist, because now it was a public life. In some way it was open to the public, or at least threatened with questions from the public. And I wasn't ready for that kind of self-consciousness. It was very hard to integrate this new visibility. Now the world could say everything, and they did. So I had to grow up. My work went ahead of me, and I had to grow into the work. All the repercussions of the visibility challenged me and nearly crushed me in some ways. And I think that happens to everyone. I was connecting to people in a way I didn't realize at the time. Because, once again, the work was very connected to me.

ON THE WORK THAT BROUGHT SUCCESS: I began to make these head sculptures. They were wooden sculptures which I carved and then covered. I had to think about it a lot. I decided they needed to have their own skin. And I used skins. I used leather. They weren't like voodoo dolls or anything like that, they were kind of tremendously right. They felt completely right. Each one led me to another one, the same as my paintings had before. Every painting had some unsolved, uninvestigated problem that it opened up. And the same with these sculptures. It was a time of deep, obsessive involvement with work. These images are in some way very primary to me. They were really self-portraits at that time.

ON THE SATISFACTIONS: There are satisfactions in the process and also in the sharing of it. Tremendous satisfactions. I consider it my gift. And I mean that in a very grand and very major way. I consider that if you want to be welcomed at the banquet, that you have to bring a gift. And this is my gift. You can tell that I've always given the work what it's required. If you look at the sculptures, they exist on many different levels. The visual impact of seeing them—suddenly this head, which is not really decapitated, it's still and calm and there. Then there is the making of it. The work takes me so long. It becomes clear on not so much a conscious level as it does on a felt level. The viewer feels it is invested with tremendous tension. And it is my life. You know I was sitting there doing that. I was there. I'm in the work.

ON THE CREATIVE PROCESS: I usually don't start cold. Even in trying to answer somebody else's problem, like as a student, you start out from your own life experience. You try to make something work that you couldn't make work before. There's something you become infatuated with. For me, I remember a period of being completely infatuated with the particular kinds of forms and movements of cement-mixing trucks. I followed them blocks and blocks to watch them, to see all the forms. It had something to do with sculpture I wanted to make. I couldn't exactly put it into words, what it was. It wasn't easily said and it wasn't easily made. In fact I probably never really made it. But I got close to it.

It sparked me, yes. You always have to dare yourself to begin, and then you begin. And you pretty much fail. I see that after all this so-called success, that I go into my studio and it can be very humiliating. I'm kept in place, in a very humble place, because I am always trying to best myself, or even trying to just get near the thing that I am trying to do. It's pretty much of a big failure a lot of the time.

Things go into my eyes and they spark a desire to make something, say something. Make it real. Make it visible. Manifest that excitement or upset. I see a photograph, and there's something about it that fills me with awe.

I don't make an attempt to tell a story usually. I'm after the idea of using the figure in a metaphorical way, but that's not even it. More than twenty years ago I made some paintings which I named after the Greek word for "man"—"andro." And they were all of figures, falling through space, crashing, not crashing on their heads and getting fractured skulls so much as almost balancing. Landing lightly on their heads and not being able to stand up. In a way I was using the figure to express some metaphor: That you are still confronted with the figure itself and the feeling in the pit of your stomach. A kind of kinetic recognition. Empathy, if you will. It remains the same concern, in a way, and I have never really put it into words, because the words don't cover the feeling. And the feeling has to do with a sense of being human. My own sense, naturally, and the sense that I have of being a human being among other humans in the world.

ON WOMEN AS ARTISTS: I find it's very dependent on the fashion of the times, on whether the times permit women to be more assertive and acknowledge that they are as whole as men. And it does come in and out of style. We do live in a patriarchal society. And I think that men, while they can be bullies and molesters, are still very fragile—in ways that women are not. But to be an artist, you have to dare yourself, you have to find for yourself, inside of yourself and outside of yourself. You need emotional support to be who you are. It is not given for a woman. It is for a man. I think it's harder for a woman in general. I think women are suffering, even now, from the Miss and Mrs. Perfect syndrome. They are constantly placed in the position of not only having to do their work, but who said that men have to look beautiful at the end of three days of working hard? If I had any advice to give, I'd say, Just be committed to what you do. Know yourself. Not even in a self-conscious way, but be your own friend. Really be your own friend.

ON HAVING A PERSONAL LIFE: That's always dependent on the time and the needs. If the need was to have a child, then that would have been important. I would have taken the time out to do it. I work the same way. I work from need. I'm a very unserene person. And for many years, the most exquisite feeling I could experience in my life was the disappearance that I experienced when I was deeply involved in my work. I didn't exist anymore. Only what I was doing existed. You might assume that my life was painful, my conscious life was painful—and in some way it was. Now, having lived longer and having had to deal with these realities, I find my everyday life less painful and I find it more difficult to be alone in the studio.

DIANE WALDMAN

Museum Curator; Deputy Director, Guggenheim Museum

Although Diane Waldman began her museum work in graduate school at the Metropolitan Museum of Art and worked briefly at the Museum of Contemporary Crafts after graduation, it was at the Guggenheim that her professional career really began. She moved from research fellow up through the curatorial ranks to her present position as deputy director.

Among the major exhibitions she has organized are the Roy Lichtenstein exhibit, September–November 1969; the Carl Andre exhibit, September–November 1970; the Guggenheim International

Exhibition 1971, February–April 1971, a survey of international developments with emphasis on minimal and conceptual art; the Robert Mangold exhibit, November 1971–January 1972; the Robert Ryman exhibit, March–April 1972; the Kasimir Malevich exhibit, November 1973–January 1974; the Max Ernst exhibit, February –April 1975; the Kenneth Noland exhibit, April–June 1977; the Willem de Kooning exhibit, February–April 1978; the Mark Rothko exhibit, November 1978–February 1979; the Arshile Gorky exhibit, April–July 1981; and the New York School exhibit, July–September 1982. She was also responsible for Transformations in Sculpture, December 1985–February 1986. Waldman has also organized freelance exhibitions for the School of Visual Arts of works on paper of Roy Lichtenstein, Ellsworth Kelly, Cy Twombly, Robert Rauschenberg, Willem de Kooning, Michael Singer, Kenneth Noland, and Robert Motherwell. She organized an exhibition of the work of Laslo Moholy-Nagy for the thirty-fifth Venice Biennale, June–October 1970. Diane Waldman has had numerous articles in such publications as Art News, Arts Magazine, *and* Art in America, *has published essays with most of her exhibitions, and has written monographs on Roy Lichtenstein, Ellsworth Kelly, Joseph Cornell, and Anthony Caro.*

ON GETTING STARTED: I had initially planned to be a painter, and I received a bachelor of fine arts in painting. I graduated in 1956 and had to make some money when I got out of college. At that time, I didn't even know there was a museum profession. There certainly *was,* but women had virtually no place in it in those days. So I went into advertising as a fashion illustrator. I was able to adapt what I had learned in studio work to fashion. I loved clothing anyhow, and I had once toyed with the idea of becoming a fashion designer. So it all worked together.

During the time I was doing commercial advertising, I realized that I myself could not be a painter, but I loved painting and sculpture so much that I thought about the possibilities of working with art in other ways. So after being out of undergraduate school for a number of years, I went back to graduate school, to the Institute of Fine Arts, and took a combined degree, which was a master's in art history and a certificate in museum training. It was really that program, museum training, which enabled me to entertain the possibility of museum work as a professional career. As part of that program I had a fellowship at the Metropolitan Museum in the Department of European Paintings, where I worked for six months.

While I was at the Metropolitan Museum, I started to interview for jobs. In fact, I could not get into one of the fine art museums, because there were no jobs available at the time. So I took a job at the Museum of Contemporary Crafts, where I worked for nine months. I took the job with the intention of moving on if, in fact, a slot opened at either the Metropolitan Museum, the Museum of Modern Art, the Guggenheim, or the Whitney. The editor of *Art News,* Tom Hess, asked me one day what I wanted to do (I'd been writing reviews for his magazine) and I told him I was interested in museum work. Eventually he arranged for me to have interviews at the Whitney and at the Guggenheim. I was offered a job here as a research fellow. It was for a two-year fellowship. And I accepted that.

Then I kept moving up, from curatorial assistant to assistant curator to associate curator to full curator, until my present position, deputy director of the Museum, which I assumed about four years ago.

ON EDUCATION: You have to go beyond the undergraduate program. When I was starting, a Ph.D. was not necessary for the museum profession. Most of the top professionals around this country did not have more than a master's degree. And, to a certain extent, that still remains. I think that the requirements for museum work are not the same as the requirements for teaching. For teaching, one must have a Ph.D. I would say that today one must have a master's degree for museum work, but a Ph.D.—it's not the make-or-break part of the job. But what is crucial is an eye for art, a visual capacity, and, if I may use the term, "connoisseurship."

The profession is about taste, and it is about the ability to distinguish a great work of art from a less significant work of art. It is the ability to distinguish a more important painter from a less important painter. It's the ability to distinguish a more important movement from a less important movement. And that is something that cannot be taught. It's something that one has within oneself, and it's something that has to be developed through time. It's also important, I think, that one be able to write, in order to write catalog texts, in order to produce something coherent to explain to the public at large what it is they are seeing on the walls of the museum.

I think it's extraordinarily important to have some sort of liberal arts background so that you can put art in context with history. I think it certainly does not hurt to have some studio experience. The art historian often tends to approach art very dryly, through reproduction, and very often many art historians don't have a very real feeling for what goes into making a work of art. The making of a work of art is part of the process of creation. It's also important to understand who the artist is, how the process affects the final result—the image, or the idea behind a work of art. I would say there are three ingredients to education for this field: liberal arts, studio work, and art history.

ON SUCCESS: When I started out I had no concept of success. I really wanted to learn about art. And I was eager to get as close to the creative process as I could without actually being a painter. To me, that meant working with artists and producing something that was creative, which, to me, consisted of the exhibition and the catalog. Success was something I never even thought seriously about. I was just so eager to be out of commercial art into a profession that allowed me to be with artists.

And even now, "success" is not a perogative for me. I tend to prefer to think about the work itself rather than to contemplate success.

If success means that someone offers me the opportunity to travel, to look at artists in a country I wouldn't normally have access to, then I think that's a part of success I enjoy very much. Success, such as it is, has a very heavy price attached to it—a greater commitment to work and a far greater responsibility than one has when one is at the entry level in the profession.

ON MONEY: I think people going into the museum profession must face the fact that they are going into a nonprofit institution and that salaries will not be competitive with the business world. In a city like New York, the expensiveness of the city doesn't dovetail with salaries, so you have to be prepared to make sacrifices. Even fees for lecturing and writing can't compare to the fees you would get in business or in the political field. But, of course, the fees I get at my level now are far better than I got in the beginning. I lecture and write on a limited basis because I'm so involved with the museum that everything else has to fit in wherever it can around the job.

ON THE FUTURE OF THE MUSEUM PROFESSION: I don't think the concept of the museum is changing. I think every museum has a twofold obligation. One is to protect and conserve and show a collection, which is static. And the other—for a museum that is active, not just a repository for works of art—is to engage in contemporary exhibitions. I think that type of program will continue.

However, what *has* changed has been the cost involved in the acquisition of great works of art, or even of important works of art for a collection. It prohibits most museums from collecting what they would like and makes us dependent on gifts, which are not easy to get. Unless there is some extraordinary release of funds from either the government or the private sector, museums more than likely have two options. One, which a number of museums have taken, is the blockbuster concept, gambling that an exhibition that proves to be a huge public success will allow them to mount smaller, serious shows with appeal to a small audience. I think basically that that concept is self-defeating. The demise of Broadway as a viable outlet for creative shows is a result of that kind of thinking. And I think it could very well happen with museums if it gets out of hand.

The other option is museums have to continue to insist on showing creative scholarly works. They have to keep enlightening their audiences and continue teaching them to appreciate art. I think they have to make their needs known, make their financial needs known. I think they have to keep insisting that the cultural life of this country is as important as it is commonly thought to be in Europe.

ON THE SATISFACTIONS: My satisfactions are very personal ones. They have had a lot to do with the fact that I work very well with artists. Every one of the artists I've worked with seems to have enjoyed their experience with the museum. And that's been an extraordinary pleasure for me. I've enjoyed the idea of working in a space that is always challenging, never static. It's an organic space for me. And to a certain extent, it's always a new space because, regardless of the size, the objects I work with and the space have to be reconciled in a way that benefits the art and the museum. I love just being in this Frank Lloyd Wright building. It's like getting up every day and breathing fresh air. I feel as if I'm working in a sacred space. The building alone is extraordinary. And it's extraordinarily satisfying for me to be in it.

The artists, no matter how difficult, are ultimately very rewarding to work with, because we have the same objectives—the best possible exhibition. It's also marvelous to be able to visit collectors who, in some instances, I wouldn't ordinarily have access to. For example, when I did the Max Ernst show, I was able to visit collections in Belgium I hadn't seen before. Many of the Belgian collections ranged from cyclatic art and included primitive art, to the art of the early twentieth century, and some of them actually went up to and included the most avant-garde art, which at that time was minimalism. It was like walking into a minimuseum, meeting the most passionate of collectors, and seeing how well they lived with and loved their art. It was an absolutely amazing experience. Those are some of the experiences I don't think anyone could ever duplicate except by being in a museum situation.

I can also say that, for me, the fact that I'm not in commerce, that there's no profit motive involved is an advantage. It's as close to an art object as I can get. And I have no other motivation involved in my process than the art and the artist.

ON THE PROCESS OF MOUNTING A MAJOR EXHIBITION: The sculpture show* came together over the course of about ten or fifteen years. In 1970–1971 I put together the last Guggenheim International. That exhibition was really about minimalism and conceptual art. It was fairly austere, but a very riveting show in the sense that many of the artists in the exhibition were asked to make work for the space. It was greeted with more than some suspicion by the public, but with a lot of enthusiasm by the art world. From that time until now I worked very heavily with painting, my primary area of interest. But as I worked with painting, I started thinking about doing a more classical sculpture show, classical in the sense that it would be a show of objects rather than a show of ideas, which is what the other exhibition was about.

I just thought and thought about it. And I decided the area that most interested me was the postwar period. So that was basically the genesis of the exhibition. We applied and received a grant from the National Endowment for the Arts, but I decided to postpone it because it was exactly at the time I became deputy director. I knew how much time and effort a sculpture show would take.

Generally, what happens is that you start to do a series of trips to view or review objects, to see objects you have known, to see if they still hold up. You send out all sorts of feelers to

---

*Transformations in Sculpture, a show curated by Diane Waldman, opened in November 1985.

artists, museum people, dealers, and collectors so you can get an idea of where the objects are. Many of them have changed hands over the course of the years. It's necessary to do a lot of what I call fieldwork, to travel around to see the objects in situ. To see, for example, if a Jasper Johns' ale can look as good now as it did ten or fifteen years ago. And to think about it and weigh it in context with other works of art. That process is very lengthy. It can take anywhere from one year to five years. I happen to work fairly fast. And of course, in this instance, I drew upon all my years of being involved with sculpture.

A great deal of the success of an exhibition depends on the availability of objects. I think we've been fortunate because our relationships with other museums has been so good. Where a museum might normally be reluctant to lend an object, they will lend it to us. For this exhibition, I had very few refusals. One of the rules of thumb in lending when I first came to the museum was to expect about a 10 to 15 percent rejection, and be prepared with a backup list of works. In this case, I didn't have a problem, which was very lucky for me. Another thing I considered, and decided against, was traveling the show. I thought I'd have a better chance of getting the objects I wanted if I said it was New York only, and for just three months. Many people simply do not like to part with an object for two years, for example.

That's the biggest part of the process, the looking, searching, weeding, comparing. I must have had twenty-five photo books, which is what I use to organize my material. I had an initial list of artists, and then I enlarged the list. And when I finally, after a year, winnowed the list down, I came back to the same group I had started with. The artists were placed in separate sections in the photo books and over the course of a year I was able to see how the works of art held up. In some cases they did not wear well, just as the artist did not wear well. So I had what I called "A" books and then backup "B" books. Then, once I winnowed down the list, I drew up the master checklist, at which point we started to write a series of letters to lenders to see what I could, in fact, get. As soon as I had the majority of answers in, we had those photographs duplicated and sent them off to the designer. During the course of the organization of the show, I wrote the text. I had someone compile a chronology of sculpture exhibitions from the postwar period to date. There is, of course, a lot of work other than my own that goes into the actual realization of an exhibition and a catalog, but I would say the process took close to a two-year period, all in all.

In terms of approaching the text, I had several themes I tried to integrate into it. One had to do with the postwar period, and the emergence, for me, of a body of sculpture, which I felt was important to show and important to write about. I tried to pull together some of the main themes that had emerged over the course of the last four decades. So while I certainly didn't set it up as a didactic exercise, I tried to talk about what each generation had attempted to do. So I went into assemblage, for example, and I talked about minimalist sculpture. I even talked about earth works, because they're an important part of the history of postwar sculpture, even though I couldn't show earth works in the exhibition. And I brought it into the seventies or up to the eighties.

I dealt with particular artists in the context of how they helped to create important signposts in sculpture, and works of art insofar as they illuminate or define the change in sculpture over the course of the last four decades. I talked about the works of art as important entities in themselves. Another theme I touch upon in the text is how painting and sculpture interact. That has to do basically with my theory that the postwar period saw a resurgence of some of the themes that had initially preoccupied the artist of the early twentieth century, artists like Picasso, who took two-dimensional ideas into the realm of the third dimension. So some of his three-dimensional sculptures really refer to ideas he first developed in painting. I talk about how sculptors have gone on to use that idea, about the importance of sculpture as sculpture. I concluded with the idea that sculptors have been very free to work in the realm between painting and sculpture and that some of the most important sculpture that has been done to date has been done, in fact, by painters.

I tend to work chronologically in designing an exhibition. The chronology is implicit in the nature of the show, at least a show like this. I always break the chronology because the visual juxtapositions are more important than who did what to whom when. So, having taken Giacometti, '50s Giacometti, as my starting point, I moved basically from the postwar period to the present. What I had as an enormous aid was a scale model of the museum spiral, part of which was left by Gilbert and George,* who had used it in order to lay out their own exhibition. I had someone expand upon it and then make scale models of the sculptures for me.

One of the features of the museum that I should mention at this point is that because the museum is a continuous spiral, we can't close off a section to the public the way other institutions can. So we do an installation while the public is right there with us. And it's horrendous. But it's also fun. It's like dress rehearsal for theatre, except you're right there. But because we can never really close off the spiral, our installation time has to be very short. An exhibition like this, which might take another museum a month to set up, I installed in ten days. Without the model, I think it would have been very, very difficult. When I had some moments to play, I could juxtapose objects, getting an idea of what would really work on the ramps in terms of height and width and volume, and what simply could not. It saved me weeks.

Of course, we ran into things we hadn't anticipated, despite the model, but it helped enormously. What happens when art is actually placed in the rough juxtaposition suggested by the model is a lot of fine tuning. For example, if two Noguchis are placed together in one bay, I know they will be by themselves.

---

*Contemporary artists who work together on their paintings.

I won't square off the Noguchis and show them with the Dubuffets, for example. I still don't know exactly where the two pieces will go within the space or how they will work with the objects in the adjoining bays. There's really no way to get that from the small-scale model. The fine tuning really depends on placing the actual objects on the ramps. That's true of hanging paintings as well. It's part of the process, but it's also part of the pleasure of doing an exhibition. I don't like the absolute predictability of knowing where everything will go. I like watching objects move around; I like seeing on the ramps what I couldn't see from a model. For example, certain colors will carry down the ramps. I hadn't known that from the mock-ups because I was working with black-and-white mock-ups. When you see it, the impact is just breathtaking.

ON SUSTAINING ENERGY: I think part of my renewal process comes from the fact that I have refused to stay with one movement in any one area of specialty. I mean, I consider the twentieth century my field, and obviously within that field there's a lot of play. I think that where a critic like Clement Greenburg, for example, can define a movement like color field painting and redefine it, I think that's absolutely commendable because it sets a standard of quality not only about art, but about criticism. I feel that a museum professional should be broader. I think it's been the fact that I went back and forth from the very youngest art to a master like Max Ernst, for example, back into the avant-garde with an artist like Robert Ryman, then back into an area of more traditional history with an artist like Gorky or Rothko, then back into an exhibition of new talent—this has kept me rejuvenated. I don't feel I need to compartmentalize my thinking and stay with one aspect of art. That would really wear down. I think the fact that I keep changing has kept me interested in art.

ON HAVING A PERSONAL LIFE: There's a very fine line between a personal and a professional life. And I think that the more you want to excel in a profession, the harder it is to make time for a private life. So you have to be on your toes all the time. In a society that's still very geared towards men, women have the responsibility of sustaining relationships and handling a lot of pragmatic things. I think it's extremely difficult. I don't have children, so I don't have that additional responsibility. My husband is a painter and I want to be available for him. I want our time together to be not about business, not about the art world, but about us. It's very difficult to come home after a day of work and shift gears.

I think I've been very fortunate, insofar as I've had, in Paul, someone who has been very understanding and supportive. I think a lot depends on the understanding between two people and how much license they allow each other to pursue individual goals, and still interact with the other. It's very difficult.

ON WOMEN IN THE MUSEUM FIELD: I think the field is much more open to women now, but you're still a woman working in a man's world. So to the extent that you are dependent upon men in positions of power, it isn't all that different from other professions. The difference I think in this field is that there are women working at every level along the way to whom you can relate—except at the level of director. And there, you still run into the fact that the majority of museum directors around the country are men. It's a fact of life. I think that will change gradually. I don't know if it will even out, but it should change. For one thing, in the more traditional museums, it was expected that a director be a man. I think that's broken down, to an extent, so trustees, for example, no longer look askew if they see a woman in a top role.

ON ADVICE TO YOUNG PEOPLE: Anyone going into any profession, man or woman, should be himself or herself. I think it's important for young people to know themselves. It's very difficult. And that, too, is a learning process. I think women can make a career in this profession. I'm one example. So the doors are open to women as well as men.

I think it's important, as I said, to want to be with artists, if you're working in the art of the twentieth century. I think it's important to want to write, to explain why one thinks an artist or a group of works of art is important. And it's important to understand that many hours of work are necessary to achieve one's goal, whatever that goal is. I did not, when I first came into the museum, think about being in the position I'm in now. I thought about excelling in the job I was doing, that I was hired to do. So my advice would be to know yourself, excel at what you're doing, and be absolutely committed to a career.

ROY LICHTENSTEIN
Painter/Sculptor

Roy Lichtenstein is considered one of America's foremost artists. His highly visible career as a painter of the first rank began in the mid-sixties as part of the pop art movement. In the more than twenty years that Roy Lichtenstein has been associated with the Leo Castelli Gallery, his innovative work has earned him an international reputation. Numerous one-man shows and group exhibitions of his paintings and sculpture have been organized by every major museum in the world, and his works are represented in major private collections. Mr. Lichtenstein lives and works in New York City.

ON GETTING STARTED: I drew as a child, as every child does, but I guess I really got started in high school. One of the courses they didn't have in my high school was art, so I'm sure that spurred my interest. I went to Parsons for Saturday classes in watercolor. This was probably in '38 or '39. I also went to the Art Student's League. In the summer of 1940, I think, I studied with Reginald Marsh. But it was only for the summer. I probably saw him in accumulated half-hour days, so even though it's part of my biography, it's a little overblown. Anyway, then I went to Ohio State and majored in art. They had a program that gave a degree, and not too many colleges at that time gave degrees in art. I wanted to get out of New York, just for fun, probably. There was no New York art scene in 1940. There was regional art, but I didn't know much about it at the time. I could draw, kind of, and I had no idea what anything meant.

I had a vague idea I wanted to be an artist, but I eventually became more and more driven. I knew that it was not a profession you'd be likely to succeed in a monetary way. People don't think that way now. More people succeed, but it is still such a slight fraction of those who try.

I think I learned a lot about art from Hoyt Sherman, who was a painter and a teacher, mostly a teacher, at Ohio State. He was my mentor and he was my biggest influence. But other people too, at Rutgers later on—Allen Kaprow. He introduced me to people involved in happenings, which were going on just a little bit before pop. At that time I was still, in my mind, in abstract expressionism, but these kinds of things put me in touch and conveyed certain ideas.

I came back to New York after graduation from Ohio State. I was painting in an apartment, but I really hadn't the faintest idea of what I was doing. I mean I had this idea that I would paint and then go to the galleries. But in those days, in sharp contrast to today, the galleries always thought you were too young. They'd say, "Well, when you're 40 or so, and you've had some experience. . . ."

I was doing all kinds of different things at the beginning. It was sort of "student work"—from Mondrian-like things to expressionist things. I brought stuff around to two galleries in '48 or '49. One was called the Chinese Gallery, and the other was Carlebach. The Chinese Gallery closed before they actually gave me a show. But a few years later Carlebach remembered me, and so my first show was there under the el, at that time on Third Avenue. I showed cubist versions of cowboys and indians and knights. I was very influenced by Paul Klee, Braque, Miro, and Picasso. Actually I've had thousands of influences.

I had about seven shows before I went with Leo Castelli in 1962. That's when I think serious things really happened.

ON THE CREATIVE PROCESS: My latest work is expressionist in part. I've made important changes in color and method. I'm methodical in what I do. I hate that, but there's no way out of it. It's the way I am. I don't believe one should be unnecessarily methodical; but, rather than methodical, you have to be centered, otherwise you can't achieve anything. You need a combination of security and growth. Without security you can't grow.

When I'm painting, I'm not thinking of the meaning of the painting. I'm just putting something in that looks good. "Looks good" has a lot of history behind it, but right at that moment it just "looks good." The mark should be lighter, darker, redder, bigger, over to the left further, or whatever. But while I'm working on it, it has very little to do with the meaning of life or the meaning of painting, or where I'm headed, or any of those things. I'm just interacting. That's why I don't think other considerations like fame or money or galleries or whatever have anything to do with painting, really. You can't be thinking of that while you're painting.

I usually get some idea while I'm working on other paintings, or early in the morning when I'm opening my eyes. Something just triggers an idea. Generally it comes out of something else I did. I don't think you can just get ideas. I think you do have to work, and part of the purpose is to interact with the painting. So I don't really know where my ideas come from, but they're not the whole thing. I mean you want to make a unity of your work, and, of course, it must express something. Ideas just come to me; I don't know how.

ON SUCCESS: I suppose success has helped, because I can have more help and more space. But then you never know what you might have been or might have done through desperation. Maybe you'd be driven to greater heights. I think there's no way to know what could have happened if things hadn't worked out as they have. I might have quit, which I doubt because I was happy. I was teaching and painting. Sometimes I think I did more painting without all this help than I do with it; but that could be in the nature of the paintings.

ON MONEY, THEN AND NOW: No one in their sane moments thought you could ever make a living in art or that you could become famous as an artist or any such thing. Though I'm not really sure how Dove, Hartley, or Marin, or others were doing, there were almost no Americans doing well when I started. Kline, de Kooning, and others had enormous problems in becoming known. They were known to a few people and that was in the late forties. And they certainly were not making money then. Even at their height, they were making what beginning people seem to make in galleries now. But, of course, the value of money is different too. Two thousand dollars could go a long way then. My first salary at Ohio State when I was teaching was $2300 a year, and we lived fairly comfortably on that—although we lived like students. I was definitely not unhappy with any of that. I enjoyed it. I was perfectly willing to teach and paint, and that's what I thought I would do. You had some sort of fantasy of success, but you didn't take it seriously. It was just so difficult for an American artist then, particularly a serious one. There were society artists and other kinds of artists who could make some sort of living on their art, but for serious work, it was only Europeans who were being looked at.

By the sixties, of course, Americans had success and recognition. It was realized that America was where the art was being done. Americans were beginning to be recognized, but they couldn't compete with Europeans yet. In the world's eye, you knew that the abstract expressionists were really doing something important and the real art was being done here, and that was fine. Everyone talked about money and they didn't have any and so on. But that was not what you were painting for; it really was not. I don't think you can proceed that way today, either.

ON STARTING OUT TODAY: There are such pressures to succeed. I hear the whole expectancy of success is there. I imagine it is. It's related to things like rock groups and sports figures, where a few kids can make a lot of money. And there are a few artists who do make it and therefore the myth continues. There are many more people going into art today and probably more succeeding in a monetary way. The odds I think are the same as they were, I would say this is simply not a field to go into for money.

ON SUCCESS: By "successful artist" I mean gifted and driven. Of course, no one knows exactly what makes these qualities. Luck plays a big part, in the sense that one is lucky to have talent, to have drive, to be in an environment conducive to art, to have insight, to be usefully intuitive, and so on. Although I don't think one's perception of oneself is a good indication; if you're driven to art, in spite of the fact that you're advised to "forget it," then I think it's fine. But I think you should just think you're interested in art and not think you're interested in being successful or famous.

ON CREATIVE PERIODS: I think the early sixties was a very creative time. So were the fifties. I know this sounds sort of self-serving, but I think there hasn't been much since then until the eighties. I don't mean there weren't individual artists doing interesting work between times, but there wasn't the kind of ferment there was in the fifties and sixties and the beginning of the eighties. It's hard to know where that will lead. I think some good artists will come out of the current scene.

I think a lot of it is that magazines, newspapers, galleries, and collectors were established in the fifties and sixties. There was a demand for articles about artists. You couldn't keep writing about the same people. You had to find new artists and I think a lot of it is that. The whole stage has been set for people to be recognized, whether they were good or mediocre. And when times change, as they will, it becomes more apparent which artists have done something important.

ON THE RELATIONSHIP WITH A DEALER: Leo Castelli has been extremely important to me. We've been very close. I think he has a great ability to perceive artists who can be successful. He picked Rauschenberg and Johns and Stella and so forth. That's why he's sought after. And the artists with him are looked at in a way they may not be in other galleries. However, I think it's still the artists who make the galleries. Even in Leo's gallery there are artists who are not terribly successful financially, so he can't make a success of just anyone. There really have to be collectors who genuinely want the work and critics have to want to look at their work. It can't be phonied up too much. Certainly there are artists who succeed and later on turn out to be not very good, and, of course there are some artists who are overlooked.

In terms of work, you can tell what Leo likes and what he doesn't like, but he makes an effort not to influence. He definitely does not try to tell you that you should do little paintings or big ones, none of that business. No, he doesn't interfere with the process at all. He stays with artists through thick and thin, though. Through the bad periods and the good. He'll continue to support for a very long time some artists who have little success. So he's very good about those things.

ON THE SATISFACTIONS: Well, I find satisfaction (or frustration) in the work. That sounds pretty corny. It's not that one hates being known. It has its moments. But that isn't the real satisfaction. You don't go around all day thinking you're famous. It just doesn't enter into things as much as people imagine. I work pretty much all the time. It's not all satisfaction, though. I mean most of the time it's frustrating, but that's the point. That's what you like to do. I like everything about it. I don't always feel I've got it working, but you get little moments when you think this is really good. Maybe the next day you realize you were wrong, and then you try again. It's those sorts of things. You really want to think you're doing something significant.

I remember when I first thought of the cartoons* and did them. I really felt that the work was important, and I didn't really care whether I had a gallery or not. But when you're doubtful, that's when you most think you need that support. You're worrying about your ability... that's the time when the fact you have a good gallery is proof of your abilities, or something like that.

I think the more you're satisfied with the work, the less you worry about what else is going on. I remember that very clearly. But since 1961 I've had the same gallery and it hasn't been an issue.

ON CREATIVE BLOCKS: I'm not blocked very often. Sometimes, though. But when I am, I just keep working and doing things and drawing and throwing stuff away. I hate to be blocked, but I think it's an interesting learning time. Even though I don't like it, I try to think of it as useful. You're forced to try for something significant. You have to have times when you're blocked and then overcome them. Otherwise you'll never transcend your own level of taste.

ON INNOVATION: You can *not work,* of course, and therefore not produce anything; and if you do work hard, there's still absolutely no guarantee that any important art will come out of it. Sometimes your little insights are real inspiration. But maybe that will never happen. I mean, it doesn't happen to most people.

---

*This refers to a series of paintings based on cartoon images; Lichtenstein took a frame from a strip, transforming it by subtly reorganizing it, increasing the size while maintaining the appearance of the original.

ON EXHIBITING: This may or may not mean anything. I don't think it's really a major part of art or anything like that. It plays some part, of course. Exhibiting your work is a way of communicating it to others and of getting critical feedback and of seeing your work in a more ideal setting.

ON WOMEN IN ART: I know that women are not represented as much as men are, even though more women take art to begin with. I think fewer women really go into art in the same way. It's a hard life, really, living in lofts and strange places and trying to work, until you have some success. I really believe, though, that there are very few galleries which aren't open to women. I think most galleries would gladly take anyone they think can paint. It doesn't make any difference. It does look as though there's prejudice in some way, because there aren't many women in the field. Obviously, somewhere along the line there's a block. I don't know what it is. It might just be expectations engendered from early childhood. It's very hard to know for sure where that occurs.

ON ONE'S OWN PERCEPTION OF ART: Well, you never know, of course. If I said that my perception of myself and my work was entirely clear, you would know there was something wrong. I think when pop began, some people understood it much better than I did. I had strong feelings about it and I liked what I did, but there were people who understood the genre more completely. Most artists are probably wrong in their evaluation of themselves. The few artists who survive history were probably seeing themselves more clearly.

ON POP ART: I liked the new colors and textures and the way things looked. I liked the directness, the strident style, the apparent lack of nuance. I liked what it said. I could see that it was a ready-made style for modern painting. It dealt with the way things were printed and communicated in the modern world. But it was entirely different, from my previous sensibility, which was more expressionist. Now I think I can express both, and that's what I'm doing. I can paint in either style, or any style, I think.

ON CRITICS: Sometimes critics clarify things. Sometimes they have interesting insights and phrase them in a better way than I would. So it gives me something to think about. But I trust my instincts more than stated ideas, whether the ideas are stated by a critic or by me. I don't know if criticism feeds back to the work, particularly. It probably does in some way, but it doesn't dictate the work. It's about telling me the meaning of what I'm doing. Sometimes you just sense that what you do is meaningful, but at the moment you don't exactly know what the meaning is, or you can't express it in words anyway.

ON PERSONAL BREAKTHROUGHS: Well, I think that the cartoons were a big breakthrough, and then everything stems from them in some way or another. Different individual paintings and periods I like better than others: The "mirrors", "The Entablatures," the "still lifes," etc., I think the brush strokes* were interesting. I did them in 1965, but I'm using them differently now. The dots and diagonals† examined printing. It's looking closer, saying something about the way we see reproduction. Using brush strokes to create images examines and comments on painting and, by extension, art.

ON A PHILOSOPHY OF ART: I have one, but I don't think I could say it so it would communicate anything of importance. You must be able to create a visual unity and express something meaningful. Form and content. I guess. It's not that complex or

---

*This refers to a series of paintings of extreme closeups of brush strokes, showing high ridges of paint with occasional drips.

†Lichtenstein focused attention on the dots and diagonals that make up a printed image by exploring an image in extreme closeup.

different from anyone else's philosophy, but it's *my* definition of those words that's crucial. It's undoubtedly different from another person's definition. I might be able to explain what I mean, given enough time.

ON ADVICE TO YOUNG PEOPLE: Artists can come from anywhere, really. I think art school and college are OK. They give you a legitimate purpose. If you're just painting, you're considered loafing, but if you go to school, society views you as a legitimate person—a student—and I think that helps. It gives you the time and place to learn and you're in contact with other people—students and faculty—who may have some idea—probably wrong—of art.

I wouldn't take anything too seriously. Well, I'd take the whole thing seriously, but I'd weigh what everyone says. Evaluate what you hear. Try to discover why two marks joined on a page may be art, or not be art. You can do it all on your own, but I don't know anyone who has. Everyone I know went to some sort of art school or college.

I'd say stay away from art. But if you can't do otherwise, Great!

4

Graphic Design

In the visual communications field, the title "graphic designer" applies strictly to the artist whose major responsibilities are in pure design. Graphic designers work on creating logos—symbols or trademarks for corporations. They design book jackets, record album covers, and letterheads. The "stars" of the profession are asked to set the style and format for a magazine, to establish a "look" for a prestigious series of books, or to redesign a corporate image. The graphic designer has a very strong sense of how to organize a page using print and/or visuals. While art directors are often graphic designers—or at least have strong graphic skills—the true graphic designer seldom sees his or her role as that of art director. The function is a more personal form of art and design. Ideally, a graphic designer works in a less collaborative environment, although all commercial art today is in some way collaborative.

People who are considering careers in the visual arts are often confused by the crossovers in responsibility and titles in the commercial art field. Part of the confusion lies in the assumption that if you can design an ad, you can design a book as well. Of course you can, but it is quite beside the point, since the chances of your doing both are very slim. An advertising portfolio focuses on persuasion in print and television. A graphic design portfolio focuses on promotion through logos, record jackets, book jackets, booklets, and brochures. Schools have compounded the confusion by the way they have defined commercial art in their curricula. Twenty years ago, *all* commercial art was defined as graphic design. Illustrators, designers (whether they designed books, magazines, or newspapers), and art directors (whether advertising or editorial) were trained as graphic designers. They took a few specialized courses in their major area of interest, but at that time the specialties were far less defined. As a matter of fact, jobs themselves were less defined, so people worked in several areas, often taking on responsibilities that they didn't think of as particularly interesting but that came with the job.

As the field of the commercial arts became more diversified, specialization became more necessary. Today the field is highly specialized, even though the job titles don't yet reflect this. The artist whose skills are in a variety of different areas has to focus his or her interest, at least in a portfolio, to get work. The aspiring advertising art director will not get a job at an advertising agency with a design portfolio. Whether the ads are beautifully designed is far less important than whether they persuade the viewer to buy. Design in advertising is in the service of selling the product. Design in graphic design must stand on its own as good design. The ability to handle type and to organize a page so it is clear, easy to read, and beautiful are all considered when looking at a design portfolio, but it is ultimately the aesthetic choices and the level of taste that will get one the plum jobs. However, any outstanding portfolio in either advertising or graphic design will be seen by people in both fields. Excellence is always in demand.

Schools today make a far greater effort to develop artists in the areas that most suit their talents and personalities. Someone with strong skills in design who's more introspective will probably work comfortably as a designer in a studio or design firm. A more outgoing person who enjoys collaboration and conceptual thinking will find more job satisfaction in advertising.

Graphic design is less open to crossover into other art careers than advertising art direction because the design experience is primarily focused on the printed media. Still, within that range there are opportunities for career changes. Continued learning is the key. Designing books requires understanding publishing. Designing record album covers presupposes an interest in the music business. So if you have several driving interests in your life, pursue them all. The earlier you are aware of what you enjoy doing, the more time and effort you'll be able to put into learning how to be good at it.

Book Design

A graphic artist may well choose book design as a career. A book designer's talents are used to enhance the appearance and format of the printed word. Book designers work with the material between a book's covers; they can be responsible for the cover or jacket design as well.

BASIC RESPONSIBILITIES The book designer generally works on a salaried basis for a publishing firm. After a manuscript is completely edited and the specifications for the book are officially approved, the designer takes the manuscript and the visuals and designs the book around the specifications: the given number of pages, number and kind of visuals, and cost of typesetting and printing. The total number of typewritten characters is determined, a typeface is chosen, and a layout is designed, often on a grid system. If the book designer is responsible for the cover as well, a jacket design must be created. More often, a freelance designer is hired to do the cover. In New York, one of the world's centers for publishing, all book covers for "trade" publishing (fiction and nonfiction for the general public) are designed on a freelance basis.

Art directors in publishing houses (who might also function as book designers) are responsible for hiring an illustrator or photographer, if one is necessary, for the cover. They also make the choice of a book-jacket designer, if they are not planning to do the jacket themselves. The decision on what kind of type, what kind of visual, what tone or attitude the cover will convey is based on the book's content. Book designers, as a normal part of their professional life, read a great many books.

SALARIES Salaries for staff book designers vary, depending on the size of the publishing house, the city or town in which its located, and how profitable a company is. Generally the salary range here is lower than that in advertising—at both ends of the scale, but salaries in book design, as in other fields in the visual arts, are flexible—what the traffic will bear. If a company wants what you have to offer, the chances of your getting more money are better. If there are many applicants for a staff job, the company can usually pay less. But if it is a job you want, take it, show what you can do, and once you have, negotiate for a higher salary from the inside. The same goes for freelance work. Freelance book-jacket designers generally receive a fee per jacket design. If you want to work for a particular art director or publishing house, do a book jacket at the quoted price, and if the director likes it, your chances of negotiating for more money are better.

EDUCATION AND TRAINING Book designers need basic graphic design skills, and most four-year graphics programs will provide them. But again, as with all graphic design careers, the chances are you will design other things besides books, even though books may be your major interest. Most designers, regardless of their area of specialization in graphic design, take on freelance work that ranges from hang tags and labels for designer clothes to posters and catalogs for exhibitions. This means that to prepare exclusively for a book design career is to limit yourself. Develop as many skills as you can, let your obsessions lead you to new areas. As a designer, everything you enjoy, everything you know, all you read will be used in your work.

Magazine Design

The design of a magazine is a very important assignment for a graphic artist; it is most often given to freelance designers with massive reputations and experience in the magazine field. Although theoretically a good graphic designer should be able to design a magazine, artists with a vision for a publication that is fresh and new as well as readable are not that easy to find. The titles of magazine designer and art director are used interchangeably, but in real fact, the designer's role differs substantially from that of the art director. In the visual arts, as we've mentioned before, there is a crossover in job responsibilities as well as in titles, but there are some specific demands in each category. When looking for work, be aware of that fact and define your terms, or you may be talking about a very different job than that advertised.

BASIC RESPONSIBILITIES A magazine designer is called in when a new magazine is in its planning stages or when an existing magazine needs redesigning. If the magazine is new, the designer consults with the editor and publisher about editorial objectives, the market, and any ideas that clarify the objectives; of course, the main discussion centers on the content planned for the magazine. These meetings could take several months or more before a design consensus is reached. When Milton Glaser designed *New York* magazine there were no other city magazines being published. His innovative direction continued to be an influence as other large metropolitan city publications sprang up all over the country, each borrowing something of the original format. *New York* is a prime example of effective magazine design; it is suited to its purpose, to inform and celebrate New Yorkers and New York City, part guidebook, part newspaper, part catalog.

Once the format for any magazine is determined, the typeface selected, and the attitude toward photography and illustration established, the problem is to keep the freshness alive through content. In theory, the designer's role is finished at this point, although often the continuing contribution of the designer, even on a limited basis, can be helpful to keeping everyone on track. The art director then runs the day-to-day business, buying art and laying out individual stories. A good magazine holds the design from issue to issue but still allows considerable freedom to interpret content in an interesting way.

The second instance where there is need of a strong designer is when a magazine is considering a redesign. In this case, the content is generally set and the market determined—what is needed is a fresh look. Or the market needs expansion and the look needs to appeal to a broader audience. In any case, the problems in redesign can be as varied as changing the size of the magazine, changing its logo, or completely reformatting the publication.

Creative control in magazines has traditionally been held by the editor and the editorial staff. They determine the content of the articles and retain approval on art and artists. But recently, with a more visually sophisticated audience and art professionals who come to a magazine with editorial skills, the designer and art director have gained more status and now usually share creative control. Many art professionals will tell you it happens only in the best of all possible worlds. Editorial people will deny there was ever a question about equality. They probably both exaggerate.

On magazines where there is a great deal of visual material to handle, where stories require individual design and treatment, the art director's input is crucial. On magazines like the *New Yorker* or *Harper's*, where type is the major component, it may appear to be otherwise. However, any magazine with high visibility invariably hires only top designers.

We have been discussing mass-market magazines in the main. But there are many small magazines with limited budgets that can provide real opportunities to learn the design field. You can usually explore and experiment with the form and exercise more creative control than on more visible magazines. Many experienced professionals occasionally take on assignments to design small magazines for that very reason. Money, in such instances, is a secondary motivation. It is always surprising to discover just how many small, special-interest magazines are published by institutions, companies, and even individuals.

SALARIES Design directors of national magazines are hired on a freelance basis and are paid a fee. The fee is often determined by the designer, who estimates the amount of time his or her services will take. With a new magazine, the investment is considerable and the design is crucial. In such cases, the publisher is generally willing to pay whatever is necessary to have the right person. Redesign of a magazine is also handled on a fee basis, and again the actual amount of the fee is dependent on the time and work involved to solve the problems. Small magazines generally have low budgets, and whether the publications are produced in-house or are given to outside freelance designers, one should not expect to get rich designing them. Fees are negotiable and designers generally balance the amount of money they can earn against how much they want to do a particular project and how beneficial it can be to their careers.

EDUCATION AND TRAINING The same kinds of skills and talents needed to design books are required of magazine designers. A basic four-year graphic design program at a good art college will teach you what you need to know. But again, if magazines have a special interest for you, seek out opportunities to learn by working with one. Banks and organizations produce newsletters for their employees. Most of them can use a fresh design. Offer your services, even for free. It's always amazing what you can find to do if you aren't asking for pay. And a printed sample or samples can look very professional in a portfolio. Also there may be summer jobs available at a magazine. Use your initiative and don't be afraid to ask.

While in school, make sure you take courses in production; knowledge of the mechanics of typesetting, engraving, printing, and bookbinding will come in handy. Typography and photography classes should be included in your curriculum. In graphic design, the more skills you have, the better. You never know when you will need them. It could make the difference between getting a job and losing it. Learning to work on the computer is essential today. Not only should you master the design capacities of various computers, you should be able to use the computer to help you organize materials. Most companies are fully computerized, and those that aren't yet are rapidly making the transition.

CORPORATE DESIGN

This is a field that has really come into its own in the last twenty years. Every company of any size appreciates the benefits of establishing its identity through a graphic representation. However, few people who run such companies have any idea how difficult it is to produce such a program, or how expensive it can be to do it well. Few corporations maintain extensive in-house graphics departments, so they tend to rely on consultants with their own companies. These companies can have as few as three people on staff, or they can have fifty or more people on staff. In recent years, many design companies have developed somewhat the same internal structure as have advertising agencies: a creative staff, marketing staff, sales staff, and traffic and production departments.

In general, corporate design work requires the services of more than one person. The scope of a program to establish corporate identity can be very broad, the presentations quite elaborate. Many require film, slides, charts, and many, many versions of a design—or many different designs, for that matter. When a presentation is imminent, small design companies may hire freelance artists and production people to get them through the busiest times.

Designers who are involved in pure graphics, who like working out symbols and systems, are temperamentally suited to working in this field, and those who are most successful are those with very strong organizational as well as communication skills.

BASIC RESPONSIBILITIES The kinds of work a corporate designer might be assigned range from designing stationery to developing a complete corporate design program. The designer, of course, prefers the work with the largest possible scope. Occasionally, however, a designer will take a small assignment in hopes that more substantial contracts will follow.

A designer often begins a complete design program by coming up with an appropriate logo, or symbol, to represent the company. That logo, once accepted, is applied in a variety of different ways to "mark" anything and everything that represents the company.

When a major change is considered by a corporation, design firms are asked to bid on the job. In this field, as in others, there are publications highlighting the works of noted designers; corporations also hear of designers by word of mouth. In most cases, each company asked to bid meets with the corporation principals to be filled in on the company: its purpose, the products it may represent or manufacture, etc. The more information the corporation can offer the design firm, the more effectively the firm can function, and presumably, the more appropriate the design program will be. Sometimes a fee is offered by the corporation to cover some of the costs in making the presentation. Other times, the design firm considers such initial expenses a part of the cost of doing business. If the firm gets the job, the initial monies can be recouped, otherwise, they're simply written off to good experience."

Once a design firm has been chosen, the logo is finalized, often at the time of the initial presentation. How the logo will be used is also determined. The designer is responsible for seeing to it that the campaign produces one cohesive graphic image of the company, from the stationery to the signs on the building.

In a first job, whether in a small or large firm, you might find yourself working on applications of an existing logo or symbol. This might require many, many drawings, some of which may be used, while others will never see the light of day. Small companies provide excellent beginning opportunities, as you get the chance to do a great many different things. Small companies cannot afford to hire someone as a backup, they need a person who has the ability to learn quickly, and to do whatever is required.

In a large company, you might be assigned to an account and asked to satisfy their graphic needs: a bulletin, brochure, or booklet. Sometimes you might even be assigned to compiling information or finding visuals for a company's annual report.

SALARIES Corporate designers, like advertising art directors, can earn very high salaries if the clients they represent are large and successful. Corporate design firms hire many designers, and salaries are dependent on your experience and on the quality of your portfolio. Small design firms tend to be owned by a designer who will do most of the important design work. Salaries will be paid according to what that designer can afford. As we have said before, these are excellent first jobs. Learning and working with very good people can afford you an eviable opportunity, regardless of the salary. (You can always search out freelance work to make up the difference.)

EDUCATION AND TRAINING If you are interested in corporate design as a career, in addition to your basic graphic design curriculum, take some advertising courses. Learn to think conceptually, get some business skills. Take as many courses in photography and film as you can fit into your schedule. Many of your presentations will require use of audio-visual techniques. A course or two in speech will be useful, since you will need to express your ideas clearly and simply to groups of people throughout your career. An understanding of the computer is essential both for design responsibilities and for organizational efficiency. Make sure you understand how to use several different makes of computers before you leave school. And remember, your real education begins only after you have left school. The best education comes from working with excellent people at the very beginning of your career.

Other Careers in Graphic Design

Book, magazine, and corporate design are the major graphic design areas in that they provide the majority of jobs for people in the field. However, there are a few specialized areas that should be noted. They are fields that do not support great numbers of artists presently, but may in the future. For example, a field like computer graphics will very soon offer wide-open career possibilities for artists with the requisite technical inclination and skill.

The following specialized areas are offered as majors in some schools if not in others. However, most schools will offer a single course or a couple of courses in one or all graphic design specializations. Within a broad graphic design undergraduate program, take as many kinds of design courses as you can. It will help you understand some of the options available to you.

COMPUTER GRAPHICS Computer graphics technology has developed rapidly since the early 1960s; computer-generated images now have such properties as shadows, light-source direction, texture representation, transparency, translucency, and many others. What this means to the visual artist is the opportunity to add another tool to his or her creative arsenal, as well as the possibility of creating entirely new imagery. Today we see computer art on the covers of *Time* and *Newsweek*; we see it on the nightly news and in such films as *Star Wars*. Computer graphics is also a major part of business and industry. Boeing, for example, has produced simulated cockpit designs to show pilots what they will see outside and inside an airplane while approaching an airfield. Architects can generate full-color renderings of a building to be viewed from any angle and any height.

As a career for artists of all persuasions—fine artists, commercial artists, and technical artists—the possibilities in the computer field are limitless. The problem, however, is with making the technology and training available. Because the technology is advancing so quickly, by the time the designer or artist graduates, the state of the art will have improved dramatically. Many schools, colleges, and universities are not able to provide the computer capabilities necessary for proper training. And for the artist who might want to specialize in computer graphics there are limited resources for professional instruction.

For a career in computer graphics, as in all of the graphic design areas, a broad background in graphics, illustration, film, and video can be important. For the fine artist interested in creating computer-generated personal art, a complete fine arts background in painting, sculpture, printmaking, and art history is recommended, as well as access to computer training of course.

GRAPHIC SYSTEMS DESIGN This is another specialized offshoot from graphic design, and as is true with the others, there is no traditional route by which to enter the field. In many instances, graphic designers simply fall into their first job and are offered a second after successfully completing the first. After a few assignments designing systems, they become specialists.

Systems design often involves long-term projects. Graphic symbols and signs can unify a building complex and can make it easier to find your way around shopping centers, zoos, museums, and subways. Systems designers also work with architects on designing interior and exterior environments—suggesting placement of trees, benches, and water fountains, helping to determine the colors to be used, etc.

Successful designers in this field get most of their jobs through contacts with architects who understand the need to incorporate graphics into their planning. However, graphic systems design is still an area where some further education is necessary if the building, construction, and architectural communities are to appreciate the need for graphics in environmental design.

TELEVISION GRAPHIC DESIGN With the introduction of the computer, the nature of television graphics has changed over the past decade. The computer has simplified some of the designing and, in special instances, has increased the creative possibilities. Television graphics emerged out of print graphics, and for a long time it was considered the stepchild of the graphics profession. That attitude has begun to change as more, and more exciting, graphics are seen on television and in film.

Where the computer has made the most difference at the network level is in news and sports graphics, where the images have changed from the once simple titles to moving, twirling, colorful minifilms that introduce sports events, nightly news shows, and specials.

But as successful as some of these lively computer-generated images have been, they are not appropriate for all programming. Television graphic designers today not only have to be equipped to design the technologically sophisticated imagery, they also have to be able to conceptualize—come up with creative ideas for a particular program without benefit of technology. Title cards still have to be designed and visuals need to be executed; even though the computer may be able to come up with a chart or graph or illustration, the television graphic designer still has to be able to produce graphic work in the traditional way—with hands-on skills.

The technology of computer-generated imagery is advancing at such a rapid rate that by the time a book is published on the subject, it can already be outdated. But if a designer understands the basic principles behind design by technology, and continues to stay abreast in the field, there is little chance he or she will find creativity hampered by new advances. On the contrary, most new technology will offer even greater possibilities.

Graphic designers with a feeling for film and video might consider television graphics as a career. However, as with all design, a group of the basic principles is a necessity. Good design is good design, whether it is on a flat page or is moving through space. A future television graphic designer might consider taking electives in film, photography, video, and the theatre arts. Television is show business whether you design graphics or produce shows.

PACKAGE DESIGN Package designers are basically graphic designers. Their careers often begin in a basic design job, but through working on a variety of assignments, they discover an interest in three-dimensional design and design problem solving.

A "package" can be anything that contains a product: the wrapping for a bar of soap, a bottle to hold perfume, the box that contains the bottle, a tube that contains toothpaste, and even the box that contains that tube. Most often a package designer is given an existing package—a box, a bottle, a tube, etc.—to redesign by changing the color or the type, by using an illustration or a photograph, in some way creating an attractive image that can be seen on the shelf by the consumer and distinguished from other packages. A package designer must also accommodate all the necessary information, legal as well as advertising, on the package.

If a package designer is also an industrial designer, he or she may be asked to come up with a three-dimensional prototype of a new box, bottle, tube, or container. Art directors are occasionally asked to design a package, in which instance, they usually do so with a two-dimensional model, but often a package that looks fine on paper won't pour correctly or open easily. A package designer with industrial design training ensures that practical considerations, as well as aesthetics, are built into the package.

Package design is highly specialized and clients tend to use proven designers. Launching a new product is an expensive proposition, so clients tend not to take chances with a graphic designer, even one with a reputation if the reputation is not specifically in packaging. Occasionally, a company will have its own package design and product development organization, but since the stakes are frequently so high, freelance designers with expertise are usually either called in to consult or are given the complete assignment.

Again, the way one moves into a specialized field is by getting experience in the general graphic design field and taking every opportunity to do the work that will result in an actual sample to show. The more samples of packages you have to show, the more opportunities you'll have for further work.

EXHIBITION DESIGN The graphic designer who wants a larger canvas on which to exercise his or her abilities might consider the specialized career of exhibit designer. At one time only architects, display artists, and industrial designers were assigned exhibition work. But today graphic designers are also offered these opportunities. In addition to a broad range of graphic skills, exhibition design requires an ability to handle spatial relationships, three-dimensional design, and oversized visual elements. The most interesting work, for the most part, goes to the few specialists in the field.

When a very large exhibit is planned, say for a world's fair, a convention, or a museum, someone who is just a competent graphic designer will probably lack the experience to handle the specific problems involved. For in mounting large-scale exhibitions, you must know how to handle traffic flow and lighting, and you must be familiar with the state-of-the-art technology in presentation—with the new techniques used in film, video, and photography and with the new techniques and materials that facilitate the assembling and dismantling of exhibits. However, even though there is room in this field for only a handful of specialists, exhibition design can be an interesting career for a designer who likes problem solving and who has a flair for original presentation of objects, ideas, and information.

In recent years, as more of such services are needed, a few independent exhibition and display studios have come into being. They are often started by people with graphic design backgrounds who have developed enough contracts in the area to specialize.

Large corporations also hire designers in this area, usually on a freelance basis. The work is generally assigned through a promotion department that is already staffed with full-time designers but that sees the need to give out such an important assignment to an outside consultant. Cosmetic companies, for example, need counter arrangements incorporating products and advertising for department-store display. Supermarkets use displays provided by food companies in special promotions. Schools, government agencies, and small businesses use various display and exhibit techniques to communicate to their public.

INTERVIEWS

MILTON GLASER
Designer/Illustrator; President, Milton Glaser, Inc.

There is probably no other graphic designer working today who can equal the accomplishments in design and illustration of Milton Glaser. Founder (with Seymour Chwast and Reynolds Ruffins) and president of the famed Push Pin Studios, he went on to found New York *magazine (with Clay Felker) as president and design director. Since 1974 he has been president of his own design firm, Milton Glaser, Inc.*

Among his diverse commissions are the redesign of many magazines, including Paris Match, New West, L'Express, *the* Village Voice, *and* Esquire, *the creation of a 600-foot mural for the new federal office building in Indianapolis, the design of the observation deck and permanent exhibition for the twin towers of the World Trade Center, and the graphics and the decorative programs for the restaurants of the Trade Center. He has redesigned the Grand Union Company, changing architectural details, packaging, and advertising.*

Milton Glaser's many illustration projects are as diverse as his design commissions. He has illustrated the works of Apollinaire for a French publisher and has coillustrated The Conversation *with Jean Michel Folon for Harmony Books. The most comprehensive collection of his work was published by Overlook Press in 1975 (paperback edition 1984) titled,* Milton Glaser: Graphic Design.

Glaser's work has been exhibited at the Museum of Modern Art in New York City, at the Royal Museum of Fine Art in Brussels, at the Biennale di Venezia, and in the Pompidou Cultural Center at Beaubourg in Paris.

Milton Glaser has been awarded numerous prizes and awards over the years, including the St. Gauden's Medal from Cooper Union. He has been elected to the Art Directors Hall of Fame in New York, he was made an honorary fellow by the Society of Arts in England, and is the recipient of the Society of Illustrators' Gold Medal. He has received honorary degrees from the Minneapolis Institute of Fine Arts, Moore College, the Philadelphia Museum School, and the School of Visual Arts. He has taught at the School of Visual Arts since 1961. He is also a member of the Board of the International Design Conference in Aspen.

ON GETTING STARTED: I really didn't have any plans about what I would be doing. When I was at Cooper Union, all I wanted to do was funny drawings and illustration. I was slightly diverted from that work when I became interested in design and design ideas and typography. I also discovered I was equally interested in imagery that could be produced by illustration, and by design dealing with abstract ideas and moving objects on the surface, without, necessarily, creating the imagery. I could never quite decide which interested me more. At a certain point, I decided I didn't have to make that decision. I felt I could operate in an area between those interests. My fellow students, those who later created Push Pin Studios, shared my interest in blurring the definition between design and illustration.

But when we all formed Push Pin, we established ourselves as illustrators first, then we began to drift into the areas of design, typography, layout, and all those other things. The one thing we didn't do, which is something that happens early in careers, was establish a clear preference. I was always sort of in between forms, sometimes illustrating, sometimes designing. Then I found the thing that interested me most: working in areas I didn't fully understand. After doing a lot of illustration, a lot of book jackets, a lot of record albums, posters, and so on,

I began to see that doing things that were somehow a little outside my competence or outside my definition of myself was what kept me interested. At that point, maybe ten years after I'd been in professional practice, I consciously began looking for opportunities to do things I hadn't done before. Then I had the opportunity to go into art directing with a magazine, which was *New York* magazine. That was a long time ago—'68.

ON *NEW YORK* MAGAZINE: Before we started *New York* magazine, I'd done individual pieces for magazines and had been a contributor, either doing design or occasionally writing. But then, for our life at *New York*, which was seven or eight years, I basically did art direction and editorial work, conceptualizing stories and designing. During that period, I was also carrying on an independent practice as an illustrator and designer. So I was doing both art directing and illustration, and I found I liked that balance. I really like doing all of that at the same time without clearly defining it. I knew I was involved in the visual world, in one way or the other. But I found I could get excited and interested by changing what I was doing from day to day, more than by being consistent. I enjoy doing something for a week at a time, and then jumping off and doing something totally different.

ON SPECIALIZATION AND DIVERSITY: It's hard to make any recommendations, because it has so much to do with the constraints of the profession. The traditional way you establish your identity is usually by having an area of specialization. You establish your reputation for that and then continue doing it until you die. Actually, some people find they're very satisfied doing that. There's a wonderful essay by Isaiah Berlin called "The Hedgehog and the Fox, or Dostoevsky and/or Tolstoy." It's about the difference between people who do many things well and people who do one thing well. The hedgehog does one thing. It goes into a burrow and protects itself. The fox does many. It can be outside, inside. It can run, it can hide, it can double-back, and so on. The premise of the essay is that artists are either hedgehogs or foxes. And I have two models in mind, two artists who have been most influential on my life. One is Morandi, with whom I studied etching in Bologna in the fifties, a man who could do one thing, was only interested in doing one thing—the sublime paintings or etchings of, basically, still lifes or landscapes or bottles. Picasso was my other, I suppose, mentor; he wanted everything, he wanted to devour the world. An idea was not safe with Picasso in the room. It's not even a question of choice; I think it's a question of temperament.

ON EDUCATION: I think the more education I've had, the more background I've had in things other than design and illustration and art—things like psychology, anthropology, behavior, language, semiotics—the better I've been able to deal with questions of communicating information. But I would say that, in general, education in the sense of knowing things about the way life works is useful to people. But, it is not necessarily art education as we've conventionally thought about it.

ON SUCCESS: I suppose you have to be very clear on what you yourself finally mean by success. I mean, you can be successful in the eyes of your peers and not make any money. You can make a lot of money and not do very good work. In the beginning for me success meant getting into shows and having my work seen and having it sort of approved. It meant seeing it be effective and, in some cases, copied. A measure of your success is how influential you are on people in your profession. I think what that does is give you strength to go on. I mean, it's hard to go on without some kind of success; you know, to feel you're just sort of beating your head against... that nobody gets it.

In the early days, the success we had at Push Pin, for instance, was basically an aesthetic success. It was certainly not financial, because for ten years at Push Pin we made no money at all. We were getting paid like a junior art director in an advertising agency. We were drawing $65 a week for the *longest* number of years. And everybody else, when we got out of school, was earning three or four times that. But we had a different kind of success. We had the success of being influential, or being well received, of having an important position in shows, and so forth. So when you talk about success, I think you sort of have to define it a little more precisely.

ON MONEY: If people want to make a lot of money, this is probably not the business to go into. In advertising, maybe, but if you're a designer, an independent designer working for yourself or working on staff—you don't make a lot of money, though you maybe make more than a checkout clerk in a supermarket. I do think you can make money if you operate a successful design organization. You cannot do it as an independent. No one working for themselves can make money anymore, unless they do something I don't know about. But you can run a business and make money.

ON HOW A DESIGNER'S LIFE CHANGES OVER THE YEARS: The first ten years always are the easiest, because you don't know what you're getting into. And it's exciting. You're building something, and you see it. Then you move from aspiration, trying to get someplace where the struggle is of interest, to stabilization, the middle thing. Then it's stabilized and the work becomes more routine, and you're no longer a bright, up-and-coming personality, and it's harder to sort of keep the edge because the people who are coming behind you are now being celebrated for what you used to do. So you're now in the middle, the second ten years, which is a maturing period where you really have to evaluate your thing. And the last ten years. I think there is a great possibility for bitterness in the last ten years, of feeling you haven't made it, and of realizing you're not going to, that you're never going to be as big as you wanted to be nor have the effect you wanted to have. There's a great possibility for disillusionment, essentially because of the misunderstanding of the profession you find in schools and in early life, where people think it's just fantastically glamorous, an endless climb upward, etc. I guess you have to begin with delusions about the professional life just to be able to proceed. But I do think you'll find, when you question people thirty years later, that there is bitterness about the lack of opportunity, about the difficulty of doing innovative work, about how extraordinarily hard it is to find first-rate clients.

But by doing many different kinds of work, you can be rechallenged by things you don't know. You sort of go, "I don't know how to do that," so the element of risk still exists. There are not many people who survive that process without getting tired or getting indifferent or bitter. And the few that do are the ones we celebrate, I guess. Finally, after you do it for thirty years and you're still around, doing good work, they say, "The guy still has it. He's still there. He's still willing to commit to it." And that's evident in the work. I think it's hard to be innovative at the end of thirty years, but you can still be good.

ON SUSTAINING CREATIVITY: I think that's very personal. Some people... Rossini sort of stopped writing in his thirties and never wrote a decent piece of music again. De Chirico had six fabulous years, and people question whether he ever produced anything afterwards. A lot of people get used up. I don't know how you do it. I think it's accident and personality. And the personal things that happen. Disasters occur that are unplanned for. It's not all willful. See, one of the great illusions we have left over from the sixties is that everything is possible, that there's no limit to human growth and potential, that all you've got to do is believe in love or truth or go into meditation or whatever it is—and you can do anything. This notion of endless expansion is very mischievous, because it also produces tremendous disillusionment when suddenly people feel the limitation of their own personalities, the limitation of their talent, the limitation of their lives. So I don't know how it happens. I don't know how people stay in there and sustain their interest.

ON THE FUTURE OF THE DESIGN BUSINESS: I think a lot of changes are happening. I don't know what they are. Most technological things have an effect you're not capable of evaluating until after they happen. It's hard to do this sort of forecasting about what's going to cause change. Certainly where the work is, where the opportunities are, and the nature of how things are done—all that is going to change very dramatically, but I don't think anybody knows how.

I know I don't know about my own career. Personally, I feel very much between forms. I've felt this way before. I sort of like feeling that I don't quite know what I'm doing, because I'm not that purposeful. The only real purpose I've had was to see how far I could suppress things when I didn't know exactly what I was doing.

I've just finished this restaurant, which was a very interesting experience. I designed a lot of lights, which I had never done before. Suddenly in the last year I've been designing lamps, almost by accident. So I've designed the lighting for this restaurant called Aurora. It's a nice restaurant and I learned a lot about light in a very interesting way. I'm very interested in environments and spaces, too, and the idea of sort of doing places. It's almost an extension of my magazine experience. I did supermarkets for a long time—I got very interested in how people responded to space and shopping. And I like that crossover between information and environment and experience. So I'd like to do projects of that kind, but I don't know where the opportunity is for me. That comes by accident.

ON THE SATISFACTIONS: There are a lot of satisfactions. There are two levels. One is to sort of work in a community. I have an office with many people. It changes in size, but it varies from twenty to thirty-five people. I like to work in a community where I basically sort of function as a coordinator/art director, running a business kind of thing. We do annual reports and we do the regular sort of graphic-arts studio operation. I have a partnership with Walter Bernard upstairs; we do editorial work. We designed the *Washington Post* and we launch new magazines and that kind of stuff. And that's a whole sort of corporate thing. That's very satisfying, particularly when it works and the level of work is good.

Then I like the work I do entirely in isolation, by myself—that's basically drawing and illustration and posters and things that are personal imagery and have nothing to do with others. I like the balance between them. It's very important for me to do those two things. If I did either one just by itself, I would not be happy. When I don't get enough time to do illustration or work that is personal, I go nuts. But I couldn't only run a business. So for my disposition and appetite, I have to do both. It's always been a juggling act for me. And when I get the balance right, it's just what I want.

ON THE CREATIVE PROCESS: I find all aspects of it interesting. I like the experience of doing it; and I also like the effect it has when it enters into the world. I don't like work that's ineffective. If I do something I enjoy doing, and I find it doesn't work the way it's supposed to work, I feel very unhappy. I like the experience of doing work, and I also like the feeling that it's well made in terms of its intention, that it fulfills its intentionality. And when I have both things, together, that's the work that's most satisfying.

ON WORKING FOR AGENCIES: I very rarely work for agencies. At agencies, the problem is that it's all predigested stuff. Some art director does a sketch based on something he saw you do or saw somebody else do or saw Magritte do. Now there was a time I could do that. When I started, I would do literally anything. But I can't do it anymore. For many reasons, I think—partially, because it doesn't make sense to do work that you don't enhance, although that's the basis for most professional lives, you see. If you're dealing with an art director, the art director's job is to conceptualize the work. But I've done my own art directing for long enough so I don't need an art director.

It's not that I don't need one; it's basically that I can't work that way anymore. So the only jobs that I do well are where I do the conceptual work. For instance, on the Perrier advertising I did recently, Joe LaRosa said, "We have a new thing on Perrier. Do some sketches for me, I'll pay you for the sketches, and if we use. . . . " That's fine. Great. But if somebody comes up with a drawing based on something I did in 1958, or even cuts it out of my book and uses it as a sample, I can't do that. But that is the profession, you see. You have to understand that in an agency, the art director must do that. Because he has to first show the work to his client, get approval. There can't be any other way. Which makes it very difficult for first-rate people, I think, to be anything except sort of renderers. There's some satisfaction in doing that. I'm not putting it down. In fact, 95 percent of the work is that. If you can afford not to do that, though, it's better for your health.

ON DEFINING YOURSELF: Well, I've had a very fuzzy definition for many years, which is why people don't exactly know what I do. Or what I am. It's an advantage in some cases. It's also a disadvantage in some ways. In functional terms, people don't know what to call you for, so they don't call you. Now, for instance, we got into the magazine thing because we are magazine specialists. We get calls every day, recommendations every day. Here I get very few jobs. I get some very big jobs, but I get very few jobs. And it's because my outline is very fuzzy.

ON DRAWING: Actually, if I had to pick the singlemost thing, I don't think there's anything more wonderful than finding out you did a drawing that was better than you thought you could do. If I had to reduce everything and say, Okay, pick one, then, yes, I love to draw. I really do. I still am astonished at what happens through drawing. I just can't believe it. So that really is it finally, if I had to reduce it. But I wouldn't want to do that really, because in truth, it's a mosaic. I like everything I do.

ON CREATIVE BLOCKS: I'm not blocked very often, no. I depend on my unconscious to come up with it and it always does. If you trust your unconscious, your unconscious rewards you. I am surprised that my unconscious is so cooperative. I've got twenty minutes to do a job, I'll do it. Guaranteed. I know my unconscious self is smarter than I am and I trust it, and it happens. I don't want to exaggerate. Sometimes you do get blocked on things, usually when you have a lot of time to work on it.

ON WOMEN IN DESIGN: I think, basically, the profession always had good opportunities for women. The thing that's prevented more women from rising to prominence has really been raising families, getting out of the field during the period of professional development. Generally speaking, on most levels, except perhaps on the corporate level, I think it's one of the best opportunity areas for women. I've never heard the kind of sexism you hear in other areas about preferring a man to a woman to do a particular job. It happens to be, and I don't think I have any illusions about it, one of the very few places where the opportunity for men and women is talent-oriented. Talent does out. It comes up. I've never seen somebody suppressed for sexist reasons.

But the other thing, women in terms of their career development have historically taken time out to raise children. And it's at a critical time, at the building part of people's lives, the sort of late twenties/early thirties. It's hard to reenter in the mid-thirties and build a career. I think for that reason you don't see the same kind of prominence among women, except maybe in the area of illustration, where women can work at home. It's also a diversion of energy. Men can be totally obsessive about their work, and do nothing except that and have women support the effort, which is the traditional way. But again, I think it's structural and not sexism, in this case.

ON HAVING A PERSONAL LIFE: I'm very vocationally directed. I don't have children, so I've been able to devote more time to work probably than someone who does. And I work all the time, but I'm very conscious of balancing it out. I love to lead the good life as well. And I have good friends.

ON EDUCATION: There are still the rudimentary ways of learning this profession. It's just learning how to draw, by trying to match an image with what you see in front of you. Remember, there was a period during the sixties when that was discredited. During the sixties, it was so hard to teach anybody anything, because people would say there was no relevance between drawing something and the new technology, blah, blah, blah. Well, the same thing applies now. It seems very hard to justify why you have to learn how to look at something and sort of make it come to life on a piece of paper when you can do it with a computer, with a camera, etc. Still I know of no better way to understand the world than to draw. For one reason or another, the same old stupid academic procedure of learning to draw in the most rudimentary way to conceptualize the world is the starting point. You don't get anything by starting with computer graphics and keyboarding it. I don't know why that's true.

In education; it seems that the only thing that matters is the peculiar relationship between teacher and student. And it doesn't even matter what subject is being taught, strangely enough. So it's not a question of curriculum. But I don't know of any better way to begin this profession than by learning how to see. And the way you learn how to see is by replicating the world in some way. So the starting point seems to be the same place.

ON A PHILOSOPHY OF WORK: I don't think I have a single philosophy. I do believe that work is central to people's life in terms of their self-definition. And I think everybody wants to do meaningful work. They want to do work that has an effect and that they're proud of and that represents them well in the world and that they feel is the best they can do.

I've tried not be cynical about my work in the sense of keeping at the top of my consciousness the fact that I want to feel that I do honest work. And that the reason for my work is basically to produce a kind of effect that is even, in a modest way, life-enhancing—that the work I do has some benefit for the people who see it. And that provides a basis for me to live in this world. I live very well in the world. I've had financial success, judged by most standards, and I've had the approval of a meaningful audience. Of the two, if I had to pick one, I'd say the approval of an audience has been much more important to me. When I chart the direction of my life, I realize that financial success isn't the reason I was doing anything. I think everybody who is serious about this work considers the financial aspect secondary to the sense of doing work that is useful to the audience that sees it.

NEIL SHAKERY

Graphic Designer; Partner, Pentagram

Neil Shakery has a broad range of experience in a variety of areas, ranging from animation to package design to graphics to art direction. It was as an editorial art director that his work gained national recognition, first with Toronto's Canadian *magazine, then in New York with* Look, Saturday Review, *and* Psychology Today. *He has won both gold and silver medals from the New York Art Directors Club, the Society of Publication Designers, and the Society of Typographic Arts. His work has been recognized as outstanding by the American Institute of Graphic Arts, the Type Director's Club, and* Communication Arts *magazine. In 1978 he became a partner in the New York office of Jonson, Pedersen, Hinrichs, adding his name to the firm's name and moving to their San Francisco office in 1980. In 1986 the company joined Pentagram, a London-based design corporation with an international reputation. His reputation as a designer and spokesman for the profession has been further enhanced by his commitment to teaching, his extensive lecture schedule, and his appointment to the executive committee for the Stanford Conference on Design.*

ON GETTING STARTED: The first job I had after school was in animation. Some people from the National Film Board in Montreal came to my school and offered me a job. It was totally unexpected. I stayed for two years, but the problem was it was too slow for me. Temperamentally, I didn't feel right for it. So I left and went to England and wound up working in a graphic design firm, not unlike this one, although it concentrated on packaging. Then I went back to Canada to continue working in design. A friend I'd gone to school with became art director of *McLeans's* magazine in Toronto. I worked with him for two years, then went on to another magazine. But while I was in Canada, my wife and I used to visit New York every year. When we actually decided to move, it wasn't really for professional reasons. I was very dubious about whether I could even get a job, let alone a good job.

ON TAKING ON NEW YORK CITY: Canadians are very intimidated by New York. Before we moved, I went down with my portfolio. I'd written letters in advance to all the places I'd really like to work and tried to set up appointments. *Look* was a magazine I really wanted to work for at the time. They were doing really exciting stuff and they were the first people I contacted. It took about six months to get my green card and everything. When we finally got there, Karin* got a job right away. I looked around and there wasn't much work available, but I finally got a job at an advertising agency. It was a pretty boring place, but one day a photographer came in and said he'd been over to *Look* and that Will Hopkins had just taken over as art director. So I picked up the phone, called *Look,* and asked for Hopkins. He said he'd been looking for me for weeks and hadn't known where to find me. He said, "Get over here!" I did. And he offered me the job.

About two weeks after I started, I got a call from Milton

---

*Karin Shakery, Neil's wife, is an editor and writer.

Glaser who had interviewed me earlier. He wanted me as art director for *New York* magazine, which was just starting up. He couldn't believe I was working for *Look*; he said I had twenty-four hours to make up my mind. I don't think I slept all night. *New York* wasn't so impressive when it first started, and I thought, "Well, this thing may only last six months." So I stayed at *Look*, and all in all I think it turned out to be a reasonably good decision.

ON EDUCATION: I think a good, basic art education is essential. I really think a lot of schools try to teach too much specialization. If you have really good basic training, that's what will develop your eye. A lot of schools try to teach you the latest thing that's going on. It changes too fast; besides, I think you pick up a lot of those practical applications afterwards, anyway. I have a feeling that designers are generally very badly educated. Many of them suffer from that. I think the ideal thing would be to have a general liberal arts education, and *then* go to art school, because then you know something. But not everyone can do that.

ON RUNNING A DESIGN BUSINESS: What makes running a design business so complex is that you have to wear so many different hats. You're not only the designer, you've got to be the employer. You've got to be a businessman. You have to know a lot more about budgets and production costs. When you're in editorial, you don't have to worry about it. You have a budget, and you know just how much you've got to spend on illustration and photography. And basically, the printing and all that stuff is set up for you. You don't really get involved in all the details. When we do something here, we're concerned about the paper costs, the whole manufacturing process, all the points along the way. I think that's what makes it interesting.

As an editorial art director, your editor is your client. It's a constant, ongoing relationship on a day-to-day basis, whereas in this business, we all have twenty-five different clients and you have to deal differently with each one. So it's much more demanding and chaotic. The deadlines are unpredictable; you're working on several accounts at once, all the time. So it demands you be much more efficient and organized than on the editorial side. Not that a magazine's not hard work, but it's predictable, and you can deal with it and work out how you'll handle it. In this business, you never know.

ON PRESSURE: A lot of people don't work terribly well under pressure, and we work under it almost constantly. I'd say, generally speaking, that this is a lot harder business than, say, being a magazine art director. I worked as a magazine art director and worked very hard at times, but you could pick your spots and pace yourself. Here you can't control it. You really have to respond spontaneously. It's just bang, bang, bang. I think that the end result is just as good or better, but it's not for everybody.

ON WORKING WITH EDITORS: I find that a lot of designers don't understand the need for a well-rounded education. Editors are, in general, much better educated and the lack of solid education puts the art director at a disadvantage. I learned an awful lot from working with editors. Negotiating, for example, in the process of trying to sell a design to the editors —that was an experience that is really valuable now. In dealing with clients, I'm able to sell them what I want, to negotiate, to offer rationales they'll accept.

ON THE SATISFACTIONS: I think the satifaction is on more than just the creative level. It's running a successful business, having a successful relationship with your staff. It's having more control of your work. We are much more involved and on a much deeper level than just being designers. When we sell a job to a client we have to ensure that the thing comes off looking terrific. The other thing that is very satisfying is that a lot of things get very beautifully produced. They're on good paper and there has been money spent on it. One of the things I found depressing in publications was that you had no control over the printing, and the paper got worse and worse as budgets got tighter. To produce good material, good images, and to have them destroyed in that printing—that was depressing.

ON THE WORKING PROCESS: The first thing is to get as much information about the assignment as you can. It sounds obvious, but a lot of clients don't understand that. They think you can walk in and all they have to do is say, "Here's a job, design it." We have to say, "wait a minute, we can't design anything until we understand your business. What do you think you need? Who are you trying to reach? What's the message? What are your priorities?" Sometimes we have a hard time convincing a client that we need to do that. Once you feel you understand what's required and what the client wants, you try to work incrementally. From a basic stage, we try to communicate with the client in a very conceptual way at every level until we find a solution that works for both of us.

ON THE QUALITIES NEEDED IN A DESIGNER: Obviously, we're looking for good design talent and experience. But there are a lot of other things, too. People who are organized, articulate. We want designers who are responsible, who have a practical side to them. Dealing with clients is one of the toughest things to do. That's where a solid general education comes in. You go into a corporation and have to deal with some pretty heavyweight people, many of whom are very well educated. The work alone can't sell itself. You have to be able to explain what you're trying to do and you have to do it well. So more than anything, I look for intelligence in a designer. People come in with some pretty slick portfolios, but they're not very smart. If you're a dumb designer, you produce dumb design.

ON PORTFOLIOS: What I don't like to see is people who bring in what they think they *ought* to show. I want to see people bring in what they *like* to do. There's a big difference. It really distresses me when I see art students coming out of school and all they have is an imitation of what they've seen and what they think will sell. I would much rather see a much less commercial portfolio and get an idea of who this person is, and what they're really excited about. I want to see something really personal in a portfolio.

ON THE FUTURE OF THE DESIGN BUSINESS: It's growing in proportion to the growth of business. If business recedes, then I think graphic design will. It's not a business that's going out of fashion or losing its potential. It will probably always have as large a share of the market as it has now, or more.

ON MONEY: Sometimes, I kind of feel like a shoemaker. You make one shoe and you get $10, and if you make another shoe, you get another $10. There's very little gravy involved here. The money doesn't necessarily accelerate. You reach a certain level and there's sort of a plateau you can't go beyond. You have to respond to what the market will bear. You can't say, "Well, now I've got ten years' experience, I should charge twice as much." Obviously, when you start out, you can't start at the same level as experienced designers, but once that plateau is reached, that's pretty much it.

There are some designers who become stars and command a lot of money. Robert Miles Runyan, Saul Bass, Milton Glaser have developed this sort of massive reputation, so that even outside the business their names are recognized. There aren't many people like that. I'd say there's certainly a decent living to be made, but it's hard work.

ON FINDING THE RIGHT JOB: I think people make the mistake in believing everything is predictable. They think, "I'll do this, and it will lead to this, then I can do this." Most people I know are doing something today that they never expected to get into in the first place. It's strange to look back on it, but I went down a couple of dead ends, and I had a couple of jobs I really didn't like. But the good thing was, I got out as fast as I could. I would say, never stay where you're not happy. A lot of people get into a situation they don't particularly like, but stay in it. Then suddenly, five years later, they realize that's all they can do. I think it's very important to work where you feel right temperamentally.

PAULA SCHER

Graphic Designer; Partner, Koppel & Scher, Inc.

Paula Scher's work as an art director and designer has received some of the highest accolades of her profession: gold medals from the Art Directors Club of New York and the Society of Illustrators, four Grammy nominations for Cover of the Year from the National Association of Recording Arts and Sciences, and numerous awards from Communication Arts, Graphis, Print, Novum Grabrausgraphik, *and the American Institute of Graphic Arts.*

Her personal vision as a designer has been recognized by the Museum of Modern Art, the Library of Congress, and the Maryland Institute of Art, where her works have been collected and exhibited. She is currently on the board of directors of the American Institute of Graphic Arts and teaches a senior portfolio course at the School of Visual Arts.

Scher has designed two new magazines for Time, Inc., and has written and designed The Honeymoon Book *and* The Brownstone. *After fifteen years as a successful designer, she opened her own design firm to expand the scope of her talents. Koppel and Scher handle the accounts of such clients as Manhattan/Blue Note Records, European Travel and Life, Swatch Watch, and Champion Papers.*

ON GETTING STARTED: I came to New York and got a job at Random House. I thought I would get to illustrate children's books, but instead I designed the insides of them. I thought my ability to see was an ability to illustrate. I had terrific ideas—I just drew them badly. Sometimes the ideas were so good, they could sell the terrible drawing. Then I realized it would be that much better if I could contribute the really good ideas and let someone else do the drawing. That's how I became an art director. I learned design from having to design the type on record jackets and book jackets. I did it badly before I learned how to do it well, and that's the truth.

Fifteen years ago, when I was starting out, this wasn't a very popular business yet, and you could learn on the job. Now students coming out of school know exactly what they're going to do, and it's a very crowded field. They have to specialize. I was lucky because I had the opportunity to fail in professional situations for a number of years before learning how to succeed.

ON EDUCATION: You should go to school, definitely. You have to, unless you are just absolutely naturally, brilliantly talented. Without a graphic history, knowing what's available in terms of typography, style, approach, there's no way you can start. You have to absorb the vocabulary. It was a cruder language when I started, but today it's a very sophisticated one. I think to be a good designer or art director you have to be well read and relatively well educated. You can't come up with ideas if you don't have anything to draw on. And you won't have anything to draw on if you live your life in a vacuum.

ON SUCCESS: When I first started out in this business, getting married and having a family was my idea of success. I never thought I'd work my whole life. I never thought I'd own a business. I never thought I would be that good. I never thought I would compete with the top designers for jobs, and sometimes get them. I had no expectations at all. Now I have no other expectations *but* that. It's reversed. There were two factors at work. Somewhere along the way it dawned on me I was going to work the rest of my life. Then there was a genuine passion for the work. I am one of the few people who really did exactly what I set out to do. I went to school to do this. I wanted to do the kind of work I'm doing. I wanted to work on the kinds of projects I work on. I'm glad my work looks the way it looks. I wouldn't want it to look like anything else. I have a lot of women friends who work very similarly, which is sort of interesting. We're all pretty passionate about it. I had no idea I had this kind of energy and strength. At 20, I didn't have any assessment of what kind of person I was.

ON MONEY: You can support yourself. If your idea of making money is having a reasonable income or living very handsomely with nice taste in a middle-class society, you can. If your idea is that you'll become massively, massively wealthy and accumulate millions of dollars, the answer is no. There is absolutely no potential for that. The best you can do is come up with a book idea or a product. Milton Glaser made all his money selling *New York* magazine stock; he didn't make his money designing. That's the reality of the business. You won't get wealthy, but you can earn a living.

ON THE QUALITIES NEEDED IN A DESIGNER: Smart and talented is a good way to begin, but interestingly enough, I don't think real success in this industry is directly related to talent. And I'm talking about people who are very, very good, not people who go where they're expected, do mediocre work and continue to do it. The people I'm talking about may not be naturally talented. But they're ambitious, they have perseverance, strong concentration, and they can articulate what it is they're doing. This is a highly verbal field, believe it or not, even though it's visual. Nothing you make can be produced or printed unless you can get a client to approve it. If you design a book jacket, a publishing company has to approve it, so you have to talk with editors. If you design a magazine, you're dealing with the publisher or editor-in-chief, and he or she has to understand what you're doing. If you do a record cover, you deal with the artist or the head of the recording company. In everything you do, you're going to have to tell people what you're doing, explain why it's terrific and why they should use it. We are commercial artists, creating art for commerce. Somebody is using your art to make money. The book jacket sells the book. The record cover sells the album. So if you can't tell clients why this thing is going to help them sell the product, you'll never be able to sell a particular piece of work you've done. That means, no matter *how* brilliant it is, you've produced nothing.

ON WORKING FOR YOURSELF: It's very complicated to explain. I felt much more secure with a corporation. You assume a paycheck is coming on Friday, so whether or not you're busy, your salary is covered. You have medical benefits, you feel like you're part of a family. When you go on your own, you have none of those things. But the reality of the situation is you're less secure in the corporation because you essentially have one client. If that client goes away, you have nothing. On your own, you work with many clients. If one leaves, there are six others, so at no given time are you really less secure. If you accept that view, and apply it personally, you have the wonderful option at any given moment to tell somebody to go to hell. It doesn't mean you do it, but you feel you're more in control. Whatever you decide to do, it's your decision. You can carefully wait it out and decide *not* to tell them to go to hell... *this* time. Or you may find you've just replaced them and then you can tell them off and not even be angry at them. In a corporation, the only time you can tell them to go to hell is when you've already made the decision you're going to quit your job.

ON WORKING FOR OTHERS: I think everybody should work with people they admire. You can learn an enormous amount by seeing how they work. Get experience. See what your options are and see what the world is like. Everyone should do that for a certain amount of time because there's no way of knowing what you're dealing with if you try to do it on your own right out of school. But how long you work for others really depends on your own personal fears and also your personal strengths. I mean how much work can you command on your own? When I started doing this, I had a considerable reputation. If I'd done it very early, it would have been more difficult. On the other hand, if I *had* done it earlier, I would have needed less money to live because I wouldn't have been making that much money.

ON THE CREATIVE PROCESS: Well, it's always so magical. All jobs are different. There are two ways I work, because I work as an art director and I work as a designer. When I work as an art director, the idea is the most important thing. What you're doing is creating a graphic dialogue with an audience. You're trying to find the best way to say something. My function is to come up with it. I'm good because I write as well as design. So I don't merely sit down and make something pretty. Sometimes I do, if it's the job. Sometimes I tell a story or make a pun. Or I attract attention. Sometimes I offend, deliberately, depending on the situation. Figuring out how I'm going to do whatever I choose is fun. The problem is already solved at that point. Then I begin to put sketches together. Sometimes I do it myself, sometimes I give it to my staff, and then we make presentations and the job goes on from there. The fun part of the job is really over when the idea is together and I know what I'm going to do.

But when I'm functioning as a designer, I may be just creating some form of visual impression. It tends to be more decorative when I do that. I'm usually working out of some style. I may do a constructivist thing, or I'll do something that looks very Bauhaus, or any variety of ways. I can sit and sort of move things around for hours. That's a whole different process. Then I'm working more like an illustrator works, or a painter. It's more putting things down, picking them up, looking at them. That's fun, too. They are two opposing ways of working and I work both ways. Most people don't.

ON SPECIALIZATION: I think the business is going to become more and more specialized the bigger it gets. I think it's unfortunate. I think magazines look lousy as a result of it. They pigeonhole people in these jobs and sometimes they're not even good at them. And we're stuck with looking at the results. But it's the nature of the business. There's a difference between what I think is realistic and what I think is right. I don't advocate staying in one area. I work very hard not to. It took a long time. But I'm the exception, not the rule. I don't think most people do all kinds of things. I can work on a corporate identity project, on an advertising campaign, a record cover, a book jacket, and a poster and design the inside of a book—all in the same day. But I'm really lucky.

ON HIRING STUDENTS: I hire all my students right out of school. Everybody who works here is a former student. They think like me, they respond like me. They're all different human beings, but they're very much indoctrinated in my way of work. It's great, because we can start projects sometimes and pass them around the room. There have been record covers seventeen different people have designed, because someone got busy on a new job and said, "Okay, finish this one off." We all have similar typographic sensibilities. A sense of humor is real important. Terry* and I indoctrinate them in that. It's a method of behavior. The style for this place is irreverent, arrogant. You're supposed to think; you're supposed to be fast. You can tell if somebody's going to be right the minute you meet them. Only one person has left us in a year and a half.

ON QUALITY: Sometimes I do just one piece a day at work. As a matter of fact, I do that a lot of the time lately. I think nobody admits this, but the fact of the matter is I have to do 150 pieces a year to do three really good ones. Then when you take a period of ten years, it's like, "God, I can remember thirty pieces of your work that are outstanding." But what about all the others that were blatantly mediocre? What we *don't* do is

---

*Terry Koppel, Paula's partner in Koppel and Scher.

really bad work. It's good B-/C+ work. To do the As, that's like the magic moment—something happens that you can't predict. But then I have high standards. When I say "good," I mean really, really good.

ON SUSTAINING ENERGY: I do free work all the time. Steve Heller and I just did this project for *Print* magazine. They gave me the cover to do. I drove myself absolutely crazy. I wanted to commit suicide over this, because I didn't have a good idea. I finally got it. I didn't want it to be purely a design, because I figured if somebody didn't like the style or genre, it would only exist for those who did. I wanted to do something very broad and very funny so everyone could appreciate it, no matter what it looked like. It's absolutely the hardest thing to do, like a pure idea. I really was miserable over it, because you only get one of those things. On the other hand, I had a pile of jobs in here at the sametime that paid a lot of money. I did them with my elbow and they looked like it. But I call my shots. I'll wait for a situation where I think it's right and then invest the energy. Otherwise I don't have any energy and I can't do it.

ON WOMEN IN DESIGN: I think it's easier as a woman to begin in the business, because it's accepted that women will work as "number 2." I think it's overcome-able by numbers, ultimately. Maybe in ten years there will be a lot of "number 1s." I also think women have to have a strength of personality, conviction, and a sort of stick-to-it-tiveness. If you do very good work, ultimately everyone sees it and ultimately you'll get credit for it. Then it's undeniable. If you have a strong personality and can get your ideas across, you can overcome the prejudices. It's just that everybody hates you, calls you a "tough woman" or whatever.

I think life is more difficult for women than for men. Women live closer to their feelings. I think they are prepared to acknowledge those things that are unfair, foolish, inhumane, not correct, not as they appear to be. I think men are characteristically denyers. I think they are raised to be denyers. They're not fazed by the same things that faze women. That's one side of the coin. Men and women operate differently. Men tend to be more protective of each other, and they're less likely to acknowledge sexism when it exists, which in itself is a problem.

I think it's difficult to live in this particular generation and at this particular time, being a successful woman, because they think you're a freak, and there isn't really a place for us yet. I don't belong to the club really. I think it's going to take a lot of women coming into the field before it happens.

Male designers are businessmen to a degree; they deal so much more with clients, so their whole mode of operating and their style is different from, say, illustrators. In any situation where there's a woman present as a peer, it's very unnerving for a lot of them. That's because of their expectations. Most men know women only as assistants, as secretaries, as wives, and so who are you? Should they talk business with you? They're confused.

ON INTUITION: I have to say that what I've done and probably will continue to do is impulsive and instinctual. My instincts tell me it's a good time to do this, or I'm going to try that, or something smells right, then I sort of go that way. I go totally with my intuitive sense when I'm meeting the client for the first time. I spend about five minutes in the room just sort of smelling it out, with no plan of operation on how to deal with him. Then I try to decide what I'm going to say on the spur of the moment, doing it completely off the cuff, and then designing for him that way. I would say it's 90 percent a gut reaction. Really, it's all intuitive.

ON A PHILOSOPHY OF WORK: You're only as good as your last piece.

LOUISE FILI

Book-Jacket Designer/Art Director; Pantheon Books

Louise Fili's highly personal book and book-jacket designs have focused some much-deserved attention on her talents as a designer. As art director/designer for Pantheon Books, her influence can readily be seen as each new list appears in the stores. In a vastly competitive market, her books stand out as originals. She teaches graphic design at the School of Visual Arts and is a consulting art director for Writers and Readers in London. As a freelance book and book-jacket designer, she has worked for firms such as Simon and Schuster, Congdon and Weed, Harcourt Brace Jovanovich, Clarkson Potter, and others. Among her books are Italian Style, The Malik Verlag, American Illustration 2, *and* Shoulder to Shoulder. *Her designs have brought her gold medals and other awards from such organizations as the New York Art Directors Club, the American Institute of Graphic Arts (AIGA), Insides, the Type Directors Club, the Society of Illustrators, and Print Casebooks. Most recently Fili and her husband, Steven Heller, were awarded a grant from the National Endowment of the Arts to design a catalog and exhibition for William Addison Dwiggins, one of America's first graphic designers.*

ON EDUCATION: I took a very circuitous route. I didn't go to art school. If I had to do it again, I would. My parents wanted me to go to a liberal arts school, so I went to Skidmore and majored in art. I soon discovered there was something called graphic design. I was always interested in lettering and since I didn't really know how to paint very well, design seemed the thing to do. I took as many graphic design courses as I could and did a lot of independent study. I soon ran out of that. I realized that going from Saratoga Springs to New York City was going to be too much of a leap for me, so I wangled my way into leaving school early and did volunteer work at the Museum of Modern Art and went to the School of Visual Arts for my last semester.

It was great, very good for contacts. Even before I finished my semester at Visual Arts, I had a job. I actually graduated from Skidmore, although my degree has never been of any use to me at all.

It's not bad to have a liberal arts background, it's just that it was that much harder for me once I came to New York. And even once I had my first job, it was still a struggle to get where I wanted to be. I knew it was the way of the business to just hop around from one job to another, so that's what I did, but it could have been easier than it actually was.

ON GETTING STARTED: I was at my first job for about five months, a small advertising agency, and I hated it. I learned everything I needed to know about advertising and less. From there, I went to work for Marty Pedersen,* who had a very small studio at the time. It was me, him, and the receptionist. That was good because at least I had a broader range of things to work on. I stayed a year, then left to look for another job. I was freelancing so as not to call it being unemployed.

Then I came to Knopf, one of the divisions of Random House, as a book designer. They brought me in just to do one picture book, which was wonderful. They paid me a weekly salary. I stayed until the book was finished. I did that with other books a couple of times. Then I realized it might be nicer if I had a stable job with benefits, though I didn't want to be locked into publishing, much as I liked it. I needed to be doing other things.

I worked for two years with Herb Lubalin.† I got to do a lot of things, but I discovered I liked doing book jackets best. When

---

*Marty Pedersen is the new publisher of *Graphis*, an international design magazine, and was a principal in the noted design firm of Jonson, Pedersen, Hinrichs & Shakery. An interview with Neil Shakery appears earlier in this chapter.

†Herb Lubalin was a noted graphic designer whose major contribution to the field was innovation in type design.

I realized that my freelance work was getting more interesting than work at the studio, I left. I started looking around for my own space, but in the middle of that, this job came up at Pantheon. I wasn't sure I should take it, but thought it might be good for me. As it turned out, it *was* good for me, and I'm still here seven years later.

ON CHOOSING A CAREER: It helps to get a background in a lot of different things. First of all, it's pretty hard to know exactly where you want to be until you try it all. Looking back, it seems very straightforward that I wanted to do books, but I didn't really think so at the time. I thought I wanted to try packaging and advertising and all this stuff, and when I did I really hated it. It wasn't just the work, it was the kind of people you had to work with, the way you had to work with clients. The thing I like about publishing is that your client is right here. It's all internal. What I hated about working in a studio owned by a big name, like Herb Lubalin, was that clients wanted whatever you sent over to come right out of *his* Pentel, so you had to play these little games. Also, whenever there was a problem, they'd always bring up money. "There was a mistake and we're not going to pay for it." All this passing-the-buck business doesn't happen much in publishing because it's all part of the same team. There are little factions, but it's not nearly as bad.

ON BOOK DESIGN AND BOOK-JACKET DESIGN: If you wanted to learn book design in school, it would be pretty hard. There are very few courses. There are book design departments within publishing houses. They do straight type text and occasionally a picture book. It's technical and very detail-oriented, and the creativity can be limited by a strict budget. It requires a lot of imagination and patience.

For book jackets, however, I think it's important to have an overall understanding of design. It's dealing with logo types or making your own logo types, working with illustration or photography. It's also having a certain intellectual sense of what's inside your book. With record albums you can do just anything; in fact you have to. But with books it's important to have an idea of what the tone should be, even if you don't read the book.

ON THE PRESSURES OF SELLING BOOKS: I'm always coming up against this. In general, if a book doesn't sell, it's the fault of the jacket. If it does sell, it has nothing to do with the jacket. It's as simple as that. I rarely get positive feedback from the sales department. I only hear if things aren't going well. If they want a book to do well, if they're hoping for a best-seller, then everybody has something to say. They're afraid to put off any particular group.

I'm lucky at Pantheon because it's known for a list of books that rarely become best-sellers. They are usually books that originate from obscure but very respected political or sociological writers. So for that kind of thing, I don't have to do a big selling job on the covers. But when we do something like Studs Terkel or *The Lover,** the kind of thing they're expecting to do very, very well, then everybody has something to say.

ON SUCCESS: I had very strange ideas about success when I started out. I remember I vowed to be a success by the time I was 25, or else. Then I remember the day I turned 25, I thought what does this mean and now what do I do? But once I decided I was interested in book jackets, I knew I had to learn everything about them. I realized that I had to do things with book jackets that have never been done before.

It isn't very easy because you're limited in size and the type of printing and all of that. But I did try to explore as many different possibilities as I could with jackets, and I tried to push the limitations as far as I could. I tried to do some new things. We

---

*An international best-seller from France, by Marguerite Duras (1985).

started doing paperbacks and I had them printed on matte stock which hadn't been done before. Have you seen *Marx for Beginners* and *Lenin for Beginners*? They've done very, very well, especially on college campuses. A British publisher had orginated them, and they had these covers that were a little boring, and each book was done by a different illustrator, so it was hard to tie them together. I used this brown-wrapping-paper stock. They did stand out on the shelf. They were different. I've tried to do as much of that kind of thing as possible. And I'm still trying. I guess success is trying to do something different that will still hold up five or ten or fifty years from now. So I really won't know for another forty years or so if I've been successful.

ON MONEY: If you're really interested in making money, this isn't the place to be. I do a great volume of work. I do my job here, plus I do a lot of outside work, most of which is the same kind of thing. But considering I kill myself to do all this freelance work to supplement my salary, I end up with a total salary of something pretty normal, like what I should be making to begin with. But, the trade-off is that in a job like this I do have a lot of freedom. I can work with a lot of different types of illustrators and photographers, and I can always try new things. I'm so interested in typography, I know I'd never be able to work at a magazine or do corporate design where you're so limited in the type. That's what I live for. The great thing about my job is that if I see a typeface I like, I can find a use for it. I don't know too many other jobs where I'd be able to do something like that.

ON COMBINING ART DIRECTION AND DESIGN: The dilemma I'm in is that I'm trying to be both art director and designer at the same time. It can be done, but I think it's very hard to do both at the same level of quality. Before I came here, I was really just a designer, and I could spend hours just fine tuning something. Now that I'm an art director, a lot of my time goes into directing art and administrating. I enjoy working with illustrators and putting something together made up of different elements—illustration, lettering, retouching, all of that. I also like having control over the jacket, which wouldn't happen if I were only designing as a freelance job. In trade publishing, mostly because of budgets, it's pretty unrealistic to be an art director who doesn't design. I mean, I do freelance out some of the jackets, just because there's such volume, and my assistant does some, but I still always keep the best ones for myself.

ON THE FUTURE OF BOOK-JACKET DESIGN: It's going to change, just as all design is. There are designers who are working on computers and have been for several years now. I think book design and jacket design is probably going to be one of the last fields to get involved in that, just because we're always the slowest to get anywhere. But it will change. I did design one jacket on a computer, and it was very bizarre. I could see instantly how it's going to affect the way we design, because it's such a different way of approaching the process: You're designing on a keyboard rather than with your hands. The most apparent thing I've seen in the ten years I've been publishing is that there's been an enormous decline in quality in books in general. The type of printing and the materials are just not what they used to be. When I was doing picture books when I first started, it was not unusual to have colored end papers or two colors throughout the book or duotones or whatever. Now it's practically unheard of. There isn't the same kind of money to spend anymore. On jackets we haven't felt it as much, because the jacket really has to sell the book. So there's still some money to be spent, but not a lot.

ON THE SATISFACTIONS: When I can work with the very best materials and the best people and get the best kind of printing and have the most freedom—that brings satisfaction. But it's a combination one doesn't always find.

For me, it's the combination of process and product that I find interesting. They don't always balance out. I can have this wonderful experience in the process, and it's very exciting. Usually once you get started in the process, you know whether or not it's going to be a success. It can be very exciting, but the process can be dependent on so many things. And people. I have to get a letterer to work on it, or a retoucher, or whatever. Then if it's a complicated printing job, I have to rely on a printer. Sometimes the most carefully thought-out process doesn't always come out the way you want. And sometimes it does.

I never wanted my own business or to be an art director or whatever, I just wanted to be a good designer. There are a lot of corporate designers who are businesspeople. It's great, because they know how to run a studio, but it's not design. And it's not what we, as students, coming out into the world of design thought it was going to be. I may be old-fashioned, and I may not be practical when it comes to business, but that's still how I see design. It's doing work that gives me personal satisfaction. I push my students toward that. Developing a personal style. And to constantly maintain that. People say to me, "When I go into a bookstore and pick up a certain book, I know it's one you've done, and when I turn it over it has your name on it." That's what I'm looking for.

ON CREATIVE BLOCKS: When I'm blocked I usually take a walk and then look through all my reference books. I'm constantly going through my own posters and through design books from the 30s and 40s. There's usually something there. If not, then I try doing tissues and then I'll just let it sit for a little while, if there's enough time. When I go back to it in a couple of days, something usually comes up.

ON SUSTAINING ENERGY: Well, as long as I'm working on at least one project that interests me, that usually keeps me going. I think working on many different things at once is the only way to work. If I only worked on one or two at a time, it could really slow me down considerably. But this way, there's always something else to jump over to. If one thing isn't working, then I'll just go on to something else, and eventually I'll get the energy back to face the one that was hanging me up in the first place. Sometimes I have to realize that not every jacket is going to be a winner, and I just have to do it and get it out—just tell myself that's the best thing to do with it.

ON THE CREATIVE PROCESS: As soon as I hear about a book, I have some kind of idea about how I want to approach it. As an art director anyway, I'll know if I want to use an illustrator or a photographer, or if it's going to be type. If it's going to be type, I immediately start thinking about how I want it to feel and what I want it to look like. Usually what I do is to get whatever references I need right away. I rely quite heavily on my references, which is why I have so many books here. I also have a lot of books at home. I'm constantly going through them, looking for unusual typefaces. Then I sit down and start tissuing. I tissue over and over again, going from something very rough until it sort of turns into something. Usually what happens is that I'll just keep doing the type over and over again until it sort of focuses into a typeface—and then I find out the typeface doesn't exist. It's happened many times. Then I end up having it hand-lettered. To find the closest face is never going to be right. On the Marx/Lenin series, I did a very loose format and I did it over and over and over. Suddenly, the word "Marx" kind of appeared. It was an existing typeface, but the weight didn't exist. It was between the medium and the bold weights. I looked at medium, and it was wrong; and I looked at bold and it was wrong. So I ended up having to have each one of these hand-lettered.

Once, I did a book on Edward Curtis' photographs of Indians. I was trying desperately to think of a cover. I knew exactly what type of face I was looking for: a wood type that was very bold and condensed and kind of spikey. I kept tissuing it over and over again, and it turned into a face that just didn't exist. I started looking at all of the wood type books, and I couldn't find it anywhere. Then I was walking past a Korean greengrocer, and I saw a sign with the typeface I wanted. It was a sign on the side of a crate for persimmons. I asked them if I could have the sign and I ended up starting from that.

ON ADVICE TO YOUNG PEOPLE: It's not a glamorous profession. A lot of students think it is. It's a lot of work. I always tell students that if they want to be a designer, just like anything else—an illustrator or a photographer or anything—they have to want it really, really badly. When I came to New York, I was just hungry for graphic design. It was such a dazzling world that I just immersed myself in it. And that's what I always recommend. If you're interested in books, then you should go to bookstores, constantly, and look at everything that's been done and constantly question it and see how you could do it better. And once you reach a certain level of success, that's not the answer either. You always have to be working at it to stay on top, because styles change and you can't be doing the same thing over and over.

Also, a lot of students don't realize that just getting along with people is very important. One of my best students a while ago was a fantastic designer, but he couldn't take any criticism. He was very moody and I hear he's having a very hard time, because he can't keep a job. If anything has to be changed, he quits. And that's not what it's about. Everything is about compromise, trying to understand the client's point of view. It's taken me a very long time to understand it. I'm very protective of my illustrators and anyone who works for me. Whenever I show a jacket design and I get any kind of flack, if it were only my design, I'd probably fight less. But I'm very protective and if they have anything to say about what someone else had done, I get very upset about it. But I've tried to understand where they're coming from, and in turn I try to make the artist understand why it has to be changed and how it's not a compromise. But a lot of it is, regardless.

ON HAVING A PERSONAL LIFE: I consider myself lucky to share a life with someone who has similar interests, because

I would find it difficult to be with someone in a totally different field. Because this is my whole life. Everything relates to design in some way or another, and you have to get your inspiration from somewhere. I don't think you can just get it from looking at a type book all day. The way I plant my garden is graphic design, the colors I paint my kitchen are colors I'd use on a book jacket. But I'd hate to think that's all I do.

ON WORK AS A SATISFYING PRIORITY: I think it depends on what age you are. What I'm finding in my thirties is that I physically can't work the way I used to. I never thought this would happen. When I was in my twenties it was very different, because I was just starting out and I felt I had to prove myself. And I did, and that was the only thing to do, and I don't regret it. But I can't work the way I used to. I don't think it's as important. Before it was a certain kind of volume I was having to produce and having to change jobs and aspiring to better things. Now I feel I'm at a certain plateau. I still feel very competitive. I want to be producing a certain quality of work, not necessarily quantity.

ON WOMEN IN DESIGN: I have to say that being a woman made it that much more difficult. Sexism in this business is not that obvious, but it's there. It's there like it's there with everything. When women are starting out, it's not that different from men, but women can only get to a certain point and that's it. To try to get beyond that, a woman would have to start her own business. But, chances are, if clients want to hire someone with his or her own business, they'll more readily go to a man, because they think a man is more reliable.

I try to warn my female students. I tell them, "I want you to know what it's going to be like when you start looking for a job. It may not affect you in your first year or your second year, but you're going to feel it eventually. You'll be doing the same job as a man's doing, but you'll get paid less and you won't be treated as well. You're going to see it happening." It's happened to me. It's very subtle, but it's there.

TONY CACIOPPO
Computer Graphics
President/Creative Director, Trilogy Design at JSL, Inc.

Tony Cacioppo began his career in broadcasting as a graphic designer for the CBS Evening News. *His talents as an animator and director moved him up to more comprehensive assignments as art director, animator, and associate producer of such shows as* CBS Reports, CBS Special Reports, *and* CBS Evening News. *Among his achievements were developing new title sequences for network news and designing and developing production methods using various in-house electronic systems. In 1983 he opened his own film, video, and computer-animation studio, Trilogy Design, where he continues his work in television and film graphics. He has been awarded two Emmys by the National Academy of Television Arts and Sciences—for Outstanding Programming Achievement and for Individual Achievement—as well as numerous awards for excellence in film graphics. Tony Cacioppo studied at Hofstra University and at the School of Visual Arts in New York.*

ON GETTING STARTED: I graduated from Visual Arts as an illustrator/designer and my first job was in a very small studio with Ron Chereskin, who's now into fashion. But I was frustrated by putting hours into a concept and having somebody react to it in a moment. After all, a musician can play a song as fast or as slow as he wants and kind of string people along. That led me to try to animate my work. I went to all the networks with my designs and graphics. I tried for about eighteen months to get into the networks. At CBS I got the best response. They kept telling me they liked my work, so I really pushed myself into the job. I called them and said, "You say you like my work and I need the job." I guess I happened to make the call at the right time, because they hired me the next day as a vacation replacement. It was an excellent place to work. They gave me every support. I really learned animation there. I went to school. I took night classes at Visual Arts on how to use the camera. But because the networks are so unionized, though I could design I couldn't actually do hands-on manipulation. I wanted that kind of experience so I could know how I might better design for this process.

ON GETTING INTO THE BUSINESS TODAY: Definitely get a graphics background. A design sense is a design sense whether you're putting up wallpaper or designing a car. Animation is also a very important ingredient in the new computer-graphics area. There's a basic of movement, the Disney people knew, and every animator knows, called "ease it." There's an ease to speed. But a lot of computer graphics consist of simply taking a joystick and moving things. Without real understanding of how things move, there's an unpleasant feeling of inertia. But I think my company has a head start. I'm an animator, an art director. My partner has been an animator for thirty-five years, so we really know how things move, how they should move. You see, it's not reality. When a ball bounces in animation it should compress as it hits. You exaggerate that shape so it feels right. It doesn't look right if you stop it frame by frame, but in animation it does. The little tricks of the trade are very beneficial in computer graphics. So I'd say an animation background is very good. Learn to do things the old-fashioned way, frame by frame by frame. It helps.

ON COMPUTERS: You should have enough experience with computers to be comfortable with them. But people who feel that computers do it for you are ignorant of the process. You don't just press a button and come back to find the Mona Lisa! It's a very grueling process.

As far as computer background goes, we started here with a little Apple computer, just to get the language, what you call syntax, the grammar of writing a program. Of course, it's frustrating. You're hacking away at it for hours and hours and you see one line on the screen. It's really a process of pushing yourself against a brick wall for a long period of time, before you suddenly realize you're on the other side of the wall. It's not a dramatic process. It's something you keep pushing and pushing and eventually a light goes on and you say, "Oh, that's what they meant," and it might be something you picked up three or four months ago, but it's helping you today. Sooner or later, the little blocks all fit together and you're more confident.

ON MONEY: "There's definitely money to be made. Basically, I do the same work today I did eight years ago, but the process is totally different. The money has kind of rechanneled itself. The optical houses were the big money-makers in the city, people who put different film elements together. Commercials were done on film. All the composition of these images and special effects were on film. Now, with video technology, the process has become more immediate. An art director wants to be able to sit in the session and say, "Bring this element in. Move it. No, I don't like it. Let's do it again." That's an essential change for the industry. So the optical houses have been drying up, and the film industry has been drying up, not in features, but in commercial activity. More and more money is being put into video production work.

Computers, logically, have a more friendly output to video than to film. There are ways of laboriously scanning across each frame of film. But it's not economical. The real output of most computers is to video. Coupled with the change in technology toward video, and the immediacy of getting things done, computer graphics is one of the fastest growing industries. My clientele keeps growing. If I do one job, I get a job from three other people who need computer graphics. It's an expanding field. There are a lot of people coming out of schools who understand the theory of computer graphics but they don't have hands-on knowledge—yet. That's inevitable. Every college can't have every piece of equipment.

ON THE FUTURE OF COMPUTER GRAPHICS: New York is definitely the center. I would say there are six to ten really big graphics houses that deal in computer graphics. There are lots of postproduction houses that have the equipment, that have the money to buy the equipment—the $200,000 Quantel Paint Box or whatever—and they don't have the people to run them. The industry and technology are there, but there's been a lag in the personnel to operate it. I think that's quickly closing up, but there is really a need for more people.

What has happened at the universities really has my mouth open. You see incredible graphics being done by universities. They have equipment to do things that cost $6000 to $7000 a frame. Academically, it's viable as a learning experience. But it doesn't make practical sense in commercial production. Far too expensive. But, Lucas Film is exploring the possibilities in this area. And what they produce is highly sophisticated. George Lucas—the director of *Star Wars* and many other films using advanced computer-graphics techniques to create special effects—is involved with hiring every genius to work in his environment, an R&D kind of attitude. Lucas is developing high-definition television, computer graphics, computer animation; I think, ultimately, there are going to be satellites beaming feature films in a video format, very-high-definition video films. So the commercial business, as I see it, is going from film to video and will, eventually, erode even the feature-film business, leaving huge areas for computer-graphics people to fill in.

ON FILM VS. VIDEO: A century from now I don't think we'll be dealing with film. It seems safe to say that we'll see it in the Smithsonian. I love film. It has a beautiful quality to it. Aesthetically, I prefer it. But video is getting closer and closer. I think the reason for the difference in the beginning was that when video first started, it was pristine. The people who went into it weren't filmmakers. So it had a different look just because of that. Now more and more directors are former film people who have seen the writing on the wall. They've contributed greatly to the improved look of video. A lot of it is lighting. Having a great lighting sense in film is going to carry into video. What have been known as film techniques are really just production techniques. I think that's being taught more and more in the schools, both in film and video production classes. The look is much higher quality now.

ON WORKING FOR YOURSELF: I prefer it, because I direct my own destiny. There are mornings when I resent it. The last year I've found myself designing business deals more than I've ever designed anything in my life. Now that I realize that's what I've been doing, it's easier for me to deal with. When you're starting out, you have to wear many different hats and you can't resent any of them. Selling, for instance—I've always resented it. I once tried selling encyclopedias, but I would get so involved with a person's life, I was willing to give them the books. I mean, I just couldn't sell. But now I'm selling me and selling something I believe in, something I love.

ON SUCCESS: Success is doing something you love, getting paid for it, and having another life beside it. My family is the most important thing to me and that has always been my success beacon. That's what I wanted. I also wanted to have a good time at work and be with people I enjoyed. Fortunately, I've had that. But, I've also had times of being out of work and depressed, just like everyone has, I'm sure, making those phone calls and waiting for your bread. But, success, as I said, is being able to do what you like and to continue to do it. To be able to do that as an adult means you have to make a certain profit. That's the part where a lot of compromise has to be made.

I consider myself successful because I've accomplished goals I keep setting for myself. To me, that's very important—that I constantly assess where I am and where I want to be.

When I was in art school, success to me was to have a piece

printed in *Graphis*. That was it. I thought, oh, if I could just be one of these people whose work I'm drooling over and be that kind of inspiration to someone. As I got to CBS and was nominated for Emmy awards and things like that, success became less tangible. It's good to be recognized for what you do, but success is a more personal thing than that.

ON WORKING FOR OTHERS: I had a five-year plan when I got out of school. And that was to work for the biggest corporation I could and make my mistakes with their budgets. I worked for CBS and there was no lid on the budget. I mean I was able to go and deal with new technologies. I think that's an important aspect of working for somebody else. You need to explore first, in any field, and inevitably you're going to make mistakes. If it's your own limited capital you make mistakes with, it could ruin your career. My recommendation is to work for a strong corporation at first.

ON THE SATISFACTIONS: I do get a lot of pleasure out of what I'm doing, but it really is that last moment when it's come together in the control room. I've come up with a concept or a look, and we've figured out all those little puzzles of how to make it work. All along the way there are triumphs to celebrate and feel good about, but it's really crossing the finish line that does it.

ON HAVING A PERSONAL LIFE: I have found that people maybe fifteen years older than I am were caught up in another set of circumstances when success had another tone to it. It's from their warnings that I'm trying to balance my life. People will say, "Geeze, my kids grew up and I never saw them." I guess there's a lot of balancing going on in society between women and men and family life. It's affected my personal life, making me want it and to really work toward it. I also don't think there's any way to do it without being conscious of it. It's very easy to work seven days a week in any business. I don't think that makes you a better person at all. I think it's the converse. It tends to make you focus on the wrong things.

I'm very convinced that to be creative you have to have some good times in your life. I like to have those experiences to draw on when I need them. I think you really have to work to get them.

LANCE WYMAN
Graphic Designer, Visual Communications Systems
President, Lance Wyman, Ltd.

Lance Wyman made his international design debut as design director for the Mexican Olympic Committee for the 1968 Olympics in Mexico City. He created a special Olympic alphabet and symbols that identified cultural and sports events and that were applied to everything from the stadium to directional signs, uniforms, posters, and other promotional material. This design achievement led to designing a graphics system for the Mexico City Metro, a graphics system for the National Zoo in Washington, D.C., a graphics system for the Jeddah International Airport in Saudi Arabia, a graphics system for the Minnesota Zoo, and in 1982, a graphics system for the Central de Abasto, the new central supply market in Mexico City.

There have been numerous exhibitions of his work, both in the United States and abroad, among them exhibits at the Center of Industrial Design at Centre Georges Pompidou in Paris, at the Biennale of Poster Art in Warsaw, at the AIGA Gallery in New York, at the Smithsonian Institution in Washington, and at the Cooper-Hewitt Museum in New York. Lance Wyman lives and works in New York City.

ON GETTING STARTED: Two months before graduating from high school I was interviewed by our school paper, and they asked me what I was going to do. I really didn't know, but I said, "Well, I'll probably pursue an art career." That was it.

Then I kind of had to do it. At that time Pratt was probably the best school around. I got turned down the first time I applied, and I went to Fairleigh Dickinson University for a year, but I finally got into Pratt. It was really my first exposure to design, and I didn't have any idea about the different types of design. I wanted to go into advertising, but after the first year, I chose industrial design. I didn't really want to do that either, but it was closer to something that made sense to me. I represented Pratt at General Motors between my junior and senior year and met a fellow who was in the graduate program at Yale studying with Paul Rand.* It was Paul Rand's influence that eventually got me into a graphic design career.

ON CHOOSING A CAREER: I think it is a personal quest and students have to deal with it on a personal level. Art school isn't necessary, certainly, but it's helpful. I think the school is responsible to some degree for making opportunities available and presenting programs, but students have to go through the searching-out process on their own. When you're in contact with other people your age doing the same thing, you share in a process of creative pollination. Probably the basic way you see design is formed during school. It's not necessarily the best way, but it's certainly a proven one. I think each person probably has a specialty or at least an ability to perform really well in one area. In the beginning you might not know what it is.

ON PORTFOLIOS: The portfolio is probably the prime tool a student has to express his or her work. Usually we look for a portfolio that shows an interest in the type of work we're doing.

---

*Paul Rand is a noted graphic designer who created the IBM logo and set a precedent in the field by applying that logo to every aspect of the corporation's internal and public communication—letterheads, print advertising, promotion—to present a unified corporate image to the world.

I think it's important for designers coming out of school to realize that it doesn't hurt to specialize and to put 100 percent effort in a single direction.

ON SUCCESS: When I started, there were role models, especially in the industrial design field. I worked for one of them at the George Nelson office. And others like Cheramayeff and Geismar, offices that probably started in the late fifties and early sixties. They represented success. They were the offices doing first-class work, the competition. You'd have to be as good or better to succeed. Now the whole design profession is much more diverse and there are many individuals and small companies doing excellent work. Success can be established on a more personalized level now.

I've gone through periods when I've been as successful as anybody in the world, and I've gone through low periods too. I hope I'm starting to come to another peak now. After spending a number of years in a career you come to respect the peaks and valleys as the reality of working. I think the definition of success is very individual.

I want to be happy about the work, and I want the work to be successful. They kind of go hand in hand.

ON THE FUTURE OF GRAPHIC DESIGN: It's never been headed anyplace other than individuals communicating with each other. It's a matter of what techniques and forms are used to communicate at any one time. The field goes through periods of style. I try to avoid style as much as I can, because I usually deal with comprehensive programs. I like to think the design programs look better as they get older, actually. A corporate program tends to have longevity. The same goes for developing programs for large building complexes. You want the work to hold up and not be stylish, just of the moment.

The computer is certainly going to play an important role. But in communication, and specifically in visual communication, the process is about turning people on. You have to get excited about what you're communicating, feel comfortable with it, or feel that it's first-class. I think the rest of it's technique.

ON WORKING FOR YOURSELF: When you work for yourself you have a lot of freedom and that freedom comes at a price. You have to get smart to preserve that freedom. That means having diverse projects going. You don't want to get stuck with a single client or a single project being everything. When you're small, dealing with a big project doesn't leave much room for other things. Still you have to make sure you have room for other things.

ON WORKING FOR OTHERS: It was good for me in the early part of my career. In fact, absolutely necessary, because I wanted to find out what the profession was all about, and I learned a lot. Now it's a process of trying to find clients to learn from. It's not so much learning about design, it's learning about other areas of activity, like running a zoo or running the Smithsonian Institution; it's seeing the totality and presenting that to the general public.

ON THE SATISFACTIONS: I think the biggest satisfaction comes out of feeling you've accomplished the highest level of design you can. And one of the main factors, outside of what you bring to a program, is having a good client. I mean, you're going to literally bang your head against the wall if you don't have a good client, one who wants good design and recognizes it. Otherwise you start out with a battle you'll never win. I doubt whether there's much good design when designers are working with bad clients.

It's important to have your work recognized. I am still thrilled if I get a medal for something or have something praised, as in *Communication Arts*, for example. Satisfaction also comes from the quieter aspects of design. For instance, this restructuring of the central core of a new city in Mexico, I've been doing, where you really have a chance to interject quality where it's important, where people are living with design every day.

ON THE WORKING PROCESS: I begin by asking a lot of questions in a lot of different ways. I guess you'd call it research, but it takes a lot of different forms. Getting a reading on the people you're going to be working with is an important part of that: getting all the hard, calculable facts concerning the corporation, like what their marketing areas are. Sometimes you have to do market research. Next it's the process of preliminary design. I try to do it on two levels: verbal and visual. If you go into something on the visual level right off, you tend to repeat yourself too easily. But if you go to the verbal, it opens up other options and other associations to work from.

ON CREATIVE BLOCKS: That's where the process comes in handy, because you have other areas to fall back on. That's where verbalization comes in handy. You can free-associate with ideas. Usually you're blocked because you can't find a concept that works for a problem. The programs we deal with have enough parts so you can just put one part aside and work on another part. In fact, you have to, because we have to develop many things at the same time. In the end, they're really all compatible and work with each other as well as alone.

ON SUSTAINING ENERGY: You have to make things interesting for yourself. There are always the obvious things that are interesting, and then there are the queries, overviews, and associations you bring to a problem. That too can make it interesting. Sometimes there are areas other designers haven't even touched. When you get a chance to work in them, there are no role models, no successful program out there to base the solution on. It's an opportunity to give it your best shot and maybe set a standard for design in that area. I think it enriches the whole design profession when you reach out into the less obvious areas.

I think different periods of life require different types of energy. I've had times when I'm just full of energy and out there planning to conquer the world. Other times I kind of glimpse the world and I know it's not going to be so easy.

ON SPECIALIZATION: Design is a big field and is becoming more and more specialized. Our particular area is systems design, visual systems—developing a logo, for instance, that becomes the inspiration for an alphabet that unifies all the materials. It can then be applied to any number of communication needs. We designed a symbol for the Child Survival Program for UNICEF, and now we've been asked to design a commemorative coin as a part of the system. It gets us into rather diverse applications. Or, for example, for a zoo you might develop symbols for all the exhibit areas. Then a map is designed so people can find their way around, one of the many specific uses for those particular symbols.

ON A LARGE DESIGN OFFICE VS. A SMALL ONE: If you decide to put together a large office, you stand the chance of being pulled away from the designing aspect. I like to design. I like to stay close to the board, close to a small nucleus of a design team to accomplish as much quality work as I can on a project. The largest team I've worked with in an office structure was about fourteen people. Even then you become more of an administrator, more interested in where the next job is coming from, because you've got a lot of mouths to feed, so to speak.

ON MONEY: Yes, you can make money. But I doubt you'll ever become rich unless you open a big office. If you want to use design as a money-making profession, try management. You could buy design, become part of a corporation that buys design services to develop corporate-identity programs. There are professions where money is made more easily, but making money in any profession takes a lot of effort. You have to be damn good to make a lot of money, and money has to be your main interest. A lot of people in the design world are out there fighting for the big money.

ON HAVING A PERSONAL LIFE: Personally I found going into the middle of my life that my profession occupied too big a part of my personality. It's not that I didn't have a personal life—a family and a home. I do. And while I am happy with my profession, I think on a psychological level it was shaping too much of my identity. I had to go through a process of breaking away from that. I think my fear was that doing so would diminish my ability to create and design.

ON THE ROLE OF THE DESIGNER: I think as a designer economics is the key, because you have to remember that a designer is always rendering a service. Whether you're illustrating for a weekly publication or designing signage systems in a building complex so people can find their way around, it's service. You can't get away from being a service. The diversity of those services depends a great deal on the ability of an economy to foster service areas where designers can be used. Ours is a specialty area. I'm in a profession where still, to a large degree, the sign manufacturer designs a lot of the signs you see in buildings. Designers are just now getting into this in a more serious way. More public awareness, more public demand for good, effective design develops the market. Competition creates that demand.

ON ADVICE TO YOUNG PEOPLE: You should maintain a level of confidence in your abilities and try not to let that be knocked out of you by bad working experiences. I see it happening. People come in here with portfolios. "This was my student work," they'll say and it's all pretty good, because they were taught in an environment that fostered clear-cut approaches to design problem solving. They had good teachers, developed techniques, and so forth. Then the schoolwork stops and you start seeing this real schlocky stuff in a portfolio and you say, "Well, what is this?" "It's my freelance work," they say. All of a sudden, you see a complete letting go of any kind of design principle. If you set out hoping to have design principles, you really have to be responsible for maintaining them.

5

Illustration

ILLUSTRATION is the commercial art that is based most closely upon the traditional form of figurative drawing and painting as practiced in the fine arts. This fact creates a unique dilemma for illustrators. The work they produce must not only meet the minds and needs of other people—a definition of commercial art—but it must measure up to the same criteria applied to the work of fine artists: It must demonstrate the ability to draw and an understanding of composition and of light and shade, and it must reflect a unique vision. It is an almost impossible task to satisfy the demands of both fields. Illustrators struggle with that task daily, and with extraordinary results. The frustration level, however, is very high. And the complaints of illustrators about the restrictions imposed on them by an assignment are intense. As professionals they will do what is asked of them to the best of their ability. As artists they would like to be given the opportunity to use the "best of their ability" to create work that is both artistic and satisfying.

Advertising and Editorial Illustration

The illustration field is divided into two distinct areas: advertising and editorial. However, almost all successful careers, even in advertising begin with success in the editorial field, in work done for books and magazines, where each piece of art is signed, as in fine art.

Editorial illustration carries with it more prestige than advertising illustration; however, it also pays far less well. Most illustrators would prefer to do only editorial illustration because it allows an artist more expression and more freedom than advertising. But when the choice comes down to a couple of hundred dollars for an editorial job with unlimited freedom, and thousands of dollars for an advertising assignment, economics usually wins. But the truth is, not all illustrators can get advertising work even if they want it, since it requires a style of painting or drawing with appeal to a broad market. It also demands a very flexible temperament, because in advertising you are often required to execute someone else's idea and are seldom asked to contribute more than "style" or "technique."

The advertising illustrator is involved in the process of selling products or services by creating appropriate images for the market the client is trying to reach. Advertising illustration is a very lucrative specialization, the highest paid in the illustration field. It is also very demanding work, with short deadlines, last-minute changes, and two sets of clients—the art director and the art director's client. A strong, effective agent is an essential ally for an advertising illustrator.

Recently illustrators with a very distinctive personal style, primarily editorial illustrators, have sought fine art outlets for their work. Others have given up illustration for a while to devote full time to painting or sculpture. But there is a strong prejudice in the fine art world against artists who choose to work in both areas. No doubt the prejudice begins in the art schools, where the commercial artist who makes art for money's sake is perceived to be less pure than the fine artist who makes art for the love of it. But as the fine art market expands and becomes more profitable, the galleries, the critics, and the collectors create an atmosphere where fine artists too can think of their art in relation to its market value, thus bringing the definition for fine art more closely in line with the definition for commercial art.

Fine artists like Andy Warhol and Robert Rauschenberg are

being commissioned to do covers for *Time* magazine in much the same way editorial illustrators are commissioned to do work. And younger fine artists growing up with less rigid definitions of art, "fine" or otherwise, actively pursue illustration when they need money. There are indications that the line between the fine arts and illustration is becoming sufficiently blurred to allow artists and illustrators to cross over in both directions. The more options there are for all artists, the better it is for everyone.

But, whether you are an editorial illustrator or an advertising illustrator, your talent is all you have. Art directors and designers often have the option of using other people's talent to enhance their own. The illustrator works alone. Doing the kind of interesting, original illustration that gets noticed and ensures success takes sustained involvement and commitment. It takes passion for the art. In the early years—the first three or four years out of school—learning new things, getting work, seeing work printed, earning money are incentives enough to keep you going. Lots of money can keep you going longer, but illustration is highly competitive and the ability to continue to produce excellent work comes only with an understanding of your own needs and drives as an artist.

It is obvious that illustration is not for most people interested in art careers. Artists who have commercial skills and talent and who like the process of collaboration with an art director will find advertising illustration satisfying. Artists who have a more personal vision and who enjoy the process of working for the printed page will find editorial illustration satisfying as well. Those who like working for an audience of children will gravitate toward doing children's books. The few cartoonists who are committed to their art and the handful of illustrators who like the moving drawing may find animation the most appropriate career for them. But the dilemma of most illustrators, regardless of specialization, is coming to terms with how they can use their talent to make a living without sacrificing personal satisfaction in their work and a deep interest in the traditions of drawing and painting.

BASIC RESPONSIBILITIES The illustrator works with an art director in both the editorial and the advertising fields. In editorial illustration, a manuscript is provided. In advertising headlines and copy are discussed. Some art directors present illustrators with layouts or specific directions, suggesting visual ideas. Many art directors leave the visualizing to the artist.

Work usually begins with a preliminary sketch, which is submitted for approval and discussed with the art director before the illustrator goes any further. Size and color limitations are determined; the illustrator must be able to work comfortably within those restrictions. The time allowed for the completion of a job is set by the art director and, depending on circumstances, can be anywhere from overnight to several weeks.

SALARIES Few illustrators are salaried; most operate as freelance artists and are paid on a per-job basis. Most magazine and book publishers have standard fees, depending on many variables. However, there are exceptions to the standard that can be applied at the art director's discretion. In the past decade the Graphic Artists' Guild has made great efforts to set standards for fees and has achieved some success in this direction. However, illustration still pays mostly what the traffic will bear, and unfortunately that hasn't changed greatly over the years. As we have indicated, advertising offers the highest fees, and advertising illustrators make substantially more money than editorial illustrators. In some cases, the difference can be as much as $50,000 to $100,000 a year. However, no beginning illustrators can expect to make even a living wage in a large city until his or her work starts getting recognition.

EDUCATION AND TRAINING In addition to a general art curriculum, an emphasis on the areas of drawing and painting is essential to the education of an illustrator. Courses in photography, advertising, and the history of illustration, can also be very helpful. And you have to learn computer skills.

As you go along in school and begin to discover more about

your talents and preferences, an advisor can help you plan your curriculum to reflect your specialty. If for example, you discover an interest in medical illustration you will need instruction in science and anatomy. If your college does not offer the courses you need, you should look for them elsewhere.

Whether you attend an art college or major in illustration at a university, you will prepare a portfolio of work to use when you "make the rounds," that is, when you approach art directors at magazines, newspapers, publishing houses, and advertising agencies. Most art institutions have special courses for illustration majors designed to help them create a "selling" portfolio, to show them how to present their work in its most professional form.

Specialty Fields in Illustration

Editorial and advertising illustration provide most of the employment for illustrators. As we have discussed, artists can work in both areas, and many do. But there are specific skills and styles, as well as temperaments, that make working in one easier than in the other, and specialization usually evolves naturally out of inclination and opportunity. Other factors are at work in forcing an artist to specialize. There is hardly an illustrator who would not like the opportunity to do a variety of different jobs in different media—the problem lies in finding the opportunities. Hence illustrators who have done several children's books and have liked doing them, continue to do them, and have little opportunity to be considered for a magazine cover.

CHILDREN'S BOOKS Children with artistic talent are fascinated by pictures and by storytelling, and many artists consider becoming children's book illustrators very early on in their lives, usually even before going to a professional art school. The problem with this field, however, is that work is limited. Children's books are expensive to produce, and consequently, few of them are published compared to the number proposed. Occasionally, well-known children's writers will request a particular illustrator, or a publisher issuing a particular series will commission freelance work.

If you wish to pursue this field, the best way to break in is to write and illustrate your own book. Although this is time-consuming, you should consider it an investment in your future career. A completed book can give an editor a clear idea of your story sense, both in pictures and words, and will be proof of your commitment and determination. Even then, do not be surprised if it takes a long time to get your foot in the door. Your best bet, if you can pull it off, is to convince an established children's writer to work with you on a book.

The educational field has a few more opportunities for illustrating preschool and early childhood materials. Scholastic, Inc., and the Children's Television Workshop put out regular publications for children of various ages; most of these are illustrated and the work is commissioned on a freelance basis.

Women students often think of the children's book field as one they can enter, even though they marry and have children. Although it seems to be a logical part-time career, like all art careers it requires time, talent, and focus. It is very difficult to be successful at anything you do on a part-time basis.

Children's book illustration, like mainstream editorial illustration, is relatively low-paying. Most illustrators are paid on a fee-per-book basis rather than per illustration. Unlike the writer, the artist does not always receive royalties and the fee received sometimes represents the complete payment.

A few agents handle illustrators who do children's books, but they are specialists. The general agent seldom handles children's book illustrators except in special situations. Naturally, with "name" illustrators, agents can negotiate fees higher than the going rate.

Despite the financial disadvantages, many artists like doing children's books. Being able to do a series of drawings or paintings, as well as being able to hold a finished book in your hands instead of just a tear sheet does give you a very satisfying sense of accomplishment.

GENERAL BOOKS This is not a primary specialized field, in that adult books seldom require illustration. Those few that do are handled through the channels of editorial illustration. On occasion, a large publisher such as Time, Inc., will publish a series of books requiring illustrations. In such cases, well-known illustrators are usually given the assignments, and, because of wide distribution and market potential, the fees paid are generally higher than in the rest of the industry.

COMIC STRIPS AND CARTOONING There is a long history of illustration in comic strips, from *Superman* to *Peanuts*. Within the last ten years, personal styles have become more apparent in this area. The field, for the most part, continues to focus on the young people's market, in syndicated newspaper strips and in comic books. There is growing interest in serious content conveyed through the traditional comic form, and the trend toward "comic" art for adults seems to be increasing, although the field is still very limited.

A specialized comic magazine, *Raw*, published in New York by Art Spiegelman and Francois Mouly, has spearheaded a change in attitude toward the comic form. It is creating an outlet for artists who want to use the comic form as a serious platform. It is difficult to predict whether *Raw* will open up the market for the comic form or whether it is simply a unique publication for our time. Artists who work in the medium or are interested in doing so submit completed stories or ideas; if accepted for publication these are paid for on a freelance basis. There is very little money to be made in it as yet; most of the artists who do make money have an established reputation.

Students interested in becoming traditional cartoonists will need a portfolio when they approach the comic book publishers who hire staff artists to work on established strips. There are outlets for single cartoons at various magazines, notably the *New Yorker* and *Playboy*. They pay per cartoon accepted, and both magazines see portfolios of new work, although they do use some artists on a regular basis.

A few colleges offer a cartoon major within the general illustration curriculum. If the school you choose does not offer one, look at all the work being done in the field currently—and in the past as well. Research the early political artists such as Daumier, look at Walt Disney, read *Pogo* and *Doonesbury* as well as all the Super Heroes. Find a copy of *Raw*. Immerse yourself in the full range of what is known as "series art" and find a direction that's personal to you. It is a field where what is considered successful today was often avant-garde when it was introduced.

ANIMATION This is a highly specialized field that requires both illustration and filmmaking skills. You must be able to think in movement rather than for the static page.

In many colleges, animation is a part of the film department curriculum, and although this makes a great deal of sense, development of the necessary drawing and painting ability may be neglected in the film curriculum. Make sure you get some experience in both film and art if you plan to work in animation.

The computer has made animated filmmaking far less expensive. Many of the Saturday morning children's cartoon programs are now composed of computer-generated images designed by artists. Computer animation has many applications in industry as well, being used to create logos for television network titles and for movie titles. The computer can also translate working drawings for automobiles and airplanes into three dimensions, showing how the machinery will function.

If you are interested in animation, try to get a job with a studio. Most animation studios are in large cities, where they can easily solicit work in advertising and promotion and are available to the news, sports, and entertainment departments of television stations. Perhaps you can even be a part of making a rare animated feature film, but, that is a rare opportunity. At present, animation is a limited career option for artists; it hardly even supports the people who currently work in the field. However, rapidly advancing technology may make a substantial difference in career opportunities before long.

The best way to go about getting a job is to make a short animated film in school or on your own. It is your resumé. Your skills and your talent will be evident on the film, and if the film is very good, you might even get a job.

There are many areas of illustration that we have not covered here—illustrators contribute to the production of filmstrips, slide presentations, and television storyboards, to name a few applications. All of these require the same basic skills as needed for editorial or advertising illustration.

ILLUSTRATION AGENTS

Many freelance illustrators have agents, who take the artist's portfolio to various clients. The agent receives a commission on each assignment he or she gets for the artist. Commissions range from 20 to 40 percent, with the average being about 25 percent. Most agents handle three or four artists, sometimes more.

INTERVIEWS

WILSON McLEAN
Illustrator, Freelance

Wilson McLean's stylized, distinctly personal imagery have made him one of the most highly visible and highly paid commercial illustrators in the country. Such advertising campaigns as those that introduced Perrier to this country and that redefined the Holland-American image have won him every major award the graphic arts industry offers. Among them are gold and silver medals from the Society of Illustrators and awards from the American Institute of Graphic Arts (AIGA), the New York Art Directors

Club, and Communication Arts. *Mr. McClean lives and works in New York City.*

ON GETTING STARTED: I had no idea you could make a living doing drawings. I didn't know what an advertising agency was. I was like a blind man, just stumbling away. All I knew was that I could draw, and it was the only thing I could do, and I liked to do it. So I started out at 15 going into local silk-screen shops where I lived in England, outside of London. They did very primitive ads for local cinemas and butcher shops. I was a typical working class kid who wanted to find work, but didn't want to go into a factory. Eventually I got a job doing retouching and lettering and some design, but no drawing. They promised me I could do drawing, but really I was gofer and a messenger. In those days in England it was very difficult to move out of that because you had your national service for two years. I was really trapped for what amounted to five years. I came out of the Army and I was still no better off than when I was 15. No more experience. But I drew and painted all during that period. So whatever talent I had was getting a little better by practice. I began to look at magazines and books and I collected things. I'd tear things out, and I really learned from the torn pages of other illustrators' works. I also went to evening classes. I studied figure drawing, oils, still lifes. That was the course I set myself—drawing, which included fashion, because I didn't know what I wanted to do at that point—and painting, because I was interested in it and enjoyed that the most. But I didn't ever consider painting at that point because everybody knows you can't make a living as a painter. Illustration was different. That was somehow tangible.

By the time I was 22 I was working on the staff of a national magazine doing pasteups, layout, and an occasional drawing. It was there I began to see serious illustration for the first time, and the stuff I mostly admired was American illustrators' works, which were in magazines like *Colliers* and *Saturday Evening Post,* and in women's magazines like *McCall's*, which in those days did wonderful stuff, unlike today. That was really my school. At 24 I started working as a freelance illustrator doing book jackets. Well, I did everything. The jackets were for crime stuff, cowboys, Gothic romances—anything. I did fashion drawing, pen and ink. I did charcoal. There wasn't much call for charcoal, but colored pencil drawing. I knew how to use all the various media: cross-hatch, pen and ink, loose line drawings, charcoal pencil. I even did strip cartoons around that time for a kind of rock/pop magazine—the life of Elvis Presley, the life of other rock stars at that time. I'm talking about 1958 to 1960, around that period.

I knew I wanted to come to New York because there was more interesting work being done here, and I was rather frustrated by what I was doing in London. You had to be a jack-of-all trades, do everything to pay the rent. You couldn't specialize in any one thing, in any one style, even. I was doing well in London. I was established by the time I was 25 or 26. I spent the next couple of years just consolidating my position and socking away money in the bank whenever I could—I was raising a family—and I then decided when I was 28 to come to New York and start all over again, here.

ON EDUCATION: I don't think art school is necessary for everybody. I think it's absolutely necessary for some people. But a lot of people in art schools are wasting their time there. My son has a bent toward art, but he's going to a liberal arts college with a strong arts program. When he graduates, if he still feels strongly about being an artist, he can choose to go to art school. But until that point, I think it's terribly important for him to get an education in other things, in philosophy and history, all of which I didn't get. I don't think most people his age know what they really want to do anyway. I think they need the time to find out and time to learn about other things.

ON SUCCESS: When I was 15, my idea of success was making £20 a week. At that time we were talking about maybe $80 or so. And I could make it doing drawings. Just incredible. Even when I was in the Army at 19 and I'd be on guard duty and I'd draw to keep awake at night, the sergeant major would come over and look and say, "Oh, you do a bit of drawin', do you, my boy?" And I'd say, "Well, that's how I'm going to make my living when I leave the Army." And he'd chortle, "What kind of money do you think you're going to make doing those little drawings, my boy?" By that time I'd raised the ante. "I'm going to make £25 a week as an illustrator." All the people on guard duty would fall down laughing. Because in the Army I was making £6 a week. They couldn't imagine making more than that. Getting printed was success too. So other people could see your work.

ON PROFESSIONALISM: One of the things I've always prided myself on, and still do, is in being a professional who does a professional job. I have very little respect for people who just knock out a job for the money, whether it's a little bit of money or a lot of money, and give it less than their best. I find that personally unconscionable. Even if I'm doing something that's trite—an ad for something I really have nothing personally invested in—I really try to make it look terrific, as professional a job as I can. That hasn't changed for me over the years at all.

ON MONEY: For a lot of illustrators, including myself, the hours are horrendous. You put enormous energy into your work over the years. You have deadlines, so you work more hours than the normal person does. And you want to be rewarded, apart from the reward of doing a picture you like. And often you're doing a picture you don't like, but you're doing it to pay the rent. After twenty years or so, you end up wanting to be able to ease up. You can in other businesses—and I'm a businessman; I'm an illustrator, but I have my own company. In other businesses you can take time off without suffering for it. Illustrators can't do that. You have to keep your nose to the grindstone. The minute you walk away from it, the money stops. Everything stops. So you have to keep in good health, because that's where the money's coming from. I don't think about this very often because it's a little disheartening to think that I can't really walk away from this, not for any time at all.

You can't get rich as an illustrator anymore. Once upon a time you actually could, like you could get rich as an actor or a writer. But, if you're talented, good at what you do, have lots of energy, don't need a lot of sleep, you can make money. You mustn't be disheartened too soon. It's very competitive. It was then, always has been; it is now because there're more people doing it; it's very competitive. You have to believe in yourself, have the kind of energy that won't get deflated. It's not for the timid, or for shrinking violets, because rejection is part of the life, especially in the beginning.

ON THE FUTURE OF ILLUSTRATION: I think there will always be illustration. But it's obviously not as important as it used to be, and it will probably get less important. With computers and videos and all sorts of other things coming in, the hands-on artisan, let's say, is going to be a rarer creature. So I think the market will shrink. But I also think there will always be room at the top for a small number of dedicated professionals who are really good at what they do. It can't be done any other way.

ON THE SATISFACTIONS: Being able to listen to jazz on my own all day long, whenever I want to, is a terrific thing. If I were working in a studio space with even some other illustrators and one of them liked country-and-western music, it would be dreadful. That sounds frivolous, but it really is important. Because I work with music all the time. Those are the kinds of advantages. The main advantage, probably, is that you're really your own boss and you don't have to deal with other people on a day-to-day basis, like most people have to do in their jobs.

The satisfactions in the work itself come harder by the year for me. There are other people who obviously would be thrilled to be doing what I do, and fifteen years ago I would have been thrilled to do what I do. But I've been doing it a long time and my standards are higher now, my needs as an artist are greater. I want to continue to grow and not just repeat what I've done six times before. Most clients want you to repeat what you've done six times before. So it's harder to satisfy oneself in the work. Probably out of a year's work, there's maybe, at tops, six pieces I like, that I'm happy with and that I won't give away or sell. Unless it's a campaign where I do five or six paintings and it happens to be a terrific campaign. Those don't come along very often, but they can happen.

ON THE WORKING PROCESS: When I'm given freedom on a job, it's generally in editorial and not in advertising, so we'll touch on that first. Say you're working for some magazine that doesn't have a big budget, but the art director wants to work with you. I'll be doing something next week like that, fortunately. I do those for myself. In a case like that, I won't even give them a sketch. I have had the kind of relationship with a couple of art directors over long periods where I've just done the picture and given it to them, but that's unusual. Most of them want to make sure everything is okay. If I have to do a sketch for them, I'll spend an hour or two doing thumbnails, and by that time I know okay, it's going to be this direction.

Then if I know I need references, which quite often I do, I have a lot of books. I'll flip through those. I have a rough file system, so I'll look through that to try to find what I want. But that will come after the idea. The idea always comes first. Then I draw a fairly loose sketch. I try to keep it loose so that the client doesn't get too tied into it at that time. Otherwise it's more difficult for you, when you're working on the finished painting, to change your mind, to go in another direction, to be flexible enough to substract or add things. If the sketch is too tightly finished, they have it there and they can say, "Wait a minute, that element isn't there," and then you're in trouble. So

I like to keep it fairly loose. Once the sketch is okayed, I stretch the canvas. I work on canvas almost all the time. I gesso the canvas, sand it down so I get the surface I want. I work in oils now, so I usually draw the thing up again on the canvas, sketching it in, and again not keeping it too tight. Some illustrators do it the old way, really work it out, do the drawing, the sketch, and then trace it through onto the canvas, and it's a very tight thing. Then they begin to fill in the areas. I don't work like that at all. But I do sketch, because sometimes the illustrations are quite complicated. I sketch in most of the things that have to go down in paint. But I leave areas free enough to move things around if I want to.

If an art director feels comfortable with me and doesn't need to see a sketch, I just begin to sketch directly on the canvas. The ideas come to me as I'm doing it and then I paint with that. I usually give myself at least a week on a job unless it's very complicated, then it could take two to three weeks. I work from ten to twelve hours a day. I don't take a lunch break. I usually have a sandwich by my drawing board or something like that, and work through lunch. I usually quit for dinner at 6:30 or 7, and I'm back to work by 8 or 8:30. I work until 11:30 or midnight, depending on how much energy I feel I have.

ON HAVING A PERSONAL LIFE: I often get younger illustrators who ask me how I have a personal life, where I get the time. The hours and the deadlines being what they are, it's hard to have a personal life. By the time you've finished a job, you're too tired to do anything anyway. Unlike other professions, it's not as if your social life and your business are wrapped up together. You're on your own, so I think you have to be very careful of that.

Certainly there are times where because of circumstances, ambition, you don't want to turn down work you think will change your life or your career in some way. You feel you must grab the opportunity because the chance may not come around again. So you wrap yourself up in it, and then obviously, your personal life does suffer.

I think, eventually, its your work that suffers if you don't take time off. In the short term, it doesn't. But if there's a continuing pattern, your work would have to suffer. You have to be able to get away from it, stand at arm's length, enjoy other aspects of your life, then come back to it renewed, as it were. I think also, if you don't get away from your work on a regular basis, social life aside, and try to look at it with an objective, fresh eye, you can get caught up in it. Then you lose sight, not only of what you're doing, but of what you want to do and how it's evolving. So I think it's very important.

ON ARTISTIC GOALS: Those are complicated. Some illustrators, myself included at this stage, see interesting creative avenues shutting down. So we're looking for other avenues to explore. Like printmaking, for instance. I'll be having two pieces printed by the end of the year, and another publishing outfit has approached me to do prints. So those are outlets, I think. We're constantly looking at another way to do what we do, to do better than what we do. It remains to be seen whether there are real possibilities for illustrators to grow into that area. There are obvious problems, and the first one is that a lot of the prints are just as commercial, if not more so than a lot of the illustrations one does. So it may just become more of the same, but different. It's printed better. It's bigger, etc., which is very nice. But it may not change anything significantly for you as an artist.

Painting is something else entirely. That's another career! And I'm a firm believer, personally, that you can't do both well. They both take too much energy. And they're different from each other. It's a bit like printmaking. Illustrators who become painters, in my view, generally are not very good or terribly interesting painters, and they end up doing, for the most part—and this is a generalization, I know—big illustrations. They don't completely change their methods, or even the character of what they're saying.

DUGALD STERMER
Illustrator/Designer/Writer, Freelance

It is unusual for a talented visual artist to excel as a writer as well. This unique combination has made Dugald Stermer a real force in the international graphic design community. Former editor and art director of Ramparts *magazine, he is presently the associate editor of* Communication Arts *magazine. He designed the official medal for the 1984 Los Angeles Olympic Games, and his clients include design firms such as Jonson, Pedersen, Hinrichs & Shakery; agencies such as Ogilvy & Mather and D'Arcy MacManus Masius; and magazines like* Time, Ramparts, California Living, Mother Jones, *and* Sierra. *He has won many awards from the American Institute of Graphic Arts (AIGA),* Communication Arts, *the Society of Illustrators, the New York Art Directors Club, and* American Illustration. *He is the author of* The Art of Revolution *(McGraw-Hill) and* Vanishing Creatures *(Lancaster-Miller) and is currently working on his new book,* Vanishing Plants and Flowers *for Overlook Press.*

ON GETTING STARTED: I never had any other notion about making a living, except through making pictures. What kind? I had no idea. Before college, I only really knew there were two kinds of commercial artists, personified by Norman Rockwell and Al Capp. Either would do for me. I had no interest in being Picasso; I didn't understand, at that time, what it was Picasso and his pals did exactly, or how they got paid. When I went to UCLA, I quickly saw that damn near everyone in the art department drew better than I did, including the freshmen—especially the freshmen. So I slid into design, graphic design, as the next best thing. I have a notion that a lot of budding artists do exactly the same thing. After all, no one in grammar school or even high school dreams of becoming a graphic designer or art director, any more than the young poet dreams of becoming a copywriter. Anyway, it took years of working as a designer and magazine art director to finally get back to the business of making pictures—in fact, to get good enough to have something of myself that people would want to buy. I was a late bloomer as an illustrator, you might say.

ON EDUCATION: A university education was appropriate for me, because drawing and writing are only different ways to carry on conversations with other people. I was curious—still am—and a university is clearly the right place for that kind of person. Art Center or Visual Arts would have put me way ahead of where I was technically then, but I fear I might have sacrificed a great deal in the bargain. Reading, writing, and learning are of great interest to me. And an art school is of little assistance in that regard, even the best ones.

ON MONEY: Sure, people make inordinate amounts of money in advertising-editorial-illustration-photography-design. And a few actually earn what they make. Those who earn it, who truly work hard for their money are mostly the illustrators and photographers. There is simply great gobs of cash being spent trying to convince us all to buy something or other, and some of that does trickle down to us craftspeople. Most of it, however, goes to the people who are in the business of convincing other people to spend more and more money. They are the creative directors, agency principals, media buyers, ad managers, and television producers. Go into those fields—or become a dentist, or a psychiatrist specializing in dentists as patients—if you want to make money. One can make money in illustration, pretty fair money, in fact, considering that most of us are doing something we would do for free if we were of independent means. But the field is increasingly crowded and competitive, with good practitioners entering it all the time, and outlets seem to be shrinking. One area we could all explore more is the self-generated market for our work, like posters, notecards, calendars, and books. Invent our world, then exploit it.

ON SUCCESS: When I started out, success probably meant something like peer approval. One of my first goals was to earn the notice and respect of the design community, first locally—meaning at that time, California—then throughout the country. I think that I never thought much of money, beyond earning enough to live on and then some. A better way to say it would be that I wanted to earn enough never to have to think about it. Unfortunately, that time has yet to arrive. I earn far more than I dreamed of twenty-five years ago. But success still means, in some ways, the respect of ones' admired contemporaries. I think that's why shows and exhibits are useful. We all like to be admired, especially by those we admire. Another benefit of a good reputation is you get offered a better class of work. Not much more money, but deeper challenges and commissions that are to some extent tailored to your approach. There's a danger that too much typecasting can lead to repeating oneself without growth. But that's also easily avoided.

After a career as a designer and editorial art director, where I've had some influence and repute, it means even more to take a more personal craft, like illustrating, and build that into a respected career. It seems as if the closer I get to developing my own voice, where I say what I want to say with pictures, the more chances I get to do that. I guess that means that success is, in part, the freedom to keep working and improving. We're successful to the extent we continue to do both.

When I was teaching, many students would invariably bring up "names" in the field, asking how they made it big, as if there were some secret that would lead to instant fame and fortune. The fact is that those very few, maybe a half dozen at any one time, extraordinary talents will make it no matter how they approach the field. They can be boorish, complacent, abusive, and generally appalling, or the opposite. And they will get work and plaudits because of their natural gifts. The rest of us must work damn hard to enter the field and especially to maintain a career. Being an illustrator is a lot like being a musician. One never truly knows how to play the violin, that's why Menuhin and Perlman practice hours every day. And there is someone sitting in a room at Juilliard practicing harder and longer, just waiting to take a few concert dates away from the masters, just as there are students at Visual Arts and other schools looking to beat out Mahurin,* god willing, for a *Time* cover.

ON MULTIPLE CAREERS: It has to do with a cottage-industry mentality with me—just do as much as you can get away with yourself. At *Ramparts* we had such a small staff, we all wore as many hats as would fit. And some that didn't. I looked at the magazine as my very own sixty-four pages to say whatever I wanted to. The other two editors felt the same, so we were always battling for space. They thought of words first, and I thought of pictures, but all of us had respect for what the other medium could do. I recognized in school that there were many things that either couldn't be said with pictures, or that I wasn't skilled enough to draw, so then I'd turn to words. As an art director I often chose words over pictures, photography over illustration—and for the most part, other peoples' illustrations over mine. I also wrote a number of pieces, mostly because they had to be written, and there wasn't anyone else around to do it at the time. I can't be specific, but there's no question in my mind that my drawing and designing have helped my writing. And I'm even more certain about the vice versa of it.

ON WORKING FOR OTHERS: I work mainly on assignment. That means that my primary task is to make my client of the moment look good. If I don't try to do that, I'm a liar and a thief. If I can also do it well, communicate an idea beyond the primary one, as defined by the client, grow in the process, and then, make a picture that stands by itself—that's great. But

---

*Matt Mahurin is a young illustrator who has had an exceptionally fast rise from obscurity to success.

none of that is what the client is paying for. There are always problems involved with doing such personal work for others, but those are only magnified when the illustrator misreads or ignores the purpose of the commission. When accepting a job, I usually try to ride the horse in the direction it's going. For the duration, I make every attempt to enjoy the ride and look forward to the destination. If I don't think I can do that, I don't take the job.

ON STYLE: To me, one's style has a great deal to do with one's temperament. I simply can't sustain my interest nor find the patience to take a lot of time on a single picture. That's probably why I work in pencil, from light to dark as it were. Others only feel comfortable by working through a picture—underpainting, glazes, media—from dark to comparative light. That takes a long time. And maybe allows for greater involvement, more experimentation in the process. I don't think people like me who work from light to dark carefully planned that approach in advance. Or that others picked oils over watercolors before trying either. We all worked around, muddled through, until we found the way of working that suited our temperaments. And if we're thoughtful at all, we continue to muddle around looking for new ways, new tools. It's like a writer trying on new words and modes of expression, maybe even turning from prose to poetry, fiction to nonfiction, and then back again. It airs out the mind.

ON THE SATISFACTIONS: I get so much pleasure out of making a picture from a blank piece of paper that it is impossible for me to put words to it. It's not that the whole process is pleasurable. Quite the contrary—much of it is painful, some of it boring, but when it takes form and life, there's nothing I've found like it. It doesn't always or even most often happen, but I always try for it.

ON PROCESS AND PRODUCT: I do think that any interesting product has an interesting process. And both the process and the product, mine and that of others, interests me greatly. Of the two, process is the more complex, and so the more interesting. It can exist without product and be fascinating in and by itself. When I'm blocked for an idea, I work on something else. I write, do another job, anything. Because I work fast, I can work on quite a few projects, so there is always somewhere to go. I've learned to have faith in my thought processes, and confidence that reflection will lead to solutions.

ON SUSTAINING ENERGY: I think that my energy comes from a curiosity that borders on fascination. When asked, "What's your favorite painting?" Picasso is quoted as saying, "The next one." I feel that way, not only in my work, but really in life, as corny as that sounds.

ON INNOVATION: Innovation is not so much important as it is inevitable for me. Every assignment, whether self-generated or from a client, calls for some kind of innovation, by its very nature. And we seem to innovate as naturally as breathing, probably out of a need to avoid boredom. Maybe I'm taking too much for granted, but to paraphrase Marvell, "The grave's a fine and private place, but none, I fear, do there innovate." Terrible nonrhyme, but good sense.

ON A PHILOSOPHY OF LIFE: The closest I can come to framing a philosophy is to say that all effort, including making pictures, has content. Even art proclaimed as being for its own sake. I think that's self-indulgent bullshit, but even in *that* case, bullshit's the content. I respond to the dialogue that pictures can help to carry on, and it's that dialogue I intend to contribute to. Art can't escape being political, social, literally meaningful. I know that this sounds insufferably pompous, but there you are. We are what we do, not what we say, or say we are. Our work is the most important thing we have, and it is best not to squander it. If that work is communication—ideas and information, even opinion—then the clarity, grace, imagination, integrity, and skill with which we communicate is what makes it effective. That's what gives it value. Besides, what else is there to do?

SEYMOUR CHWAST
Illustrator/Designer, Director, Push Pin Group

Seymour Chwast's massive talents as an illustrator and graphic designer have brought him an international reputation. As one of the founding partners of Push Pin Studios, his original vision changed contemporary visual communication and continues to influence young designers and illustrators all over the world.

Chwast works easily in all the visual arts, from advertising to film to books, graphics, magazines, posters, and packaging. He has created typefaces and has designed and illustrated more than a dozen children's books. He was publisher and art director of Push Pin Graphics. He formed the Push Pin Press which originated and produced a wide range of books. He has received every major design award, is the recipient of the St. Gauden's Medal from Cooper Union, and was elected to the Art Directors Hall of Fame. His posters are in the permanent collection of the Museum of Modern Art, the Cooper-Hewitt Museum, the Library of Congress, and the Gutenberg Museum.

ON EDUCATION: Art school is one of the few places where you can learn how to think and where you can learn to draw, which are indispensable skills to an illustrator or graphic designer. But artists need a strong foundation in the academics and humanities as well. We have to know what's going on to understand the references we read. It's possible to do it on your own, but a good foundation is very helpful.

For designers it's important to learn production skills. And a lot of schools don't teach them or at least don't teach them adequately. You have to know about pasteups, how things are printed. And schools should teach that process. Once the design is done, how does it get into print? Understanding that can help-students get a first job, since most entry-level design jobs require getting involved with production. The more you know, the easier it is to get that first job—and the better you'll be at doing it.

ON PORTFOLIOS: A portfolio is the only essential tool for getting a job as a graphic designer or illustrator. In art school you are presented a number of visual and conceptual problems. When you solve them, you have a piece for your portfolio. It's possible to make a portfolio on your own, but it probably won't be based on the kinds of essential design or illustration problems assigned by a teacher who knows what's needed on the job.

ON TECHNOLOGY AND CREATIVITY: The graphic design field is certainly growing. There's more interest in computer graphics and I guess electronic media is going to become far more important in years to come. That's something to consider. But the problem is, while we get more technological in the way we work, as our tools get more sophisticated, we're not getting any more creative. Technological advances are a problem. They become the excuse for creativity. They provide us with tools, they're only a means to an end. Creating beautiful things that are meaningful to everyone—clients, artists, the world, that's unique.

ON MONEY: If you're good, you can earn a living. There's no question about that. If you're very good, you can earn a very good living.

ON THE SATISFACTIONS: I like doing posters, animated films, packaging, illustration, especially when I can have control over it. If I'm going to be able to do something unique, where I can build my own ideas, start from scratch and build my own concepts and follow through, it's satisfying. When I work with sketches from an art director or a client, that's OK, too, but I'd say generally less rewarding.

ON THE FINE ARTS: The fine arts area seems too much like a rat race to me. I need immediate satisfaction. When I do something, I want to see it in print very soon after. That's inspiring and helps my ego. I don't have the patience to work for myself for too long building up to something. I like working with type. I like working with paper. I like the whole process of print.

ON THE CREATIVE PROCESS: Well, if an idea doesn't come immediately to mind, or if an idea isn't presented to me, I start making sketches, go through books looking for notions that will spark some idea. I love old posters, and I have a lot of books with old things in them. Ultimately the most important thing is the way people respond to whatever I do. If they don't understand it, it virtually doesn't mean anything. Communication is very important. I want people to understand what I'm doing, especially the client who's paying for it. What I like to do is to be able to come up with an idea, then define the style to render the idea, and leave myself some options.

ON CREATIVE BLOCKS: I'm blocked right now. It's really terrible. Well, I guess I have to work it through.

ON SUSTAINING ENERGY: Fear does it for me. As Mel Brooks said, "Fear that the person a little lower down on the ladder is coming up fast." Seriously, I think the best way for work to evolve, to sustain your interest is always to be a little outside the mainstream. See what's going on, but not to be victimized by the fashion of the times. Some illustrators never change their style and they manage very well. They work in a way that has nothing to do with trends and fashion. Me, I think I'd get too bored with it.

ON HAVING A PERSONAL LIFE: You have to work long hours, so you have to live with someone who is understanding or busy too. It has created problems for me, but there's less stress for me now. I used to work longer hours, but I'm more relaxed because I have some control over my life and some things come easier.

ON SUCCESS: I wanted to do good work. I wanted to solve interesting problems. I knew I wanted to be a graphic designer who had a personal style. Because I'm an illustrator as well as a designer, that gives me more of an opportunity than someone who does just illustration. I still care an awful lot about what I do and the work around me. I respond to the good things and the bad with the same kind of passion. But I still have the same problems. If clients don't like the work, they'll reject it. They don't care if I've been around for a long time. Sometimes a reputation helps, but at other times it doesn't have anything to do with it. If the client's needs aren't taken care of, neither my work nor my reputation means a damn. I guess I've been lucky. I haven't made too many mistakes.

ON STAYING IN A JOB: I've been fired three or four times from jobs, and most people go through that while picking up experience. Most people just out of school have to expect things like that to happen. Hopefully, when you get started, you won't get settled too quickly. If a job seems comfortable, it's easy to stay there for the rest of your life, but it's not the best thing. People who are entrepreneurial will go out looking for other work, even while they have a job. There are always ways to freelance in areas that will satisfy you, even if you can't do it on a job.

ON ARTISTIC CONFLICTS: I haven't had any great conflicts, although it's been a little schizophrenic, being an artist who expresses himself and being a designer where I care about things like the silverware. You see, I want everything around me to be visually something I'm going to like very much. On the other hand, I like to get down in the dirt and mix paint around and lose myself in my work, not be concerned about my environment. I want to push things around, get messy, and come out with something terrific. But then the older I become the neater I become, and I think maybe I haven't allowed myself to be as creative and expressive as I can be. So I guess there's a sort of conflict going on. That's why I wear a clean shirt but I try to avoid ties.

MARSHALL ARISMAN
Illustrator/Painter, Freelance

Although Marshall Arisman's work as an illustrator is more widely known, his work as a figurative painter has been exhibited in many galleries and museums both here and abroad. His illustrations have appeared in all major publications, and they have received awards and recognition from professional societies such as the Society of Illustrators, the American Institute of Graphic Arts, (AIGA) American Illustration, Communication Arts, *and* Graphis. *His paintings are represented in Europe by the Phillipe Guimiot Gallery in Brussels, and in San Francisco by Harcourts Gallery. In New York he has exhibited at the Grace Borgenicht Gallery, the Sindin Gallery, and others. He is the cochairman of the media department of the School of Visual Arts and director of the master's program in illustration at the same institution. He is considered a highly innovative artist whose work has a very strong personal political emphasis.*

ON GETTING STARTED: When I got out of high school I went to Pratt Institute to study graphic design and advertising. I graduated with a graphics portfolio and got a job at General Motors in their Tech Center in Detroit. After three months, I began to realize that graphic design was not personal enough for me. I wanted more contact with my hand in drawing. I wanted more isolation with the work I did. At that point, I went to Europe for a year and basically got into illustration as a way to avoid a 9-to-5, five-day-a-week job.

I really didn't know how to go about it, but it seemed possible to freelance, to make some money without working totally for somebody else. The problem at that point was that I really couldn't draw, so my first illustration portfolio was almost primitive in that it didn't show much drawing ability. But at that time it was my best effort. The first year I made $2000 and I think the second year I made $2600. Around the third year it began to occur to me that I had to stop freelancing and, in essence, go back and learn how to draw, which is basically what I did. Looking back, probably the luckiest thing for me was that I was so unsuccessful then at being an illustrator.

I took a year off, only teaching to make a living, and began doing drawings for myself; I began to teach myself how to draw. By the end of that year, my old illustration agent had opened a small gallery and I had an exhibition of my drawings in the gallery and got a good review in the *New York Times*. So I thought then I'd have a fine arts career. But the gallery began discussing plans for the next show for the next year, and I suddenly heard echos of General Motors and commercial art. I felt I didn't know exactly what I wanted to do yet. I felt I was too young to develop a style that quickly, and I wanted to do some sculpture. So I stopped the gallery situation and started doing sculpture instead.

ON STARTING OUT TODAY: It seems to me that not enough illustrators look at the field as if they are artists looking for an outlet. I look at illustration as one outlet among many for the work I do. The printed page for me is an outlet. A gallery wall is another outlet. Printmaking is another.

It's a question of how you see yourself in any situation. If you see yourself as an illustrator who is a professional artisan in a business of using your craft to make money, then I suppose the best way to start out is for you to develop as much craft as you can and develop the ability to render everything and anything.

The real truth is, if you find out that what you really want to do is work that's figurative and descriptive, and *that* is the work in your portfolio, then when you get work from a magazine or publishing house, you're being hired for what you already do. If you fill your portfolio with work you don't want to do, you inevitably will get a job doing the thing you don't want to do.

ON EDUCATION: School was very important for me. I needed to be somewhere for four years, surrounded by people who were also struggling with all these questions of what they wanted to do and where they wanted to do it. This obviously isn't true for everybody. There are illustrators who have never been to college, who are totally self-taught. That takes a great deal of self-discipline. It takes a great deal of clarity at a very early age. I didn't have that kind of clarity when I was 18 years old. My school experience was not even clarifying enough as to allow me to find out exactly what I wanted to do, though it certainly taught me what I *didn't* want to do.

In a really good art school you'll find all of the different disciplines: fine arts, graphic design, advertising, illustration, photography. And there will be electives in all those areas open to any major. If you are a graphics major you can still try illustration classes or vice versa. One other thing, there's a great dilemma in all art schools concerning the liberal arts. I feel a little bit cheated in the sense that my education outside of art wasn't that strong. On the other hand, I really needed the concentration in the art area. It would have been ideal, I suppose, had I been able to go to a liberal arts school for one year and then continue in an art school. But I think it's an individual issue.

ON SUCCESS: I think success when I started meant making money and getting recognition in the business, whether it was getting into the Society of Illustrators show or getting into the different annuals. I look at success somewhat differently today. It is a question of attempting to get in print my own ideas. I try to use the publishing industry as an outlet for my own viewpoint. But I know they in turn try to use me. I think it's a tie game. But I'm in a rather unique situation. At age 46 I have no one to blame for my good or bad pictures except myself. I've been given enough freedom in illustration so I can't blame the business for my failures. The question of success becomes, for me, whether the pictures I make are getting better—or at least more interesting, that's a better word. So now it gets much more difficult to judge success. I now get into these shows, but that's not enough. I make enough money, so that's not the issue. The issue is the work itself and how good it is. And that's a question other people have opinions on. But *my* opinion of it is my yardstick of success.

ON MONEY: Absolutely, there's money to be made in illustration. I do work for magazines and newspapers, I do some book jackets, I've done some album covers. But the primary source of my work is editorial. In terms of the marketplace, the editorial market can't be compared, in terms of money, to the advertising-illustration market or the movie-poster market. For example, an average page in any mass magazine, and this is an average, whether it's *Esquire, Penthouse, Playboy,* or *Psychology Today,* is approximately $1000 per page. An average advertising job, which might be anything from rendering a hot dog to rendering floor tiles, my guess would be a range of $7000 to $10,000.

So it's a question of freedom. In editorial work, I get almost total freedom. It's simply the way the process works. In an advertising-illustration situation, the art director and the copywriter make a comp, which means a sketch of the idea. It goes to the client. The client okays it. By the time the illustrator gets it, it's already been very hammered down. You don't get much flexibility or freedom in that situation. For me, the freedom is much more important than the money. But there's a catch here, for people coming into the business. Everyone who makes a name in the illustration business makes it through the editorial market. It's impossible to start with advertising work. So what happens is simply this: You get out of school, you take editorial work for exposure. You then submit that work to annuals and juried situations like the Society of Illustrators, *American Illus-*

tration, or the *Communication Arts Annual.* That exposure gets your name around. Once your name is known, if your abilities and desire are to move into advertising, it's possible. So you build a reputation editorially, and then if you want to take advantage of it, you can go for work in advertising.

ON PORTFOLIOS: What usually happens is, in order to get the work in advertising, you basically have to change the focus of your portfolio and direct it more toward advertising possibilities. You simply make samples in the area, whether it's rendering Coca-Cola bottles or other things that can be applied to advertising. Your samples change, and as they change, what you have to show becomes your portfolio. The portfolio designed to get work in advertising does not lead to more editorial work.

All illustration is grounded in drawing and painting, figurative drawing and painting. The best advice I have for a young person would be to find a situation that would teach you how to draw and paint, and then to continue to draw and paint. Try to make pictures about things you think are important. If you make pictures about things you think are important, you will have a personal portfolio, simply because your interests will reflect themselves in the portfolio. If you think politics are important, that concern will become the basis of your imagery and, consequently, the portfolio will then be personal.

ON THE REALITIES OF HAVING A CAREER IN ILLUSTRATION: The problem with illustration is that it is totally a freelance business. The only two staff positions I know of are at Hallmark Cards, where they employ 700 staff illustrators, and at American Greeting Cards, where they hire 300 staff illustrators. So the dilemma for the illustrator starting out is there is no staff position to apply for. In smaller towns, it's possible to get out of school and get a job doing part graphic design and using a little of your illustration ability when you get the chance. But in a large city like New York, the graphic design studios want to see specialized graphic design portfolios and so on and so forth. You cannot be a jack-of-all-trades. You must have some focus. The dilemma for the illustrator is simply economic. The student graduating from Visual Arts or any art school anywhere in the country is after the same page along with every other illustrator with ten, fifteen, twenty years' experience. So the casualty rate in illustration is very high. Nevertheless, if you have been in art school and tried other disciplines—graphics, advertising, or whatever—and find the only thing you are really interested in is your own drawing, your own painting, developing your own style, commenting on things that seriously concern you, then give it a chance.

ON THE SATISFACTIONS OF ILLUSTRATING VS. THOSE OF PAINTING: When it all works well, I am assigned an illustration, the topic of which is something I'm very interested in or think is important. I then do it. It gets printed and then I get feedback from other people. It's a way for me to communicate with the world. The work is done in isolation, but the point of the work is to make me feel less isolated. When communication really works, it works because other people agree with or understand a part of what you're trying to do. And that's satisfying.

What happens in a painting is that I don't have any guidelines at all except my own. I'll give you an example. If I start a painting with the idea of showing a dog in a landscape, and then somewhere in the middle of doing it, the dog looks like a pig in a barn, I can allow the painting to go in any direction because there are no limitations. No one tells me the subject must be a dog and it must be in a landscape. In illustration there are real lines, and there are real definitions. If I'm assigned a book jacket where the story outlined takes place in Vietnam, I can't paint a Maine landscape. In illustration you have to love describing things. In painting, I can be much more open about where the paintings go. I don't see one as better than the other. I'm not even sure if some of the illustrations I've produced aren't better than the paintings I've produced.

I think you have to get very clear that the process itself does not necessarily produce one thing or the other. It's simply a question of you trying to find out what it is you can get from each area. I find the balance is very healthy for me. I like the freedom I get when I paint a picture on my own. I like the time limit I'm given in illustration. I also like to be able to paint on a painting for six months. So they are different, but I need them both. It's much like teaching. I have ended up doing three things. I teach. I paint. I do illustrations. All three give me some balance, and they give me different things.

ON THE WORKING PROCESS: I am given something to read, a manuscript, a book, or an article. I read and try to understand it, then reread it. I start to make sketches. Once I begin to get some idea where I'm going with the picture, the next step is reference. I find out what the landscape of Vietnam looks like, which means I go to a photo book on Vietnam or I go to the picture library or my own picture file.

My approach to the page is that I like the immediacy of not being totally in control. Which means I don't have a paint process that is step by step. Some people have a painting process on which they can build. You do step A, then step B, then step C. My process is much more direct. I paint with my fingers. I push the paint around a lot. I'm not exactly in control when I'm painting. And that for me is fun. That is an element whether I'm illustrating or painting. It's an attempt to allow the accident to occur while I'm in the process of painting. That, for me, is why I'm painting.

ON CREATIVE BLOCKS: I've been panicked by not having an idea. But I have never yet been through what people call a "creative block," where they can't work on anything for a month or longer. I am an obsessive worker. I believe that growth comes out of the work and the analysis follows. Not the analysis and then the work. I think it's important for me to understand that. The more I think about something, the more blocked I become. I then have to go to work. When I get to the work, the solution somehow comes through it. So if I get frustrated and feel stifled, I try to change media. If I have been totally painting, I might try to do a monoprint. I try to switch gears on myself, to change the direction of what I'm doing. If I'm working totally from someone else's words, then I try to work totally from my own thoughts. It's just a game of trying to find a different approach.

ON SUSTAINING ENERGY: The energy is sustained by the fact that at 46 I'm beginning to feel like I'm just starting, which is energizing in itself.

ON INNOVATION: I like the connection to history. I like the classical context. I think of myself as being connected to, I hope, Velazquez or Hopper or any figurative painter. I'm not concerned with developing a new art style or a redefinition of what art is.

ON HAVING A PERSONAL LIFE: It's important because it takes you away from your work. The difficulty comes when you are so obsessed by something you don't want to leave it. And maybe the worst thing is to stay with an obsession. The importance of a personal life is simply that it drags me away from my obsession. I guess I balance my work and my personal life with the help of my wife.

ON A PHILOSOPHY OF LIFE: Well, I would say that you simply to try to stay connected to work you think is important, is useful to you in your life. If you're able to even come close to that, you have been very lucky in a world where 99 percent of the people are working in jobs they hate or have no feeling for. They get a paycheck and that's all.

ON ADVICE TO YOUNG PEOPLE: Don't be too concerned whether you're dedicated enough to be an artist. I think one of the false questions that gets asked in this area is whether you want to be an artist enough. I think that's a very hard question to answer. I think all you can do is look at what you are doing at the moment. And if what you are doing at the moment is spending all of your time avoiding making pictures because you hate them, maybe you should consider doing something else. But if you are making pictures and you are still interested in them, that's probably as good an indication as any that if you continue with it you're going to get better.

VIVIENNE FLESHER
Illustrator, Freelance

Vivienne Flesher's distinctive work in pastels, charcoal, and oils has brought her a broad range of assignments, from editorial illustration to advertising. Her clients include Rolling Stone, Vogue, Time, *the* New York Times, Connoisseur, *and many others. The illustrations she created for* Seasonal Gifts from The Kitchen, *published by William Morrow, received a Gold Medal from the Society of Illustrators in 1984. Flesher's advertising clients include Bloomingdale's in New York, Epson Computers, Elizabeth Arden, Grasshopper-Keds, and International Paper Company. She has completed two series of posters and catalogs for Canon typewriter, and several of her paintings appeared in the movie* Almost You, *a 1985 Touchstone production. Recently she was commissioned by the U.S. Postal Service to create a "love" stamp. Articles on her work have appeared in* Illustration Magazine *(no. 35) and in the November 1985 issue of* Idea *magazine.*

ON GETTING STARTED: I majored in illustration at Parsons and after graduation I did pasteups and mechanicals and just strengthened my portfolio and my determination. Finally, after about a year, I went out one April Fools' Day to look for work—an appropriate day—although I did *get* work, and it was steady. But I didn't really make a living at it for probably three years.

When I went to school I was so young. I wanted to draw and paint, and unfortunately I didn't understand completely what I was getting involved with in the world of illustration.

I reached a lot of my goals very early on and I was surprised. Now when I think back on it, I feel I could have done more. I channeled myself into illustration, which probably helped me become more successful as an illustrator. But it narrowed down my personal life. Now I feel a need to do a lot more things.

ON EDUCATION: I found I worked all the time at Parsons. I never worked as hard as I did when I was in school. But Parsons wasn't that strong in the liberal arts, so I really feel I missed that part of my education. I try to read as much as I can, and learn as much, but I really think you just need a more rounded education. I think a liberal arts education gives you so much more information and allows you to make more intelligent choices.

Some people don't need school at all, though. When I was teaching, I remember seeing kids in the class that were best left, if not alone, almost alone. The paths they were taking themselves was so exciting, there was nothing more I could give. It was more exciting to see what they could do. But other people need a stronger hand and have to be shown where to go. So it depends. I think, though, if you're going into illustration, there are some basic things you need to know. Certain rules, for instance, on how to get your portfolio set up, but they're easy enough to figure out or find out about in a short period of time. You don't need college for that. As I said, it just depends on the person.

ON SUCCESS: This is a field where success does mean something. It almost seems like there's no point in going into illustration if you're not planning to be successful.

ON COMPETITION: It's a very competitive field. One where people imitate each other, and it's not frowned on. Actually, it's sort of encouraged. That creates problems. Everybody with a similar kind of drawing ability often feels, "Well, that job could be for me, too." And unless people are somewhat secure in the way they feel, it creates problems.

ON STYLE: I think when a unique style catches on, it can support more than one artist. But in the beginning, when a person is struggling and not making any money, as I did for a long time, with a style that's somewhat unique, it can be very hard. After the sheep sort of catch on and start giving out work, everybody's doing it and you see it everywhere.

A style is hard to change in illustration, because they always want what you've done in the annuals that are four years old. I've been pretty lucky, though, and I've been allowed to do what I want in advertising. They kind of leave me alone. Sometimes, though, when I'm into a job and it's miserable, I do it as quickly as possible and think of the next job that may be better.

ON MONEY: I think you can make money. It's hard, though. In a way, I think you can make more money earlier on than in many fields. Something I have to work on is to figure out how to get money from a source other than my art.

Frankly, if people want to make money, the stock market is a better field to go into. You can make more money and it's not as hard. I guess you can live a lot more, too. You have to love illustration and want it so badly. You work incredibly hard for all your money, and then you lose your life to illustration, so you have to like it.

ON THE SATISFACTIONS: Well, often I'm very happy with the drawings I've done. When you have a deadline to meet, an assignment to fit the drawing into and you can do it and also be happy with the drawing... it's a thrill. It's exciting, too, when I'm on a bus and I can see people are looking at a drawing of mine in a magazine.

ON THE WORKING PROCESS: You have to make a schedule for yourself. I actually write things down I should do, things like when I have to start in order to deliver the job in time. Sometimes the schedule gets confused. If I need to, I work all night, though I don't like doing it. When I was younger I used to stay up all night a lot more and I liked it. I enjoyed the quietness of working and just hearing the garbage trucks at four in the morning and seeing the sun come up. But now it just wrecks me for a couple of days after. So that's been changing and it happens less and less. I want to be a little more organized and I'd like to procrastinate a little less. But I think a lot of people go through the same thing.

Rather than work, I watch TV. I just do anything I can. I clean my apartment, anything before working. I procrastinate as long as possible, sometimes for days. Then I work, usually only when the deadline is looming, sometimes even after the deadline has passed, but that's only when I can get away with it. I like it once I start working, but I don't like getting started. There's so much of a drawing that is a mess until it's somewhat resolved, and it takes so long to resolve it, that I never feel that eager to begin.

I can resolve a drawing in my mind the way I'd like it to look, but there's so much left to chance. It often takes a turn and does something on its own, so there's just no way of knowing until you're done.

When I start drawing or painting I don't like to leave it except for maybe five or ten minutes. I'll work all day long or night and that's the way I enjoy working. I don't like leaving it and coming back a day or two later. Once I get going I enjoy the process, but it's so personal and such a quiet thing that I don't even think so much about what goes on, it just sort of happens. It's a lot of decision making, and sometimes you just choose not to decide anything and you just keep going. It's exciting and tiring.

ON THE REALITIES OF HAVING A CAREER IN ILLUSTRATION: I think you have to realize that it's a business and that people aren't hiring you to be completely creative, to do just anything you feel like doing at the moment. You have to make compromises and you have to be able to compromise. So many people can't. I think there's an art to thinking quickly, figuring out how you can compromise and still live with yourself and be interested in doing the drawing. That's something you learn. But I think it happens slowly. You really have to learn because if you take your work at all seriously, and you can't learn how to compromise, it will be too, too hard.

ON DRAWING: First I have to be excited about what I'm going to do. I start thinking. I start drawing. Then once I've started I don't think so much. Sometimes the act of making a mistake lets you see what you've done. And often, in fixing the mistake you get something even nicer. Just covering up with different colors can create something you never dreamed of doing.

Drawing and color are the base of my illustration. It's the way the material touches a surface that I like. Or the way the paint or pastel or charcoal is on paper. Maybe I'll just like the mark it makes. When I was a child, I drew things I loved. I drew animals and fish and those kinds of things. There was always a way to be closer to things I liked. I would draw them for hours. It was a treat, something I could do for hours and be left alone. I find illustration interferes a lot with my drawing for fun. And I'm not pleased with that at all. Last summer I went to Europe for about two months and during that time I was able to do about five drawings I loved and they had nothing to do with illustration. I was able to have enough time to unwind and do them. I want more time like that, to draw for myself.

I find I grow less when I draw for illustration than when I draw for myself. Often you're doing so many jobs you don't have time to experiment as fully as you'd like. So you do what you know you can do and grow less.

ON CREATIVE BLOCKS: When I was just starting, it was very difficult to learn the process of developing an idea. How do you satisfy the client and yourself? It was something I learned. I learned by observing other people to see how they did it. I talked to other illustrators and sometimes tried their methods. And when it didn't work for me, I went off on my own.

ON HAVING A PERSONAL LIFE: Oh, God, it's terribly important to have a personal life. I think that's where it really gets hard for a woman. Maybe it gets hard for men, too, in that way. But I know that for a woman, especially when you're starting a relationship, it can be hard. I mean I'll get a job on Tuesday and it will be due Thursday, and it's a job I really want to do, so I have to cancel my date that night and life sort goes on hold until the drawing is done. Not everyone can tolerate it, and I don't think everyone should. It can take over your life and make a shambles of it. I've been working hard for the last three years and I've just decided that it's time to have fun; it's time not to work so much and *live*. Just observe things, go to the theatre, draw for myself, take pictures, do anything I want to do. I've paid my dues to achieve a certain success, and now with the help of agents, I can sort of sit back a little bit and do more of what I haven't done in a while.

ON ADVICE TO YOUNG PEOPLE: I think they should know how to do more than just illustration. They should be plumbers or writers or musicians. They should have other interests. Photography. Painting. Making furniture. Anything. They should have other areas of interest they're really involved in. It will help them strike a balance in their lives, because they'll need it when they start illustration.

6

Industrial Design

INDUSTRIAL design is the design of commercially produced products, ranging from hard goods such as refrigerators, stereo units, cars, and television sets to office equipment, furniture, specialized instruments for the medical profession, toys, bottles, and boxes to contain everything from detergents to perfume. To be effective in this highly complex field, you need not only art and design talents but in-depth knowledge of engineering, manufacturing methods, and production capabilities.

There is a tendency for any artist or designer to feel he or she can design a box or bottle as well as a book or advertisement, and it often happens that commercial designers, such as those specializing in graphics, or art directors working in advertising agencies, will be asked to design packages. But to produce a design that is both pleasing and can be readily manufactured in mass quantities for a reasonable cost requires an expert. The industrial designer *is* that expert. Other artists may be skilled in creating renderings of a package and presenting them beautifully, but they usually have little knowledge or understanding of the practical requirements for actually making the physical object. Consequently, when many of these designs reach the production stage, they are rejected. The industrial designer, with both design and production expertise, naturally has a far higher degree of success in this area.

Industrial design begins with improving the visual appearance of products by using materials well—shaping, forming, and finding ways for the consumer to use a product more efficiently.

The industrial designer is primarily concerned with the relationship between people and their use of a product. On the other hand, as the exterior design of practically everything we use becomes more important, no industrial designer who ignores the aesthetics of a product can be successful today. Function is as important as it always was, but form has to keep up with the increasingly sophisticated tastes of the consumer. Whether all the designing and redesigning we see in the marketplace is necessary or not, they seem to be inevitable processes in an economy where innovation, not only in product development but in packaging, is the primary tool in selling the product. Industrial design is definitely a career with a future.

BASIC RESPONSIBILITIES The industrial designer is a problem solver. He or she works with a corporation to style or package a product to attract the consumer. But the responsibility doesn't end there. After buying, the consumer should be able to use the product easily and effectively.

A designer consults with the engineers who develop the technology as well as with the people who handle marketing and merchandising. Often the marketing departments and production departments in large corporations disagree on the direction of a product. The concerns of the production department are making sure the product works; those of marketing are making sure the product sells. A designer has to understand the problems of both sides to come up with a solution that meets both needs more or less equally. Otherwise, a company will produce a toy or iron or roll-on deodorant package that is highly marketable but can't be made, or a computer or jar or light fixture that's easy to make but can't be marketed.

Some designers specialize in a particular kind of product category—for example, cosmetic packaging or cars. If you design cars, you have only three or four corporations for which to work and most of your work will consist of sketching your ideas on paper. The frustrations involved, of course, lie in the fact that very few new cars are designed each year. The aspiration of a designer to see "his" or "her" car on the production line at some time could easily remain unfulfilled. The designer who specializes in cosmetic purchasing has far greater opportunity to see his or her work in use.

SALARIES Beginning salaries for industrial designers working for corporations are moderate, and, as in most design fields, the actual figures depend on how much your talents are wanted or needed. Designers who work on their own charge on a fee basis per project. The real money in the industrial design field lies in royalties; each time a product you designed is sold, you receive a percentage agreed on when the initial contract was signed.

EDUCATION AND TRAINING A college education is the easiest, most direct method for getting the well-rounded training and background necessary to enter this competive field. Many colleges offer both four- and five-year programs that combine courses in design with courses in engineering, materials, and manufacturing techniques as well as in marketing, advertising, and business.

INTERVIEW

EARL HOYT

Industrial Designer; President, The Hoyt Group, Industrial Design and Marketing Consultants

A graduate of Pratt Institute, Earl Hoyt worked for five years with such design firms as Donald Desky Associates and Lippincott & Margulies, both in New York, before starting his own business in partnership with his wife. The Hoyt Group has been responsible for the design of many well-known products and packages seen in supermarkets and department stores across the country. They range from coffee percolators and stereo equipment to medical and *industrial equipment. Hoyt was awarded a CLIO* for the design of Carpet Fresh for Airwick Industries in 1981. For Johnson & Johnson, Hoyt designed, among other things, the dental floss container found in nearly every home in the country. His other clients include companies such as Chesebrough Pond's, Colgate-Palmolive, Carter Wallace, Gillette, and Richardson-Vicks. He is one of the most sought-after designers in the country for his strong production knowledge and for his original graphic design talents that ensure clients a memorable product identity.*

ON GETTING STARTED: My mother was a textile designer. She was Italian and she had a flair, an artistic flair. My father was a machinist. He was German, and he had precision, the how-things-work knowledge. I feel an industrial designer is kind of a combination of both of these. And I think I picked up some of the artistic flair from my mother, and the mechanical, precision-oriented interest in machinery from my dad. I'm the kind of guy that bridges the gap between the production people who are into pure mechanics and the artistic people. I work in between, back and forth. I'm able to interpret both needs and come up with a total solution—one that's aesthetic and still producible.

I was always into mechanical things. I liked the way things worked. I've always taken things apart and tried to fix them. I was always kind of an automobile mechanic, and as a kid fixing up cars, I tried styling them. In my youth, it wasn't called "styling" but that's what it was—trying to get the car to look better, dechroming it or customizing it, or what have you.

From high school, I went into the Army for two years and it was a rude awakening that you can get older and not smarter. I saw a lot of gentlemen with stripes who were 50 or 60 years old reading Batman funny books. I knew immediately I wanted

---

*The CLIO awards are presented each year for outstanding achievement in creative advertising by the CLIO organization, located in New York City.

to have a professional career of some sort. I was lucky I had an artistic background to fall back on. So I came back from the Army and applied to several art schools. I had what they called "potential." I wasn't very good at the time, but it looked like I could grow and work in the art field. I had this very strong interest in designing art, putting things down on a piece of paper. And I was inventive. So I did some research, to see if there was a profession that called for those talents. I wrote to General Motors, as a matter of fact. They wrote back and told me what industrial design was and what was expected of someone who was an industrial designer. I didn't want to be a car designer, per se, but I had some interest. Pratt, at that time, was structured to teach design, and you picked up your own interests from there.

ON EDUCATION: Well, now that I'm in business for myself and have been for twenty years, I can see very clearly that art school would not be a good background for business. I picked up my knowledge of business on my own. I think having that knowledge is extremely important, because good design and knowledge of design is a very small part of being successful in business for yourself.

Let me tell you how I did it. When I came out of Pratt, I had several jobs in industrial design. One with a consulting firm, then with a major manufacturer, to learn what it was like to be a captive designer in a company. Then I left design completely and took a job as a salesman for six months to learn how to write a proposal intelligently, to find out who you call on in a company, how you go through the sequence of events that leads to getting new business. I found I enjoyed that somewhat, not a lot, but somewhat. Cold soliciting is very difficult for someone like a designer, because designers are not built the way salespeople are built. They're very sensitive, and when they get resistance on the phone, they put the phone down and go home and cry, whereas a good salesperson just keeps going.

I had to learn how to do it. And I did. I worked at it until I felt

I could write an intelligent proposal. Then I had the guts to jump on my own. I wouldn't do it before that. I think that in order to be an excellent designer, you have to be able to get someone's attention and that's a whole different ballgame. They don't teach that at school at all. I don't remember getting anything at Pratt that related to new business development.

When I teach, I try to teach reality. It's not a formal part of the course. But I do tell them what it's like to try to get new business, who you're going to see in meetings, how to address the different people in meetings, how to design your project in such a way that you address the four or five different disciplines represented there—marketing, production, sales, the president of the company. The president sees everything entirely differently from the others. And it's very important, to have your work accepted, to know which direction each guy is going to be seeing. The production people only see your solution as something they're going to produce. They have no other interest. Purchasing is only interested in what it's going to cost. They don't care what it looks like, how it functions. Marketing only cares how the consumer is going to react to it. They really don't care what it costs as long as it's affordable. To be a successful designer, you have to know how to attack that.

But when you come out of school, you really only know how to make something look good. The rest you learn in the real world.

ON WHERE MOST INDUSTRIAL DESIGNERS WORK: Industry takes most of the graduates. They go with big corporations. It could vary from a department with two people to a department with twenty or thirty. A company like IBM has industrial design offices around the world, twenty or thirty different departments.

ON THE ROLE OF THE INDUSTRIAL DESIGNER: You have to know what materials can be used to do this certain function and how the item's going to be made. The role goes far beyond just a visual styling. It's the visual styling with the knowledge of materials, the limitations of materials. And you're going to make it look good in a way that's producible and doable. Also function. We like to use the term "human"; there has to be an interface, some way to make it meaningful for the human to attack the machine. So you're talking human engineering too. That's what we call "human factors" in our business, those which make something comfortable to use, easy to reach. Industrial designers do a lot of different things. They usually takes over where the engineer stops. At IBM, the electrical engineer invents the function of the machine, internally, the capacity of the machine. How a person uses the machine is where the industrial designer comes in—and does much more than simply visual styling, even though in the end it has to look good or you can't sell it. But that's not our only function. Volkswagen proved us wrong by making a funny-looking car that sold well anyway.

ON SUCCESS: I really can't separate the word "success" from being recognized. I've had discussions with a lot of people regarding success and fame. They tend to mix up the terms. On television, you're famous because of exposure. In our profession, success is being recognized by the value of your work. It's very important to be recognized, because it makes it easier to get the next job. Then it's very simple. Not only easier to get the next job, but to get better-quality jobs, things that interest you more. And of course, you want financial rewards for your work. I find them to be inseparable.

ON MONEY: I think if you have a good business head, you can make a great deal of money in any profession. In industrial design, there are some very, very bright people, no question about it.

Many industrial designers become very wealthy with royalties. The furniture industry pays royalties, the toy industry pays royalties. That's an interesting area because we were talking about success and what you want in success. You could be *extremely* successful financially, have patents on various things, and still be totally unheard of. You could have invented the precision valve that's on an aerosol can and be one of the wealthiest people in America. But to me that's not success, because my goal is not financial. I wouldn't mind having lots of money; it would be silly to deny that. But my idea of success is being recognized for good work. A lot of industrial designers make a lot of money, but nobody's ever heard of them. They're behind the scenes.

ON THE FUTURE OF INDUSTRIAL DESIGN: I don't see any new trends in industrial design. I don't see anything being done differently than it is now. But I think it's going to be done more thoroughly throughout industry. Everything is getting designed. There isn't a stone left unturned anywhere. This is not unusual in Finland or Denmark. They've been doing it for hundreds of years. And in the oriental countries, in Japan, everything they do is gorgeous. They're design-oriented countries. I think we're becoming that finally. It's been a long struggle. Just going to Woolworth's and looking at the vases and what have you for the last twenty years. We've made a lot of garbage in the United States. In general, I think there is a tremendous improvement in design quality of everything that's being made. And I think that's a positive, that's good.

ON WORKING FOR YOURSELF: On an occasional Monday, I'd like to give it all up and go fishing. But most days I like working for myself. I like going to the client, hearing the problem personally, going back to my office, and having the energy, the tenacity, the creativity—or whatever the word is—to attack the problem. And when I feel I have it solved, I have a tremendous pride in going back to the client. And I get very eager. I can't wait to see the client again to say, "Look how I solved your damn problem." I do like that.

ON THE SATISFACTIONS: I like design problems. I'm a problem solver. And the more difficult it is, the happier I get, because when clients can see that you've solved something that they've been stuck with, it puts you in an interesting position. Let's face it, if it's easy to solve, they do it themselves. They don't call me. I only get called when clients have tried to solve it themselves and couldn't. I get the marketing problems. "How do you dispense this new product? How do you do it cheaply? How do you close it? How do you ship it? How do you open it again?" They are problems that take tremendous inventiveness and creativity and patience, and when you solve them, it's satisfying.

ON THE WORKING PROCESS: I probably work like a lot of industrial design firms. The first part of the program is to meet with the client. This is called "orientation." You have to thoroughly understand what he or she thinks the problem is. You may have your own opinion but it's only fair you let the client know you understand it as he or she sees it.

You usually write a proposal where you state exactly what you're going to do, based on your understanding. In fact, sometimes that's the heading of the proposal: "My Understanding of Your Problem." And you just repeat back to the client pretty much what he or she said to you, but you use your words.

Then even after I get the job, I like to go through the factory, and I like to see how they're making the thing now. I also go to the supermarket or other stores and see the product in a competitive situation. This is all predesign. I haven't done any design work, not yet. We're into totally understanding what the problem is. What the client's trying to do, and how he or she is trying to do it, and how other people have done it.

With all that input, you go back to the boards and start what I call "creative design." My proposals have a phase I. Phase I is creative design. And that's whatever process you do as a designer. I have a certain way of working that I've arrived at, from many years of doing this. I do it two dimensionally, three dimensionally. I go to the library to get inspiration; I go to the museum to get inspiration; I just sit in my office and struggle; I go through research books. I have found through the years that

I want a certain amount of time to do this. I find that time is important, four to six weeks for the creative phase. That's the fun part.

In phase II, the client reviews all this work. I happen to draw very well, so for years I've made a lot of very fancy sketches and drawings. Drawings are good because they're quick. You can get a lot more ideas done quickly in sketch form. But the last five or six years, I've tended toward working three dimensionally. Perhaps because I've been doing so many bottles and forms and shapes that I find I can't get the subtleties in two dimensions. I also find working three dimensionally saves a tremendous amount of time. The client can take it in hand and feel if it's comfortable.

I work in urethane foam, which is a material that's easy to cut, easy to sand. It comes out nice and clean. And you don't have to paint it white; it is white. And it's lightweight, so you can make twenty models and carry them on a plane. And I've found it to be very successful. Clients like seeing three-dimensional shapes.

In phase II you start to reduce your designs to a workable direction. Let's say you had twenty drawings and/or models. Now you want to reduce them to three. So now you go back and refine the selected directions. This means taking the client's input, taking other people's input, like the production people, marketing, etc. Once you present work, you know a lot more about everything.

Then you go to phase III, which is the final selection of one design. That means you have to make mechanical drawings of the shape. You might make a final model.

In my work, what I call phase IV is all the follow-through work that could happen after you've finished phase III. You meet with outside suppliers who are going to manufacture it. You deal with management changes. That's an all-encompassing statement that means that sometimes when it's all done, management changes its mind. And that happens more often than not.

So in general, it's three phases: creative design, basic refinement, and final mode. Phase IV is follow-through and layers-on, color selection, the little details that pop up. Sometimes it's very large, and sometimes phase IV is nothing at all. When I write a proposal, I expect to get at least the first three phases. I don't expect clients to give me phase I and then finish phase II and III themselves. My experience has indicated to me that the job always goes sour if that happens. Always.

ON DESIGN FEES: The client likes to see the complete expected cost in the proposal. So you say, "Phase I is X amount of dollars. Phase II is X amount, Phase III is X amount." Then you put in your contingency fees and what-have-you. Phase IV is usually on an hourly basis, because you don't know what it's going to be. And the client feels that's fair and I feel that's fair. If they want me to go to Chicago for the day and check a plant, then they pay for the day and out-of-pocket, and everybody's happy. But you can't anticipate how many times they'll want you to go to Chicago to look at something. That's why that has to be on an hourly basis.

ON CREATIVE BLOCKS: I guess I've been in the business long enough now where I don't panic when nothing happens. As a matter of fact, last Friday, I just went home early and mowed my lawn. When I came in Monday, it was okay, and the juices started running again. I think basically, if you're a creative person, it eventually comes to you. Sometimes, though, I'll accept a program that's very difficult and I don't see the answer immediately. I do feel a little panicked, no doubt about it. I'm not pompous enough to think I know the answers to everything. Not by a long shot, but I'm very confident I can struggle through it and solve it. I think I probably work more that way than through some kind of divine inspiration. I just struggle through my methodology, and when I teach school I teach that methodology—how I go about trying to get ideas, relating different concepts, my understanding of how the world works. And somehow it falls together. I usually can come up with a unique, improved method of doing something.

IN RETROSPECT: I was determined to stay a small, independent designer. My goal was to have a very fine reputation so that when the work came in, it was because someone could see there was quality to what I did. Anybody can get business if they get ten salespeople to beat on doors. My ego did not allow me to do that. That may be a dumb thing, but that's me. So I've kept small. I still have only four people working for me. If I had to do it over again, I'm not sure I wouldn't have made it a little bit bigger, just so I had a little more time off. I still wouldn't want to be real large. But that's about the only thing I would do differently. I like what I do, and I've had fun for twenty years.

ON SPECIALIZATION: We're in a world of specialization. So someone who is really, really good in furniture, who has developed a wonderful reputation and made tremendous royalties designing chairs, can get business more easily in the furniture area. He knows furniture production. He knows wood. He knows all the factories down South. He knows how to weld. It would be difficult for a guy like him to try to talk somebody into letting him design an automobile. It's not that he can't, but he probably wouldn't. I'm personally going in certain directions and it helps to get very strong in specific directions because that's how you pick up work. I have strong credentials in structural packaging. Even out of a small office. So you tend to specialize, I guess, almost as a method of survival. You don't plan it that way, but it happens. For many years, I did dental equipment, and because I did, I tended to get other related products. But it took three or four years for something to be conceived, designed, developed, test-engineered, engineered, and finally put out. By the time it was on the market, you'd almost forgotten you did it. The process was too long and not satisfying to the ego.

It's important for a young person to know that about industrial design. If you want instant gratification, industrial design is *not* the profession. You'd be better off in graphics, where you might design a flier this week and have it printed next week, and get your satisfaction quickly.

In industrial design, whatever you do professionally takes years before you see it. There are all kinds of consumer testing, samples are made, and then preproduction and then production, and then you go national. It takes six to eight months for the tools to be made. They finally make them, and it takes you six months to get into the network of distribution to the stores. You can work for years before you ever see anything on the market.

ON ADVICE TO YOUNG PEOPLE: My personal feeling is to keep your mind on your work. There are a lot of distractions in the field of industrial design, in any professional field, I guess. You can spend time giving your opinions about design and getting your picture in the papers. But you'll grow faster and become more successful if your mind is on one thing, and that is solving your client's problems. I have always felt that that would be its own reward, because no one could take that away from you, once you've built that reputation. I think industrial design is a very fine profession today. And it's a very large one. The country is becoming more design-oriented, and every new product and service that's designed involves designers. It's a very secure future, with lots of opportunity.

7

Photography

WITHIN the past decade, photography has come of age. Technology has much to do with it. Cameras are easier and more efficient to use. We have refined techniques for developing film faster. Even the Polaroid process, which in the beginning was considered too facile for art, has heightened our expectation for instant images from film. Photography has become a medium through which photographers, painters, and artists can make personal statements.

Photography is now recognized as a legitimate art form, although there are many who believe it can never be "true" art because the images do not originate from the artist's hand, that even the most extraordinary photograph only documents existence, it does not create from nothing. But major museums have collections that are taken seriously. Photography has a history. It has its stars—Ansel Adams, Dorothea Lange, Cartier Bresson, Irving Penn, Richard Avedon, Duane Michals, and many others.

The interesting phenomenon about photography is the fact that it is one of the few fields in the arts where there is little backlash for working both as a commercial and as a fine artist. Its practitioners show personal work in galleries at the same time they use their talents to shoot ads for bowls of steaming soup and take on assignments for *Vogue* or *Harper's Bazaar*. Coffee-table books showing the works of famous photographers lie side by side with books that show the paintings and sculptures of famous artists. Working commercially is not perceived by either photographers or the media as compromising their artistry. In that way it is one of the healthiest artistic fields within which to work, as it allows a photographer to make a very good living while at the same time encouraging him or her to pursue a personal vision as well.

But the accessibility of the camera—prices make it possible for most people to own at least one—gluts the professional field with many ineffective and often ungifted images. Today even the simplest cameras possess capabilities that only more expensive cameras could claim a decade ago. Photographic images are commonplace. With everyone able to produce images, even good ones now and then, professional photography has to have very high standards. And it does. Being a photographer is not as simple as clicking a shutter, even if Kodak and Polaroid would like us to believe it. Photography is a complex and difficult field.

But at the same time, because most young people grow up being able to make images with the camera, for many of us, photography ranks with fingerpainting as a means of first experiencing the creative process. So it is logical that many artistically oriented people consider photography among their options for a career. This is evidenced by the number of courses offered in colleges and universities across the country. But the actual numbers of photographers who earn a living from their art has not increased dramatically. Becoming a successful photographer, like becoming a successful illustrator or designer, still takes commitment, passion, desire, hard work, and talent.

Photography, unlike some other art and design fields, offers many outlets for work. In photography you can make a name for yourself in the editorial arena, in the fine arts, and sometimes in the documentary news field. And there are other arenas in photography where it is possible to earn a living, enjoy a creative life, and remain satisfied, through perhaps not in as public a way.

It seems to be true that if you can take a good photograph in one area, you can do so in any area. However, you do not always have that opportunity until you have made a substantial reputation in a specialized field. As you will see, most photographers specialize, that is they make most of their money in one area; then with success, they are given an opportunity to work in other areas.

EDUCATION AND TRAINING Regardless of specialization, most photographers will benefit from a four-year professional program in an art college or university. Such a program will ground you in the basic techniques of camera work: lenses, lighting, developing, and printing. It will also provide you with more sophisticated theory and workshop courses to help you discover your special fields of interest within photography.

If you already know that your interests range toward advertising, take as many advertising courses as your schedule allows. Working as an advertising photographer means being able to communicate with art directors and copywriters on their terms. If you can understand how to help them achieve their aims, you are obviously more valuable. Advertising photographers can benefit from courses in business, directing, acting, illustration concepts, communication problems, design, and composition.

An editorial photographer can benefit from business courses as well as from courses in illustration concepts, design, and composition. You might also take some still-life workshops so as to understand what that discipline is like. Most people discover a talent or preference for one kind of photography while they are still in school. If that happens with you, ask a counselor to help you structure a program, particularly in your junior and senior years, that refects your interest. If, for example, your field is fashion, take a course or two in fashion drawing, draping, or styling, not with an eye to being good at it, but simply for the information that will help your photography.

A portfolio is necessary in applying for a first job, although most assistants are hired on the basic of recommendation alone. This is one of the advantages of attending a school with a professional faculty. Your instructors will know what entry-level jobs are available and if they think you're qualified, they will recommend you.

The assistant loads cameras, builds sets, works in the darkroom, scouts locations, sweeps floors, goes for coffee, and helps in any way necessary. A willing assistant will not only learn the business, but will even earn a modest salary. Some photographers remain assistants for several years, particularly if they are working for artists from whom there is a great deal to learn. Although college and art school are important, in truth, if you are apprenticed to a good photographer, you can learn a great deal more and a great deal faster. So there is some justification for considering a broader college education in the liberal arts to give yourself some breadth and depth. Photography is a communication medium, and one should have something to communicate. Many young people split the difference, taking two years at a liberal arts school and then transferring to a professional program, thus getting the best of both worlds.

Advertising Photography

This is the most highly paid of all the specialties in photography. Advertising generates the most money; consequently it pays the highest fees. The work, however, is unsigned and you do not have the kind of control that exists in editorial photography. The advertising photographer works with an agency art director to fulfill the demands of an ad layout. In some instances, you have creative input, working with the art director and copywriter to come up with the concept, but in many cases you are hired simply to execute an idea. In any case, the photographer hires models; finds locations, if necessary; helps design sets; creates the lighting; and approves props and costumes. You are always hired for both technical and artistic skills.

Within the advertising field there are two specialties—still-life and people photography, though many photographers do both. Still-life photography gives the photographer more control. It is often done in the photographer's own studio and the number of people required to staff a shooting is fewer. Still life in advertising most often refers to food product shots or to straight product shots, which are simply photographs of the client's package, be it a bottle of Coca-Cola or a carton of Tide. They can be very simple or very complicated—such as a high-speed shot of splashing milk. A still-life photographer needs a good sense of composition and an appreciation for detail. Lighting expertise is essential since most still-life photography is done in a studio under artificial conditions. Technical skill with larger-format cameras is also essential.

Photographers who specialize in taking pictures of people are very much in demand in the advertising world. The ability to choose the kind of model, either professional or amateur, with the qualities required by a client is a valuable talent. Photographers of people must be able to handle models well, and get believable performances from them, so we are talking about casting and directing abilities, much as in motion pictures. People photographers must possess personal qualities such as sensitivity to people, intuition, and flexibility. They often find themselves in uncontrolled outdoor situations where lighting is not ideal, where weather is a factor, and where they must be able to adapt to circumstances. Putting together models, props, and scenery in a studio with the client looking on is not always easy, either.

Advertising photographers, particularly in the still-life area, maintain studios, which means that staff and overhead are added to their professional costs. Skills in business are very important. The problems of getting work, getting paid, and running the studio efficiently are often difficult for creative people to handle, but photographers must be able to do so if they are to survive in this competitive area.

Editorial Photography

The editorial photographer provides much of the visual imagery for magazines and newspapers. The field is less highly paid than advertising, although at its top end, photographers earn substantial incomes. Fashion, travel, and documentary photography are the main subspecialties in editorial photography.

The editorial photographer, regardless of specialization, has the advantage over the advertising photographer in that he or she is always credited for the work produced. It is the reason why editorial photographers are known by a wider public, and why some of the most interesting work comes from their ranks. When one figuratively signs his or her name to a photograph, there is more at stake than money. The editorial photographer also has many more opportunities to develop an artistic vision within his or her work because an interest, a passion, a fascination can be explored in depth. It is no wonder that the photographers who most often show in galleries emerge from the field of editorial photography.

FASHION PHOTOGRAPHY Fashion photography tends to be more highly specialized than the other editorial areas, partially because it requires a strong interest in the fashion field and necessitates a special understanding of materials and textures, line, and style. The most prestigious work is done for the mass-market fashion magazines, both here and abroad, like *Vogue*, *Harper's Bazaar*, *Elle*, and others. The fashion photographer needs to know about accessories, makeup, hair styles, new trends in furniture and interior design as well as be skilled in art and graphic design. In order to succeed as an editorial fashion photographer, the more you know about costumes, painting, color, and scenic design, the better. Inspiration for a photograph may come from the clothes, but the environment must be in keeping with the spirit of the design. Much fashion photography uses exotic backgrounds for shots, a situation which requires a strong sense of organization, considerable patience, and above all, an ability to work with people: Models and fashion editors can be temperamental and difficult.

TRAVEL PHOTOGRAPHY Within the editorial field, the travel photographer would seem to have the most exciting job. You get to visit exotic places with all expenses paid, meet new people, experience new cultures. For the right personality, there are few disadvantages. More and more mass magazines do features on travel. There are also specialized travel magazines, including airline publications. But it is definitely not the career for all photographers. The travel photographer must enjoy *all* parts of the travel experience. The normal irritations of getting from one place to the other, the endless airports and rented cars, strange places in strange cities, spurious directions—all difficult situations for anyone—are simply part of the experience. To do all this requires organization and the sensibility of an explorer. You need a determined, even an aggressive streak to find your way around in unfamiliar circumstances. Many travel photographers work alone, so the ability to make friends, or at least acquaintances, easily is helpful. And since the most beautiful light is at sunrise or sunset and the best angle is often from the most inaccessible places, the travel photographer needs to be in good health and to have plenty of physical stamina.

Most editorial photographers will have an opportunity to do a travel story, however, when a difficult travel story comes up on the schedule, the experienced travel photographer is the one who generally gets the assignment. Shooting in the jungles of New Guinea or in the mountains of Tibet requires more of a photographer than doing a picture story on Parisian bridges or on the bookstores of London.

DOCUMENTARY PHOTOGRAPHY The documentary photographer concentrates on illustrating general interest stories, and this field is very broad. Technically, the travel photographer is a documentary photographer as well, and often is assigned some general photographs along with a travel story. But the documentary photographer specializes in carrying out most general photographic assignments. Doing the interior of a house, taking the portrait of a famous personality, following a rock star through a normal day—all are typical assignments such a photographer might be offered. His or her talents are used by general magazines, women's magazines, special interest magazines, and newspapers. Often it is the documentary photographer who provides many of the images for stock photographs. It is a career for a photographer who likes real variety.

In this category we can also place the photographers who cover international news events, very often in trouble zones around the world. They may be assigned by a major newspaper or magazine to a news desk, or they may simply be freelancers who work in highly dangerous situations, photographing wars and war-related events. These are unique careers, and the people who pursue them thrive on the excitement and the danger. Often these photographers find themselves in Ireland, Nicaragua, or the Middle East, in places uncovered by the bureau of a major newspaper or news magazine, and they sell their photographs to the highest bidder.

Other Specialties in Photography

There are other specializations in photography that should be mentioned briefly, as they provide opportunities for interesting work for the right person.

THEATRICAL PHOTOGRAPHY The theatrical photographer documents theatrical productions—the sets, the costumes, the actors, the scenes in performance and rehearsal. The photographs are used for publicity and programs and are given to magazines and newspapers.

It is a freelance career and often it is pursued out of an interest in the theatre. Often a documentary photographer who works editorially provides services in this area; however, as is true in most fields, when the best work is needed, the people who specialize are the first to be approached. There are standards of excellence specific to the field, although it is not a particularly creative career.

PORTRAIT PHOTOGRAPHY The portrait photographer must be able to render a pleasing, natural, usually flattering, study of a person. The ability to make a subject feel comfortable and relaxed is very important. A portrait photographer usually maintains his or her own studio, although a large department store may hire a portrait photographer to work on salary or commission. Other stores lease space to photographers. The portrait business tends to be concentrated in specific areas. In New York and California, the portrait photographer who specializes in models and actors' composite sheets can do very well. A photographer who likes children could gain a reputation doing portraits of children. Someone who is successful in working with businessmen will receive commissions from the business community.

Salaries for this profession are very flexible, depending on demand and on the photographer's reputation.

FINE ART PHOTOGRAPHY The area of fine art photography, as we've discussed, is often entered into by artists who work editorially. The photographer who thinks of the camera as a way to do more than simply document people, places, and events or sell things for other people, may begin to think of himself or herself as a fine artist.

Photography as a medium for personal expression is relatively recent, but we are living in a time when definitions of fine art are changing, and that which twenty years ago was unacceptable is now promoted with enthusiasm. Museums across the country now have photography exhibitions as regularly as they do drawing or painting exhibitions, and a few very well known photographers have long-term relationships with galleries, exhibiting on a regular basis. Most of these artists work commercially as well, but, of course, they can be very selective about the work they take.

Most young people do not go into a fine arts career in photography right out of school, as it is difficult to find a gallery if you are unknown and it is even more difficult to sell. Many begin as editorial photographers and develop a reputation expressing a personal viewpoint

The International Center of Photography, 1130 Fifth Avenue,

New York, New York 10128, which is dedicated to promoting the work of contemporary photographers, is a good source of information on a career in photography.

INTERVIEWS

MALCOLM KIRK
Travel Photographer, Freelance

Before the age of 7, Malcolm Kirk had traveled more than many people do in a lifetime. Born in Ceylon, he spent his early years in India, Malaya, China, and England before settling down to school in Scotland. His early travels seem to have sparked a lifelong interest in seeing new and exotic places. His book, Man as Art, *an extraordinary study of the people of New Guinea, was published after he'd spent thirteen years photographing that area of the world. Editorial work for* Omni, Time-Life Books, National Geographic, Travel and Leisure, Geo, Stern, *the* New York Times, Architectural Digest, *and* Harper's Bazaar *has taken him down the Amazon and into monasteries in Europe. He has ballooned over the Swiss Alps, trekked in Nepal, and looked through the camera's eye at Tahiti, Bora Bora, the Fiji islands, Singapore, Sarawak, Bangkok, Samoa, the New Hebrides, and Bali. He has been around the world many times over. Among his advertising clients have been E. F. Hutton, Polaroid, Bechtel, Avianca, Volvo, the Irish Tourist Board, and General Electric. In his own highly specialized field he has made an important contribution to photography, and his work has been recognized with many awards and exhibitions.*

ON GETTING STARTED: Actually, I was always more interested in travel than in photography. I happened to be down in New Zealand, studying zoology. I dropped out of the university and took a boat back to England with no idea of what I wanted to do. On the ship, I met an Australian photojournalist who seemed to be living exactly the kind of life I wanted to live—

which was traveling, taking photographs, and making money. I asked him how he'd started and he said, "Well, if I were you, I'd go to London and get trained in a good school of photography." Which is what I did.

It was a three-year course that gave you a diploma, and after the second year I realized the diploma wasn't going to do me any good at all. So I quit and decided to come to New York and learn the ropes, practically speaking. At that time, it was the golden age for photographers in New York, and I was lucky enough to get a job as an assistant to Irving Penn for a minimum wage of $50 a week. I guess I was in a hurry; I only stayed with him for three months and then worked with another photographer for a much larger salary. My intention then was to break away from him, too. I had saved enough money to do a trip on the Amazon. Before I left, I called *National Geographic*, that being the only magazine I could think of that might sponsor something like that, and asked them if they'd be interested in underwriting the expedition in return for some pictures. They asked to see some of my photographs, and I had nothing to show at all. They said, "Well, how do you expect us to sponsor you if you have nothing to show us?" So at that point, I realized I had to do it on my own. I made the trip, came back and showed my slides to Irving Penn's agent at that time, Peter Schub. He sold the pictures to *Holiday* magazine, which was then a large, glossy travel magazine. I was still kind of broke, so I went back to being an assistant again to earn some more money. But I also had another idea for going down to New Guinea, so I called *National Geographic* again and asked if they'd be interested in sponsoring me. They asked about my Amazon material, and when I told them I had sold it, they said, "Well, let's take a look at it." They looked and said, "Let's give this guy a chance." So that was my first break.

ON STARTING OUT TODAY: It's a tough, tough business. I would hate to start all over again trying to make the contacts. I think, first of all, you do need a technical background in photography. You shouldn't get overwhelmed by it, but you do need some, and I would say that taking some kind of course, for example, the one at the School of Visual Arts would give you the background you needed. Then go out on a limb and do something on your own, something you believe in. Work, do any kind of job, just save the money and go out and do it. And before you do it, contact a few magazines and see if there's any interest in it. If so, try to angle your photography toward that interest.

ON SUCCESS: When I was first starting out, my goal was to keep traveling as much as I could, and success meant just getting one assignment right after the other. I very much admire Penn. He's methodical. He's the greatest technician I think I've ever come across, and he had no formal training. I think he picked up pretty much all of his training as he went along, studying with other photographers.

As I get older, I get more conscious of the financial side of things. When I was younger, the money never really meant much to me. I enjoyed seeing my work in print. I guess I've seen it enough now that it doesn't really hold any great fascination. I'd like to do more books. I think that probably would be my greatest satisfaction, but I'd want to do only subjects I myself choose, not something somebody else chooses for me.

ON MONEY: I don't make a lot of money, let's put it that way. I would advise any photographer who is getting into the travel field to look very seriously at stock photography. I've been very lazy. I know I could have made a lot more money had I organized myself. My problem is, once I've done a job, it's finished, and I just want to push it aside and get it out of the way and get on to something fresh. I think if I were more methodical about it, I'd sit down and make all those years of work work for me through stock photography. I think, though, that it's possible to make money in travel photography. For example, Pete Turner has done extremely well, although he's combined his travel with a lot of advertising. That's *really* where the money is. Certainly advertising will come out of travel photography. There will always be some demand.

ON HAVING AN AGENT: In terms of my travel stuff, I've been most successful getting that work myself. In terms of advertising, I think my agent has done far better for me.

ON THE FUTURE OF TRAVEL PHOTOGRAPHY: When I came over here in 1954 that was really the golden age, and I'd say it started tailing off at the end of the 60s and early 70s. Now more of the articles that are published on travel tend to make use of stock photographs, and there are fewer assignments. The days of the big juicy assignments are dwindling. There's enough work to support a handful of good photographers, and a lot of people are going to drop out by the wayside. So anyone getting into that field should think very, very seriously about his or her own talents.

ON ADVICE TO YOUNG PEOPLE: I think you have to cover yourself, and certainly not look at travel photography as a means of your entire living. You'll have to look at stock photography as another large means of support, and some advertising and especially getting into some annual report work. A lot of people whom I knew while I was working with travel magazines have virtually dropped out of the field and are almost exclusively doing corporate work and doing extremely well.

I think your greatest asset is your personality. I think someone who is outgoing, who is willing to make the contacts and follow up on them—sometimes *that* talent can outweigh your actual technical and aesthetic talent. The talent for selling yourself can be your greatest asset as a photographer.

ON BEING A PHOTOGRAPHER'S ASSISTANT: The assistant does everything, the most menial jobs—sweeping up, getting copy, loading the camera, and checking to see that the meter's at the correct setting. It's good hands-on experience. If you're astute as an assistant, you can learn a lot just watching the way the photographer lights the subject and how he or she communicates with the subject and so forth. Most photographers have assistants these days, sometimes not full time, but they certainly hire an assistant by the day or by the week when they go out on an assignment. Magazines generally don't budge for that, so you're very much on your own at that point, unless you have a spouse who's prepared to come with you.

ON THE CREATIVE PROCESS: Well, I like to have time. It's funny, when you walked in here I was saying I've got myself spread very thin because after a fairly slow period things are picking up and I've got a lot of irons in the fire. I work best when I can approach one subject at a time and do a thorough research job into whomever or whatever I'm going to photograph. I like to be able to put in the preparation. It's unpaid time, but I think it pays off in the long run. I tend to get very caught up in each assignment, and that feeling lasts with me for a week or two after I get back, sometimes longer. I almost need a time when there are no assignments, just to get over one job and prepare myself for the next one. I'm certainly not the sort of person who can churn out a lot of work.

It's like a boxer going into the ring. You concentrate with a certain kind of dedication, your whole being, all your fibers are tense, you're anticipating, you're looking. . . . I think a lot of people just go in and wing it, and maybe they've got a good sense of design and they can carry it off. If they're successful, that's obviously what they do rely on, their sense of design, composition, and so forth. But when it comes to the quality of the picture, take Irving Penn again. When I first worked with him in the mid-60s he used to spend three months every summer taking one or two assignments from *Look* magazine. He would select a subject. I don't know quite how it worked. Perhaps the art director suggested something, or perhaps Penn himself came up with it. But I sense that Penn spent the winter preparing himself. You can see that preparation in his work. I'm sure another photographer could have gone out and taken dramatic pictures. But Penn's pictures, the way they were so carefully put together and the selection, you knew there was a great deal of thought in them. He went out and shot a story in Provence, a story on the foods of France, and a story on Japan. There was a sense of timelessness about those articles which I think is missing from a lot of people's work.

ON DOING A BOOK: *Man as Art* came about from the early *National Geographic* assignments I did in New Guinea. I started taking these fairly formal, straightforward pictures of painted faces in New Guinea. While some of the picture editors at *National Geographic* were interested by them, they couldn't raise enough support among the editorial staff to do a story on it. I myself believed in the material. I got other assignments from other magazines and went back until I managed to put this thing together on my own. I did quite well, I must say, with *Man as Art*. But—and I've discussed this with other photographers—I don't think books allow a photographer to make a good living. They do give you a lot of satisfaction, though.

ON STOCK PHOTOGRAPHY: You try to find out from photo agencies what sort of pictures sell best, then you go out and try to concentrate on that kind. Sometimes I travel simply for pleasure. I know I should be taking stock pictures then, but I don't because I'm more interested in enjoying myself than in working. Somebody once said, "You can't travel and photograph. It's one or the other." In stock photography you leave your transparencies with an agency, and once every three or four months, or sometimes every six months, you receive a statement showing which of your pictures has been sold. The usual split is on a 60–40 percent or a 50–50 percent basis. They send you a check at that time.

ON DOING ON-LOCATION PHOTOGRAPHY: Lighting is probably the crucial thing—being able to use both daylight and artificial light, which I do more and more. I used to set up almost all my work as 100 percent daylight. It's one of the complications, as I say, as I've progressed in the field. I find myself doing a lot of interiors that cannot be lit by daylight. I think every art director is looking for wonderful lighting and wonderful composition.

You've also got to have a pleasant personality. When you approach an art director for a job in an editorial field, he needs to be reassured, first of all. If it's a portrait of a well-known person, you can't be the sort who rubs a person the wrong way. You have to come back with meticulous captions for your photographs and be very organized about them. You have to deliver and you can't make excuses. You get the job done. You don't call the art director up and say, "I'm here, but the thing isn't working out. What do I do next?"

ON THE DIFFERENCES BETWEEN EDITORIAL AND ADVERTISING PHOTOGRAPHY: I myself feel more comfortable in editorial. Maybe it's because I've worked on that side more than the other side of photography. But it's essentially that I'm my own cameraman, my own director, my own lighting man. In advertising, you've got so many other people that are hanging over your shoulder at that instant of exposure. You've got the art director, you've quite often got the client, people making suggestions, you've got assistants around you, and you've got stylists—I tend to get crazy at that sort of situation. I can't think. If I'm on my own, I can think. So I prefer that.

ON TECHNIQUE: It can add immediate impact to the photograph, and I guess in advertising that's essential. You do need to catch the person's eye. But again, going back to Penn, I look at food photography, and I don't think anyone has come close to Penn, in terms of food photography. He had one assistant, Bob Freson, who did a marvelous book called *A Taste of France*, where you can see Penn's influence, but in terms of capturing the taste and flavor of food, nobody compares with Penn. In my field, in travel photography, too, you can jazz a picture up with gimmicky people and so forth, but I think if you're looking for real depth, a photograph itself has to be honest, it can't be manipulated too much.

ON THE SATISFACTIONS: I can't imagine what else I would do. What always amazes me is that I've done these wonderful things and people have been paying me to do them. I'd almost be willing to pay to get to do these things. In fact, I've done jobs that have earned me very little money simply for the satisfaction of getting to someplace I've always wanted to go. I still put myself out on a limb, doing things that I did when I first started off, doing work for very little money, as I say, maybe to get in with a particular new art director or a new magazine. Take those risks, and once you're in, their sense of generosity will make the relationship work a little better in the financial sense.

DUANE MICHALS

Fine Art and Editorial Photographer, Freelance

Duane Michals is regarded as one of the foremost fine arts photographers of our time, and he has a highly successful career in commercial photography as well. He has little conflict in balancing both aspects of his working life, enjoying them for their separate satisfactions and rewards. He has no studio and no agent and likes controlling his own time and the kind of work he chooses to do. Duane Michals has exhibited photographs in major gallery and museum shows in New York, Paris, London, and Japan. His exhibits and his books have established his reputation as a highly innovative artist with a clear and resonant personal vision. His commercial work (portraits, places, people, food, etc.) has appeared in all the major magazines including Vogue, Esquire, Mademoiselle, Horizon, *and* Scientific American. *In recent years he has discovered his voice as a poet and has combined poetry and photography to create powerful artistic statements. Duane Michals lives and works in New York City.*

ON GETTING STARTED: It happened purely by accident. I always say I had an aesthetic itch, but I didn't know where to scratch. I knew I should be something in the arts—write, illustrate, paint—but exactly what it was wasn't apparent to me. I went to Russia as a tourist in 1958 with a borrowed camera, and it all came together. I never planned to be a photographer. I never went to photography school, but the trip literally changed my life. I wanted to be a designer. You see, I love books and magazines most of all. And I wanted to be an art director for *Vogue* or *Esquire* or something. Henry Wolf was then the art director of *Harper's Bazaar*. Bob Benton* told me he was looking for an assistant. I had invented a magazine using my own photographs based on the notion that the whole issue would be devoted to a single subject. I did one issue on Russia. Henry bought one of the pictures, but Sam Antiput got the job. My life would have been quite different if I had gotten the job, and probably much less interesting.

ON STARTING OUT TODAY: You have to follow your instincts. It's a big category. I mean, do you want to be a commercial photographer, or what? I say, if you want something, go get it. Nobody can hire you unless they know you exist. So you have to do what we all did. Richard Avedon wasn't Richard Avedon when he was 20, and Steiglitz wasn't Steiglitz at 20, and neither was Irving Penn. We all find ourselves at 21, 22, 24 going, "What the hell am I doing? Where do I start? How do I get a job?"

ON EDUCATION: Well, it depends. I don't know if Robert Frank went to photography school, but you just get up and do it.

---

*Bob Benton began his career as an artist in illustration but is most widely known today as a film director.

There are certain people who are simply, instinctually, what they should be. Like Arnold Varga. When he was young, he was drawing and doing things right off the bat. I think he went to the Art Institute in Pittsburgh for a year, or something like that. The people who are really out there are simply already out there, doing and working. So it really depends on the person. Some people need to go to school and others don't.

ON SUCCESS: Success is always personally defined. Unfortunately, most people don't know what it is. They define it based on the public notion, the notion that you have to have all these things. Then they get it all and realize they're miserable. So I think it's very important to know what your needs are. Having been professionally poor for such a long time, my needs are to live comfortably. It's not nice, being poor. I need just enough—not too much, not too little. To buy freedom, you make an exchange. So success for me means I can afford to spend a lot of money for dinner. I have the freedom to do what I want to do. I can buy a $50 art book and not feel quite as guilty as I would if I didn't have the $50.

I am successful. I'm not bragging. I'm also bald. So it just happens to be a fact. But I also work very hard, even if I don't call what I do work. My definition of work is when you have to do something you don't want to do. I even love photographic jobs that aren't interesting, so I never feel like I work.

ON THE FUTURE OF PHOTOGRAPHY: I think it's a wonderful field. This is the age of photography and I think it's going to become more and more important. But the problems come from the fact that it's the most democratic of the arts. You wouldn't say, "My daughter can draw as well as Picasso," but people do say, "My daughter can take a picture as well as anybody." It's the technology. As the technology becomes easier and easier, photography becomes more and more difficult. People used to be intimidated by cameras. Now that it's so simple to take a picture, it's extremely difficult to break through into art. Look what's accepted as being the profound photographs of our time. It's a joke.

ON MONEY: Richard Avedon must make $500,000 plus a year. He has a studio, and probably four darkroom assistants, and an agent, and a secretary, and etc., etc. And I have none of the apparatus of doing business. I mean, I don't have a darkroom. I never had a studio. I have two functioning cameras and two sort of dubious, backup cameras. Making my living usually means working on the average of two days a week. Sometimes I work no days a week and sometimes I work five days a week, or whatever. But I'm saying it averages out to two or three days a week. My idea has always been—whether or not I realized it early on, I know it now—to free myself; so as I get older, I have no overhead. Most people as they get older, accumulate, confuse, and have to keep up. What I've done is totally eliminate, so it's very sparse. If I don't work, I don't lose money. I don't have to make $10,000 a week just to cover expenses. Years ago, Penn said to me he always admired me because I didn't go the route of the studio and all that. But it wasn't a decision. It was never a choice. It never entered my mind for five seconds that I wanted to do that.

My idea was always to make enough money to live comfortably, to be free for what I want to do, which is exactly what I've done. So I live quite comfortably. I could live more comfortably if I wanted to double my income, which I don't make any effort at all to do. I enjoy money and I have great respect for it, but I'm not cuckoo about it. Having been poor, I worry if I'm not busy, but eventually somebody calls up. But I also take jobs other people probably wouldn't because the money they pay is beneath them.

ON COMMERCIAL WORK: Most commercial jobs have definitions. They're givens. They're all ready. I don't take on jobs that are too prescribed, though. There are photographers who are brilliant at that: An art director comes in with a sketch, and he wants a woman jumping out of a plane, and her dress is going to be on fire, but you're going to be able to see the label of the manufacturer, and she's going to be smiling with a cloud up there. And they'll go out and do that. The photographer puts some kind of glassine over the 8 X 10 camera with the whole thing drawn in. It's amazing. I can't do that, so my assignments are rather loosely prescribed. I can't do product shots where I have to fill in the art director's dotted lines. Some people do it very well and get very rich at it. I can't.

I love doing commercial work. I couldn't do my own work all the time. My own work is so introspective. When I do pick up the camera, everything is there. There's no fat on my shooting. There's not a wasted motion. It's all right there. Because I'm very specific, when I finally do it, it's all perfect. And jobs are wonderful! I mean, I get to travel everywhere. I *never* pay for anything. God, I've been to Europe four times this year and I haven't paid for any of it. How could you not enjoy it? I meet famous people. I mean it's just a wonderful, interesting life. I never know from week to week what I'm going to be doing. It's always full of surprises. So it's worked out well. I'm almost embarrassed to talk about it. I love the balance of the jobs and I like the challenge of the jobs. And I like that weighed against my own personal work. It makes me feel very rich and experienced. I need time to think. Ideas don't just plop out of the sky every single day of the week. I really need time just to think about things. So having a job to do is like exercising one muscle while the other muscles are resting.

ON THE CREATIVE PROCESS: The process with me is I get intrigued by an idea and I think about it for a long time, and sort of play with it in my head. I can't walk around with a camera looking for a photograph. I mean I never walk down the street hoping to see something wonderful happen in front of me. The photograph comes out first from an idea, something I find I'm amused by or intrigued by. It's like playing with a Rubik cube.

With the writing too, I get intrigued by something. Just a little thing that pops into my mind, or a phrase I heard somebody say. And like a chorale, I seem to build on it.

ON CREATIVE BLOCKS: I just wait. You need that, I think. I'm very prolific. I'm always amazed how much I come up with. But you have to expect that to happen, so I just sort of wait it out.

ON CREATIVE RISK: I guess it's a philosophy. I think that once you stop risking, you're through creatively. I think you cannot be a creative person without taking risks. It sounds like such a cliché, but it's true. I don't care how many years Picasso was working, when he would do something really creative it was dangerous. Risky, because you don't know what you're doing. And that's the act, this going from the known to the unknown. It's always wandering into the darkness. When I began to write poems, somebody asked if I was going to publish them. I said, "Well, it could be that I'm a failed poet, but the greater failure is if I'm not up to writing it."

CHARLES GOLD

Advertising Photographer, Freelance

Charles Gold is a highly successful commercial photographer specializing in still-life photography. He is particularly well known for his beautiful food shots. Among his major clients are General Foods, Pillsbury, Schenley, Pepperidge Farm, McDonalds', Hardy's, and many others. Over the past twenty years his photographs have won him every major award in print advertising from the Art Directors Club award, the One Club award, the Communication Arts *award, and the Andy award. He has most recently completed his first book for Abrams with Perri Wolfman,* The Perfect Setting, *a pictorial essay on unusual table settings, from casual to elegant.*

ON GETTING STARTED: I went to college and studied to be a potter. I am just shy of a master's degree in pottery. But I found it wasn't what I wanted to do. By a very happy accident I got a job at Young & Rubicam as a comp photographer, doing layouts. Basically I shot Polaroids that were used as stats and layouts presented to clients, and that was the end of my responsibility. It was a very lucky thing: being in the right place at the right time for the right job. After two years, my responsibility was doing the storyboards and layouts, dealing with about eighty art directors. That was really an education. But then there began to be a lot of conflict between the client and the agency because the client wanted to use my comp shots as finished art. That gave me the confidence to go out. I've been freelancing for about twenty-three years now.

ON STARTING OUT TODAY: I think the way I started is a great way, because you learn the business end of it. But it's not a readily available route. Positions like that are very few and far between. Unfortunately, one of the big problems I had when I opened the studio was that I knew *nothing* about running one. I'd never been an assistant. I'd never had an assistant. I didn't know how to deal with one. So that was very difficult for me. On the other hand, I had the agency experience and I knew how to deal with clients. Most photographers today start out by being either freelance or full-time assistants for existing photographers. They learn the technical, a little bit of the creative and the running of the studio. Probably they have a little more difficulty learning to deal with clients. But they see the relationship when they're in the studio.

ON EDUCATION: Well, there isn't one answer. I suppose, in retrospect, I really do believe in the Middle Ages guild system—learning under someone you respect highly, and learning the artist's technique. Then moving on to someone else, learning how that second person's technique is different from the first. That's the best education. That was sort of my way. Although I didn't have a master I worked under, I worked under a lot of art directors, and that was my experience. I really think a general education is the best. I think that photography school or something like that is so dry. The people I see tend to be very narrow; young people coming out of school don't even know the great modern painters. You should have as rich a background as you can bring to what you do. Just to know how to develop film makes you a very dull person. Experience life, then you can narrow it down and try to sell corn flakes. But you'll sell corn flakes with a little bit better perspective than just knowing how to get the right f-stop and the right focus.

ON SUCCESS: When I started, success to me was peer recognition—art directors, other photographers saying, "Wow, I wish I'd done that shot." That was success. Then a modicum of financial stability. That also meant success. It's nice to love what you do. But it's also nice to make a living at it. Success for me now is also the ability to have more control over what I'm doing, knowing that I can achieve what it is that's in my mind. When I was younger it was, "I wish I could do this, but I don't know how." Now I feel very confident, and that's part of success, I think. I have more confidence and it allows me to be freer and to expand my world.

ON MONEY: In photography? It's the only way *I've* ever managed to make money. You can still make money, but it's much more difficult than ever before. Competition is fierce, which means there are fewer jobs available per photographer. And the fees, I wouldn't sit here and tell you the fees are lower than they've ever been, because they're not. But they could be higher if the competition wasn't as fierce as it is. But, sure, sure, you can make a living.

ON PHOTOGRAPHY AS A BUSINESS: You have to know all the business angles—overhead. How many people can you afford to employ? How much can you afford to pay for rent? What is your business lifestyle? Then there are certain minimum givens from my way of thinking. Other photographers think totally differently. Rent is fiercely expensive in New York. There is a proliferation of studios for rent by the day and I guess they're doing well, but the way I see it, I have to have a home and I have to have a studio. It's the way I work.

Business is knowing cash flow. Nobody ever taught me that. One day I didn't have any money, and I said, "Holy s—t." But my accountant said, "You have receivables." I said, "Well, I can't buy film with receivables." So you learn to budget your money. Even when you know something's coming in, when it does, you don't go out and buy the Rolls Royce because you don't know when it's going to come in again. The agencies used to pay in 30 or 60 days. Now it's 90 or 120 days in some cases.

How much do you allot for professional services? Accountants, lawyers. Every job you do, there's a legal document involved, purchase order. It's scary. The cost of materials. All these things. It never occurred to me when I started that I was in business. I thought I could take pictures and that would be all I'd have to worry about. Well, no one was worrying about the other part. And it took me five years of pain to realize I had to know it. I didn't go to school for it, I learned through the school of hard knocks. I guess you could take a course, but something tells me that when you're talking about people, who have a burning need to do this thing—become a photographer—you ultimately just have to go out and do it.

ON HAVING AN AGENT: I've always had an agent. From the day I went into business. It's unfair to say that agents are necessary evils. They're not evils, but they're necessary. I've always believed that. If you want to reach a certain level, then I think you have to be free to concentrate on what you do best and you let someone else do what they do best. I think it's also one of the most difficult relationships to have, because you're not a partner, you are a partner, you're not married, you're married, it's emotions, it's not emotions. It's everything. And for some reason it's different in this industry than in any other, except maybe the entertainment industry. It's very objective in other fields. But here the relationships are very subjective/objective. I guess because it's a creative process. We offer a creative service. It's not just socks we're selling.

ON HIRING ASSISTANTS: I don't care about their book. I'm not hiring somebody to take pictures. I'm not hiring a creative person when I hire an assistant. I am hiring somebody who has technical skills for which I'm paying. I want to know how well they mop a floor, how well they load film, how well they keep the lenses clean and in place, and how well they keep the studio in order. Do they think like I need them to think? How well do they set up shots? Do they anticipate my needs, take directions well, etc.? I don't care what their creative abilities are.

I've advertised for assistants and it's been awful; and I've gotten recommendations and that's been just as awful. But more often than not, it's sort of a grapevine. I think today there are lots of periodicals with advertising for assistants and spaces and all that. The *Photo District News* and *American Photographer* and zillions of others where you can advertise.

ON THE FUTURE OF ADVERTISING PHOTOGRAPHY: It has to keep going, sure. It has to. I've seen it go through many fluctuations. Television is competitive with print. It gets very strong, then it gets weaker, then it flips around. I think advertising is taken much more seriously today than it ever has been. I think we're here to stay. From a supply end, my end, I guess I've seen some headway made over the last years. When I started out, you never charged the client for film and processing, for an assistant, for lunch, for insurance. Things were less expensive, but fees were also lower. So we fought and gained the right to charge for necessities on top of the fee.

The copyright issue is the one most up in the air now. What we want, very explicitly, is the right to sell the use of a picture in a consumer magazine. If you want to use it in a newspaper, you pay me more, on a billboard, you pay me more. It's happening, but the clients are resisting. They're saying, "We want a buyout. We want to own that copyright and all the reproduction rights to it, and for that we'll give you a little more than if we bought just one right."

The APA—Advertising Photographers of America—have gotten together on photographer's fees. I'm a member and I think they're doing a good job. They've made strides, but really not fast enough for me. But I guess it's evolution, not revolution. There are too many of us for it to be revolutionary.

ON WORKING FOR YOURSELF: I couldn't do it any other way. I'd love the security of a check every week without the responsibility. Not to worry about negotiating leases and rents and employment and taxes. Just let me shoot pictures and get a check every week. I would love that. On the other hand, I love being able to walk out of here at 2 o'clock if I so choose, or not come in if I'm not shooting. And I don't have a supervisor looking over my shoulder. As a freelance person I take the chance. I can hit heights financially much higher than I ever could as a salaried employee, but you can hit depths, too, that are much lower.

ON THE SATISFACTIONS: It's thrilling. When I was younger, I used to read about more established photographers. I would hear them talk about the magic. And I didn't understand. I'd say, "When you're this far along there's no magic any more. It's dry and it's rote." But you never know. There are so many steps between when I click the shutter and get a piece of developed film back, a processed piece of film in color. So many people involved, messengers, the lab. But then, there's this mystical moment. I get the film back, put it on the light box, and there's a knot in my stomach. Then it's "I wish I had," or "I could of done more than I did," or, in some rare instances, "Like, wow!" and that's very satisfying. That never dried up. I never took that for granted.

ON THE WORKING PROCESS: In the old days, you would get a call. You would send in your portfolio, and you'd get the job. They would send you a layout. You would discuss the layout. You'd send in an estimate. That would be approved. You'd pick a date to shoot. You'd amass all the props and people you needed for the day and put it all together. Then on the day, you'd shoot. Very ordered. It doesn't happen like that any more. I mean, I am involved in shootings now where I get a call: "We have a job, do you want it?" I say, "What is it?" "I can't tell you." "What's the layout?" "I don't have it yet, but we need an estimate." "How can I estimate something I haven't seen?" Or it's "You want the job? It's next Wednesday. Are you available?" "Yes, I am." "Okay, goodbye." They've already put in their own estimate. Sometimes it works, sometimes it doesn't. The best results come out when I get the layout in advance and I have time to look at it and think about it. I discuss the job with the art director, see what he or she had in mind if it's not evident on the layout. We bounce ideas back and forth and we're prepared to go into the studio with a couple of different directions.

I like to see a layout a week or so before shooting. That way it's in my head. It goes to sleep with me, and it's away with me on the weekend. It just lives with me. Then when I come to it, it's sort of inside me for awhile and I've considered it. But you do as good a job as you possibly can under all conditions. And you hone your edge so you can do better and better under more adverse conditions.

I'm a commercial photographer. Some things I do are better than other things. Sometimes I shoot for myself, and I'd like to think it's a little more inspired than other times. But I don't really make any bones about it being great art.

ON WOMEN IN ADVERTISING PHOTOGRAPHY: When I started it was very difficult for women. I don't know why. I didn't even know of any female photographers. A few interior photographers, one or two or three, maybe. But now just in the area of still life, which is what I do, there are I guess five or six or maybe eight really very good women photographers. I think they are bringing a certain feminine sensitivity to photography that you see in the magazines more and more. I've been in positions of bidding against some of them for jobs and lost, and I've been very upset. Then I'd see the final result, and I'd say, "Well, I couldn't have done that." It's not in my realm. There are just certain things I'm incapable of that I see in some of those pictures.

ON HAVING A PERSONAL LIFE: I have sort of designed my life. I'm a studio photographer. I don't go on location often, and when I do it's rarely overnight. I go home to my family every night. I always have. And I think it's very possible to do that. I think the thing about advertising photography is that you can design it to be what you want it to be. I know a very good photographer in Maine who works as much as he wants to. He gets layouts trucked up to him or air-expressed up. He goes on location from there. He sets up his shootings and he meets the people. Or he comes into New York and has meetings with agency people. He's as successful as anybody could be. So to my mind, it's possible.

Afterword

THE *School of Visual Arts Guide to Careers* grew out of a much smaller version originally produced by Visual Arts Press for the School of Visual Arts in New York under the title of *Careers in the Visual Arts.* The first printing was in March 1973, and since then it has gone into six more printings. This first book was little more than a pamphlet; as it was continually revised to include more career information and advice, the concept gradually emerged of expanding the book to feature interviews with a variety of artists who would discuss their experiences as well as offer advice to those who were just beginning careers. The result, of course, is this co-publication by McGraw-Hill and Visual Arts Press.

The School of Visual Arts was founded in 1947 and is today the largest undergraduate college of art in the country. Visual Arts pioneered the concept of bringing outstanding working professionals into the classrooms to teach what they know best from their everyday experience, arranging school schedules to meet their special professional needs. The Visual Arts faculty numbers nearly 650 members. This allows students to have a broad choice of faculty within a curriculum that allows for and encourages many electives. At the same time, the programs require that all students master the core of each of the disciplines taught. Visual Arts also offers a broad range of courses in art history, the humanities, and even computer science. A unique student advisement system ensures that Visual Arts has all the best attributes of a small college.